Memory Unbound

MEMORY UNBOUND

Tracing the Dynamics of Memory Studies

Edited by

Lucy Bond, Stef Craps, and Pieter Vermeulen

berghahn

NEW YORK · OXFORD

www.berghahnbooks.com

Published by
Berghahn Books
www.berghahnbooks.com

Library of Congress Cataloging-in-Publication Data

Names: Bond, Lucy, 1983– editor. | Craps, Stef, 1976– editor. | Vermeulen, Pieter,
1980– editor.
Title: Memory unbound : tracing the dynamics of memory studies / edited by
Lucy Bond, Stef Craps, and Pieter Vermeulen.
Description: New York : Berghahn Books, [2017] | Includes bibliographical
references and index.
Identifiers: LCCN 2016021777 | ISBN 9781785333002 (hardback) |
ISBN 9781785338410 (paperback)
Subjects: LCSH: Collective memory. | Memory—Social aspects.
Classification: LCC HM1033 .M456 2017 | DDC 302/.1—dc23
LC record available at hkps://lccn.loc.gov/2016021777

British Library Cataloguing in Publication Data

A catalogue record for this book is available from the British Library

ISBN 978-1-78533-300-2 (hardback)
ISBN 978-1-78533-841-0 (paperback)
ISBN 978-1-78533-301-9 (ebook)

Contents

PART III. Transmedial Memory

PART IV. Transdisciplinary Memory

Illustrations

Introduction

Memory on the Move

Lucy Bond, Stef Craps, and Pieter Vermeulen

⊂⊗◊⊗⊃

Memory, it is safe to say, is not what it used to be. Previously thought to be anchored in particular places, to be lodged in particular containers (monuments, texts, geographical locations), and to belong to the (national, familial, social) communities it helped acquire a sense of historical continuity, memory has, in the last few years, increasingly been considered a fluid and flexible affair. In a globalized age, memories travel along and across the migratory paths of world citizens. In a digital age, they are forwarded from cameras over smartphones to computers and back in unpredictable loops. In the process, they redefine the relations between different generations, as geographical and medial transfers affect the uptake of memories by people who can no longer be said to simply inherit them. Meanwhile, the study of memory spans and complicates the boundaries between academic disciplines, generating a multifaceted and evolving field of research.

Memory, then, is presently conceptualized as something that does not stay put but circulates, migrates, travels; it is more and more perceived as a process, as work that is continually in progress, rather than as a reified object. In recent years, the transcultural or transnational circulation of memories has moved to the center of attention. Concomitantly, there has been a marked increase of interest in how memory travels between different media, specifically in the role of digital media in the production, preservation, and transfer of memories. Moreover, as the Holocaust begins to pass out of living memory, the question of how memories of survivors of historical traumas are transmitted to, and inherited by, members of later generations has become another area of intense inquiry. Finally, memory studies appears to be moving toward greater interdisciplinarity or, at least, enhanced awareness of the necessity or desirability of cross-fertilization between memory research in the humanities, social sciences, and natural sciences.

Attentive to these shifts, this volume responds to the need to nuance and develop our understanding of the dynamics of memory in theory and in practice. It does so not by focusing on one discrete form of mobility but by interrogating the relations between what we see as the four most salient dimensions of the mobility of memory: its transcultural, transgenerational, transmedial, and transdisciplinary drift. As the many echoes within and between the different sections of the book make clear, these four dimensions inevitably intersect with and inflect one another: new social and digital media, for instance, facilitate the transcultural travel of memories, and these transcultural memories in turn change the way the past is transmitted to later generations—who, it goes without saying, constellate media in very different ways than their elders. The upshot of these complex interactions is that the field of memory studies itself needs to find new methods to track that new mnemonic reality: in the terms we propose in this collection, it needs to take on the transdisciplinary challenge of memories on the move.

If we have yet decided to divide the volume into four sections, each naming one particular dimension of mnemonic mobility, this is only to indicate the particular dimension the contributions to that section have chosen to foreground. In actual fact, as all chapters make clear, none of these dimensions can be discussed in isolation from the other three. Together, the four sections suggest that the various modes of memory's unbounded character are best considered comprehensively and in an integrated manner. They develop concepts and vocabularies for mapping the interactions between these dimensions without—and this is a crucial point to which several of the essays in the book respond—blurring all distinctions between media, objects, and practices and without abandoning the past to the indistinctiveness of a frictionless digitized and globalized memoryscape. Memorative activity today, as this volume shows, is considerably more plural and recalcitrant—and therefore more interesting: our title, *Memory Unbound*, does not aim to declare the end of all local and specific attachments; it rather names a commitment to tracking the unpredictable mobility of objects and practices that, now that they are widely considered to be unbound, refuse to be re-bound. Ultimately, we contend, attention to the manifold ways in which memory moves across cultures, generations, media, and disciplines is indispensable for the study of memory today. In this introductory chapter, we present the four organizing dimensions of mnemonic mobility by locating them in ongoing discussions in the field of memory studies and by situating the different essays in the collection as interventions in these debates.

TRANSCULTURAL MEMORY

The chapters in the first section examine what is arguably the most familiar mode of mnemonic mobility: the transmission, circulation, mediation,
and reception of memory between and beyond ethnic, cultural, or national
groups. Analyses of this dimension manifest a significant departure from
orthodox models of memorative practice and theory, which have frequently
located memory as the geographically and culturally bounded property
of particular collectives (Halbwachs, *On Collective Memory*) or communities
(J. Assmann, *Cultural Memory*), typically delineated by the borders of the
nation-state as modernity's privileged cultural unit (Nora).

Commemorative practices have long played a significant role in establishing the "imagined community" (Anderson) of the nation. As Katharine
Hodgkin and Susannah Radstone assert:

> In nationalist movements and in achieved nation states alike, the appeal to
> memory articulates the narrative of the nationalist past, and enjoins its subject
> to recognize and own it ... Memory is thus at the heart of nationalist struggles,
> transmitted from one generation to the next as a sacred injunction ... it is also
> one of the major mobilizing forces in the modern nation state. (169)

Hodgkin and Radstone suggest that the topography of national memory
construes a "geography of belonging" (169) or, as Duncan Bell conceives
it, a "mythscape" that "simplifies, dramatizes and selectively narrates the
story of a nation's past and its place in the world: a story that elucidates
contemporary meaning through (re)constructing its past" (75). Pierre Nora
contends that such mythscapes typically comprise a constellation of fixed
sites, such as monuments and memorials, at which "memory crystallizes
and secretes itself" (8). Nora further alleges that, following the "acceleration of history" that accompanied the "movement towards democratization
and mass culture on a global scale" (7), such *lieux de mémoire* (sites of memory) have offered an artificial and impoverished substitute for the *milieux
de mémoire* (genuine "environments of memory") that had previously provided a sense of historical continuity for "societies that had long assured the
transmission and conservation of collectively remembered values, whether
through churches or schools, the family or the state" (7).

Lamenting the paradoxes of a "historical age that calls out for memory
because it has abandoned it" (12), Nora suggests that the "conquest of memory by history" is the byproduct of "our hopelessly forgetful modern society, propelled by change" (8). Highlighting the destabilizing properties of
globalizing capitalism, accelerated technological development, and cultural

postmodernism, Andreas Huyssen similarly asserts, "As the territorial and spatial coordinates of our ... lives are blurred or even dissolved by increased mobility around the globe" (*Twilight Memories* 7), contemporary society has entertained a collective search for a mode of "temporal anchoring" able to lend an illusion of security to a "culture [that] is terminally ill with amnesia" (2). Both Nora and Huyssen thus implicitly associate the rise of the recent "memory boom" in the academy, and the related cultural "memory industry" (Klein 127), with the decentering of the nation as the locus of historical consciousness in the era of globalization. However, as Huyssen expands, there is no going back to the past we thought we knew; instead, rather than reinscribing the national geographies of belonging alluded to by Hodgkin and Radstone, "the mnemonic convulsions of our culture seem chaotic, fragmentary, and free-floating. They do not seem to have a clear political or territorial focus" (Huyssen, *Twilight Memories* 7). Accordingly, "the form in which we think of the past is increasingly memory without borders rather than national history within borders" (Huyssen, *Present Pasts* 4).

This is not to suggest that national memory cultures have disappeared—nor, indeed, that national memory was ever as stable and self-contained as traditional theories of memory tended to assume. As the highly patriotic commemorative discourses surrounding September 11 in the United States suggest, to name just one recent example, the notion of national belonging continues to exert a significant influence over contemporary memorial practice (Bond; Simpson). The idea of the nation as a fairly homogenous cultural unit retains its traction as a unifying trope in the wake of traumatic events, especially when commemorative endeavors are reliant on federal funding and governmental support for their realization. However, increasingly, even where they advance a national(ist) agenda, memory politics tend to be intrinsically globally oriented. As a number of scholars have argued, in the post-Cold War period, memorative discourses have emerged as the cornerstone of a new geopolitical community, which has positioned a public commitment to *Vergangenheitsbewältigung,* or coming to terms with the past, as a prerequisite for a nation's membership of international institutions such as the European Union and the United Nations and thus as the key to participation in the global political arena (Levy and Sznaider; Sierp).

Moreover, a growing critical consensus contends that interpreting memory through the normative framework of the nation obscures the hegemonic and often homogenizing properties of national memory regimes, occluding the ways in which memories may travel across geographical or cultural boundaries and marginalizing the experiences and histories of particular individuals or collectives. Accordingly, the recent "transcultural turn" (Bond and Rapson) in memory studies has sought to highlight the elisions and biases inherent in national memory by exploring the ways in which diverse media and forms of memory may circulate between and beyond the borders of the nation-state, variously foregrounding the "cosmopolitan" (Levy and Sznaider), "multidirectional" (Rothberg), "traveling" (Erll, "Travelling Memory"), "palimpsestic" (Silverman), "transcultural" (Bond and Rapson; Crownshaw), "transnational" (De Cesari and Rigney), "global" (A. Assmann and Conrad), or "globital" (Reading) dynamics of memorative theory and practice. All of these terms will be critically evaluated throughout this volume, as it tries to fine-tune our vocabularies for capturing the multifaceted mobility of memory.

Despite the important methodological and disciplinary differences between these approaches, the exponents of the transcultural turn cumulatively espouse a number of key principles: first, they contend that memorative discourses can provide the foundation for global human rights regimes; second, they privilege comparative, rather than competitive, interpretations of the past; third, they shift attention from memory's static location in particular sites and objects to the dynamics and technologies by and through which it is articulated. This makes clear that the study of transcultural memory can never be isolated from an understanding of memory's transmedial mobility, as the many echoes between the different sections of this volume make clear.

A number of the ideas associated with the transcultural turn have already had a significant impact on cultural memory research. Advocating "a new cosmopolitan memory ... that harbours the possibility of transcending ethnic and national boundaries" to provide "the cultural foundation for global human rights dynamics" (4), Daniel Levy and Natan Sznaider assert that "national and ethnic memories are transformed in the age of globalization rather than erased ... They begin to develop in accordance with common rhythms and periodizations. But in each case, the common elements combine with pre-existing elements to form something new" (3). Arguing that the histories of "the Holocaust, slavery, and colonial domination are in fact interconnected, and by refusing to think them together (except in a competitive manner) we deprive ourselves of an opportunity to gain a greater insight into each of these different strands of history" (Craps and Rothberg 518), Michael Rothberg similarly rejects a "zero-sum" model of memory as a "struggle over scarce resources," positioning memorative activity as fundamentally "*multidirectional*: as subject to ongoing negotiation, cross-referencing, and borrowing" (Rothberg 3). Foregrounding the "incessant wandering of carriers, media, contents, forms, and practices of memory, their continual 'travels' and ongoing transformations through time and space, across social, linguistic and political borders" (Erll, "Travelling Memory" 11), Astrid Erll examines the ongoing pre- and remediation of memorative discourses in the global age, while—working across memory and media studies—Joanne Garde-Hansen, Andrew Hoskins, and Anna Reading propose that techno-logical advancements have engendered a "connective turn," "shaping an on-going re-calibration of time, space (and place) and memory by people and machines as they inhabit and connect with both dense and diffuse social networks" (Hoskins, "Media, Memory, Metaphor" 29).

Collectively, these critics construe a model of memory as a fluid, inclusive, and open-ended process, rather than a fixed and exclusionary narrative, embracing the possibility that the intersection of disparate commemorative discourses might offer an opportunity to forge empathic communities of remembrance across national, cultural, or ethnic boundaries. Such ideas, it seems to us, are of paramount importance in an era when contemporary geopolitics are dominated by manifold transnational concerns, ranging from terrorism to the global financial crisis, the threat of climate change, and the increasing numbers of migrants, stateless persons, and refugees occasioned by social, political, economic, or environmental precarity.

However, as Wulf Kansteiner reminds us, despite the recent tendency to celebrate the "dialectical, conflicted interplay between global and local memories and identities" as a "very positive development" (331), it is important not to lose sight of the hegemonic dynamics of certain memory regimes and the power differentials between different memories and memory agents in the laudable move to embrace the ethical potential of transcultural paradigms of remembrance; memory, like all cultural and social practices, operates within the closed horizons of global capital, and it cannot but be affected and animated by the constraints and the compulsions this closure imposes. Accordingly, a number of recent critiques (Bond; Craps; Moses; Tomsky) have sought to highlight the (implicit and explicit) roles that memorative practice and theory have played in buttressing a global "trauma economy," in which disparate memories are mediated by "economic, cultural, discursive, and political structures that guide, enable and ultimately institutionalize the representation, travel and attention to certain traumas" (Tomsky 53). As Judith Butler has argued, such structures perpetuate inequitable hierarchies of life, which ensure that "certain lives will be highly protected, and the abrogation of their claims to sanctity will be sufficient to mobilize the forces of war. Other lives will … not even qualify as 'grievable'" (32).

These considerations underscore the fact that the transcultural frames of memory that shape our understanding of the past are—as memorative discourses have always been—contested, contingent, and both politically and ethically ambiguous. Bearing this in mind, the chapters in this section seek to question what is at stake in negotiating the shifting scales of contemporary memory and what role memory studies might play in the ongoing mediation between the private and the public, the past and the present, the local, the national, and the global.

In "Staging Shared Memory: *Je Veux voir* and *L'Empreinte de l'ange,*" Max Silverman builds on his notion of "palimpsestic memory"—one of the most illuminating perspectives from which transcultural memory has begun to be viewed in recent years—to explore the ways in which our stories of the past may be vulnerable to interaction with otherness; remaining attentive to this tenuous possibility, Silverman argues, involves an ethics of shared memory that eschews self-sufficiency and autonomy. The chapter foregrounds the *performative* dimensions of memory, underscoring the fact that the conjunction of different pasts is an (ethically charged and aesthetically attuned) act of construction in the present, not a preformulated narrative that is automatically transmitted to the next generation. Silverman explores two recent works that both stage the transcultural dimension of the encounter with otherness—the film *Je Veux voir* (2008) by the Lebanese filmmakers Joana Hadjithomas and Khalil Joreige and the novel *L'Empreinte de l'ange* (1998) by the Canadian writer Nancy Huston—to argue that the encounters that take place in the present of these texts (of filming, of writing) are constitutive of the creative act of remembrance itself. These works stage an ethics of shared memory, which is neither voyeuristic nor solipsistic but open-ended and am bivalent for self and other.

Few recent works of art perform the encounter with a troubled past as self-consciously and impressively as Joshua Oppenheimer's much-discussed 2012 documentary *The Art of Killing*. Rosanne Kennedy's essay "Remembering the Indonesian Killings: *The Act of Killing* and the Global Memory Imperative" contributes to debates about the relationship between genocide, national and transnational memory, and history in a global media age by analyzing the production, circulation, and reception of the film. The film, Kennedy shows, draws on explicitly transcultural models in generating a memory of the Indonesian genocide: one explicit model is the Holocaust paradigm, especially Claude Lanzmann's *Shoah;* the second is provided by Hollywood films. Kennedy argues that the particular constellation of these models that the film "performs" (in Silverman's sense) provides an example of cosmopolitan memory, in which global icons and models are localized in specific national or local contexts. Yet still, and anticipating an issue that Aleida Assmann will elaborate in her contribution to this section, Kennedy contends that the most significant audience for the film remains a national one (even if it also implicates Western audiences, particularly Americans, since the CIA supported the regime that carried out the Indonesian genocide as part of the United States' own interest in ending the spread of communism). In so doing, *The Act of Killing* shows the relevance of both national and transcultural frames for remembering genocide in the present.

These overlapping and differently scaled frames are further explored in Aleida Assmann's chapter "Transnational Memory and the Construction of History through Mass Media." Assmann foregrounds the changing role of mass media, which often address national audiences, in the drift of memory within and across national and cultural borders—borders that, she argues, are more stubborn and less permeable than celebrations of transnational and transcultural mobility tend to assume. She offers a general assessment of the "transnational turn" announced by historians and theorists in various subfields of cultural studies, which aims to go beyond national identifications, investments, and interests and to explore new forms of belonging, participation, and cultural identification in a world characterized by dispersed and displaced populations with different historical experiences and trajectories. In practice, Assmann argues, the term "transnational" often covers up rather than uncovers important problems that we encounter in this new area of research. Given the growing impact of national history constructed through the mass media, the chapter focuses on the 2013 German television miniseries *Unsere Mütter, unsere Väter* (Generation War) and its reception, asking whether it stimulates nationalistic narcissism or has the potential to reimage the national past in a more comprehensive European perspective. Only by taking seriously the national frame, Assmann concludes, can a genuinely transnational method accurately describe actual memorial processes.

TRANSGENERATIONAL MEMORY

The chapters in the second section foreground the dynamics that inform the intergenerational transmission of memory. The emergence of memory studies as an interdisciplinary field of inquiry in the 1980s was driven in part by growing interest in the ways the experience of violence affects subsequent generations. Children of Holocaust survivors began to publicly explore what it means to grow up with the memory of a painful history that one did not experience firsthand, yet by whose legacy one feels profoundly stamped. The relationship between descendants of survivors and the traumatic past of which they have no direct personal experience has been described in terms of "postmemory" (Hirsch), "*mémoire trouée*" (memory shot through with holes; Raczymow), "absent memory" (Fine), and "prosthetic memory" (Landsberg).

Arguably the most influential conceptualization of transgenerational memory can be found in the work of Marianne Hirsch. In 1992 Hirsch coined the term "postmemory" to make an argument about the role of family photographs in the graphic novel *Maus,* Art Spiegelman's famous account of his father's experience of the Holocaust. The concept refers to the relationship of the children of Holocaust survivors to their parents' traumatic experiences, which were transmitted to them during childhood through stories, images, and behaviors in such a powerful way as to seem to constitute memories in their own right ("Family Picture"). Hirsch explored postmemory in greater depth in her seminal 1997 study *Family Frames: Photography, Narrative, and Postmemory.* Distinguished from memory by "generational distance" and from history by "deep personal connection," she argues, postmemory is "a powerful and very particular form of memory precisely because its connection to its object or source is mediated not through recollection but through an imaginative investment and creation" (*Family Frames* 22). "It is a question," she writes elsewhere, "of adopting the traumatic experiences—and thus also the memories—of others as experiences one might oneself have had, and of inscribing them into one's own life story" ("Projected Memory" 9; "Surviving Images" 10).

A prominent line of critique of theories of transgenerational memory objects to their perceived tendency to conflate the suffering of survivors with that of their offspring. In his article "Second-Generation Testimony, Transmission of Trauma, and Postmemory," Ernst van Alphen challenges the assumption that there is a "fundamental continuity" (474) between the experiences of Holocaust survivors and those of their children, arguing that they are of a different nature altogether. In his view, "it makes little sense to speak of the *transmission* of trauma. Children of survivors can be traumatized, but their trauma does not consist of the Holocaust experience, not even in indirect or mitigated form. Their trauma is caused by being raised by a traumatized Holocaust survivor" (482; emphasis in original). He goes on to dismiss the concept of postmemory as a form of "wishful thinking" (486). As the relationship between memory and the past is an indexical one, and as postmemory can claim no such relationship, postmemory is "not relatively but fundamentally different from memory" (486). According to van Alphen, it is important to recognize that "the deep personal connection" of which Hirsch speaks can only refer to the connection between children of survivors and their parents and emphatically not to the connection between the children's experience and the parental past (486–87). Using a term that implies connection to describe a situation that is really one of disconnection, he argues, obscures the specificity of the challenges faced by children of survivors and of the dynamics between survivor parents and their children (487–88). In his book *Fantasies of Witnessing,* Gary Weissman similarly criticizes Hirsch for blurring the distinctions between survivors and those who witness their trauma secondhand by allegedly suggesting that "the difference between memory and postmemory is primarily one of distance rather than substance" (17). In her 2012 book *The Generation of Postmemory,* Hirsch responds to van Alphen's and Weissman's objections to her use of the word "memory" in her formulation of postmemory (31, 254–55n3). While granting that "postmemory is not identical to memory: it is 'post,'" she sees no reason to stop using the term, as postmemory "approximates memory in its affective force and its psychic effects" (31).

In the same vein as van Alphen and Weissman, Amy Hungerford has questioned the notion of trauma transmission, taking particular aim at the work of Shoshana Felman and Cathy Caruth, two key figures in the field of trauma theory. In *The Holocaust of Texts,* Hungerford takes Felman to task for suggesting that "the experience of listening to Holocaust testimony produces symptoms of trauma equivalent to the traumatic symptoms produced by actually experiencing the Holocaust" (104). Hungerford also criticizes what she sees as Caruth's attempt to "cut [the experience of trauma] free of the person to whom the trauma happens" (114) and thereby make it into a generic experience that can be transferred from one person to another: "By cutting experience free from the subject of experience, Caruth allows trauma not only to be abstract in the extreme but also, by virtue of that abstraction, to be transmissible" (115). In Hungerford's view, Caruth's notion of transmissible trauma risks violating or obscuring the very specificity of history that she is officially so anxious to preserve. Hungerford goes on to question the wisdom of emphasizing the need to *remember* traumatic events that one has not lived oneself rather than to *learn* about them: "Memory (the knowledge of what we have experienced)," she decries, "is privileged over learning; in much public discourse on the subject of the Holocaust, for example, it has become more important to 'remember' the Holocaust than simply to learn about it" (155). Gabriele Schwab, however, has taken issue with Hungerford's summary dismissal of "emotionally engaged and personally inflected engagements" with the Holocaust, calling it a "politically questionable" attitude that amounts to an "emotional silencing" of the event (117).

Despite critical questions about the pertinence of transgenerational memory, research into this mnemonic dynamic has steadily grown and lately begun to diversify. Even if it was initially developed in relation to children of Holocaust survivors, postmemory is not limited to "the intimate embodied space of the family" but, as Hirsch explains, can be extended to "more distant, adoptive witnesses or affiliative contemporaries" (*Generation of Postmemory* 6). Drawing on Geoffrey Hartman's concept of "witnesses by adoption" ("Surviving Images" 8), she describes her theory of postmemory as "*retrospective witnessing by adoption*" ("Surviving Images" 10). What she retains from Hartman's concept is "the connection to and enlargement of family that this term implies" ("Surviving Images" 10). Hirsch notes that the expansion of the postmemorial community beyond family boundaries is enabled by the conventionality of the familial tropes prevalent in postmemorial writing and art, which provides a space for identification that can, in theory at least, be occupied by any reader or viewer. If theories of traumatic transfer originally focused on the Holocaust, attention has shifted in recent years to the intergenerational transmission of memories of a wide range of histories, including "African slavery; the Vietnam War; the Dirty War in Argentina and other dictatorships in Latin America; South African apartheid; Soviet, East European, and Chinese communist terror; the Armenian, the Cambodian, and the Rwandan genocides; the Japanese internment camps in the United States; the stolen generations in aboriginal Australia; the Indian partition; and others" (Hirsch, *Generation of Postmemory* 19). Critics such as Schwab and Erin McGlothlin have further extended the inquiry into transgenerational memory by focusing on descendants of perpetrators as well as victims, while other scholars have approached these dynamics from a transcultural angle. Moreover, while visual media—photography in particular—have traditionally been seen to play an important role in transgenerational memory alongside verbal storytelling, in recent years such processes have increasingly acquired a transmedial dimension as the impact of digital media technologies on modes of memory transmission has become a focus of inquiry. The three chapters in this section reflect on these new dynamic contexts of transgenerational memory from transdisciplinary perspectives.

In "Small Acts of Repair: The Unclaimed Legacy of the Romanian Holocaust," Marianne Hirsch and Leo Spitzer raise the question of transgenerational memory by focusing on a very specific topic: the work and the reception of a number of writers and artists who were deported to Transnistria, an area that was annexed by Romania during World War II and became what they call a "forgotten cemetery" in which hundreds of thousands of Jews, Roma, and political prisoners perished. While Transnistria's history fails to fit common conceptions of Holocaust persecution and murder, much of the vibrant intellectual and artistic activity that took place in its ghettos and camps also largely fails to fit the paradigms of Holocaust art or literature. This chapter aims to illuminate and restore this little-known chapter of Holocaust history, thus activating the performative dimension of transcultural and transgenerational remembrance that Max Silverman foregrounds in his contribution. At the same time, through its attention to both visual and literary media, it also asks larger questions about possibilities of repair and redress in the aftermath of atrocity and about the needs of audiences that inherit these painful histories through different media.

In "Fictions of Generational Memory: Caryl Phillips's *In the Falling Snow* and Black British Writing in Times of Mnemonic Transition," Astrid Erll defines "fictions of generational memory" as a type of literature that addresses the problem of "generation" in both its synchronic and diachronic dimensions, as it deals with generationality (that is, generational identity) as well as with genealogy (as a mode of vertical transmission). The essay combines memory theory with different strands of generation studies (in the fields of sociology, social history, and cultural studies) in order to develop tools for the analysis of fictions of generational memory. It analyzes these fictions as a truly global phenomenon and as a specific literary way to cope with generational, and hence also mnemonic, transitions—from witnesses to their children and grandchildren, from memory to postmemory, and from communicative to cultural memory (to use Jan and Aleida Assmann's terms). Drawing on Caryl Phillips's novel *In the Falling Snow* (2009) as its main example, the essay shows how contemporary black writing in Britain addresses the mnemonic transitions that can currently be observed in Britain's immigrant generations. As the members of the Empire Windrush generation are aging, the second and third generations of black Britons are looking for new ways to relate to the legacy of British immigration history. Locating themselves as distinct generations (in the sense of generationality) in this history, they seek to reassemble diasporic family memories and to unearth genealogies that reach across what Paul Gilroy has influentially called the "Black Atlantic."

In "The Uses of Facebook for Examining Collective Memory: The Emergence of Nasser Facebook Pages in Egypt," Joyce van de Bildt adds a transmedial twist to the transcultural and transnational nature of transgenerational memory underlined by Erll. Anticipating the focus on digital and social media in (especially) the third section of this book, the chapter demonstrates how Facebook pages function as a platform on which people express their different views of a shared past, evoking competition, comparison, and conversation. As a case study, the chapter explores the emergence of Facebook pages dedicated to Gamal 'Abd al-Nasser. The pages' historical themes stand for larger, more complex interpretations of the Egyptian national past, which are closely related to current social and political agendas. Since the Nasser forums are predominantly founded by a younger generation of Egyptians whose members have not experienced his period of rule, van de Bildt argues that these "historical" Facebook pages should be examined as forms of transgenerational memory and as instances of nostalgia. The chapter explicitly raises disciplinary questions, considering, like Jessica K. Young's chapter in this collection, whether social media are appropriate tools for examining cultural memory practices and how they can be complemented by other medial and disciplinary approaches to vernacular, as opposed to official, memory.

TRANSMEDIAL MEMORY

It is one of the central insights of memory studies that memories, whether individual or shared, are always mediated. In his first, foundational, study of memory, *Les Cadres sociaux de la mémoire* (1925), Maurice Halbwachs underlines that even our most intimate and personal memories are inflected by social structures: memory is inseparable from the social and linguistic frameworks that coconstitute it. More recently, memory studies has extensively researched the role of the technologies and apparatuses that make possible the storage and transmission of memory, underscoring the fact that even childhood memories, which might strike us as the most private and authentic forms of recollection we have, are triggered and shaped by mediating objects such as photographs, home videos, souvenirs, oral stories, and written documents. Moreover, as a number of critical interventions have argued, what goes for individual memories also goes for shared memories: the remarkable rise (and the particular shape) of the Holocaust in American historical consciousness, for instance, cannot be explained without referring to the broad appeal of the 1978 TV miniseries *Holocaust,* the efforts of the Fortunoff Video Archive for Holocaust Testimonies to videotape the accounts of survivors since the 1980s, and the establishment of the United States Holocaust Memorial Museum in the 1990s. In turn, this insight into the mediated nature of *all* memory problematizes any attempt to unreflexively deny transgenerational (post)memory the status of memory on account of its alleged lack of authenticity and indexicality; after all, if memory is inevitably mediated, such indexicality and authenticity are always an effect—or, indeed, an affect—never an achieved ontological certainty.

This key insight has entailed a double shift in memory studies toward a focus on processes and dynamics of memory rather than on static sites of remembrance and toward a closer scrutiny of the media of memory, which are never neutral carriers of historical understanding but actively coconstitute the meanings and dynamics of commemorative culture. Ann Rigney has described the first shift as a move from "monumentality" to "morphing" (345), from the assumption of media carriers' stabilizing and naturalizing force to a more variegated account of the different ways in which media allow memory to circulate—as "relay stations," as "stabilizers," or as "catalysts" of memory (350–52). From such a dynamic perspective, memory objects are not discrete phenomena but elements in chains and networks of transmedial interactions; with Astrid Erll, Rigney has deployed the notion of "remediation" to capture these processes. Borrowing the concept from Jay David Bolter and Richard Grusin's book *Remediation: Understanding New Media,* Erll and Rigney see remediation as "the ongoing transcription of a 'memory matter' into different media"—memory matter, that is, is essentially "a transmedial phenomenon; it is not tied to one specific medium" (Erll, *Memory in Culture* 141). What emerges from this understanding is a fluid and flexible account of mnemonic processes in which "media are always 'emergent' rather than stable" and in which media figure "as complex and dynamic systems rather than as a line-up of discrete and stable technologies" (Erll and Rigney 3). Memory, in other words, is regarded as fundamentally implicated in "plurimedial networks" (Erll, "Literature, Film" 395).

The differences and overlaps between the media that make up such networks have increasingly become a focus of attention in memory studies. Different media have different constraints and different affordances: we now know that the advent of writing in early civilization radically altered the constitution of memory cultures, allowing them to develop new connective structures less reliant on imitation and ritual for their reproduction (J. Assmann, *Cultural Memory* 3–4); later, the invention of the printing press spelled the decline of certain ancient mnemotechnics as broader audiences gained access to print material to which they could outsource their memory work (Erll, *Memory in Culture* 116–18). Different media, in other words, command different forms of attention and uptake (think also of the aura of authenticity surrounding photography), which in turn generates different media cultures and communities. Today, media culture is essentially marked by the spread of digital and so-called social media, which plug contemporary memory work into what Andrew Hoskins has called a "new memory ecology." According to Hoskins, new media saturate contemporary memory work to the point that we can speak of a veritable "new memory," a term that covers "both the media-affected formation and reformation of shared or social memory in the contemporary age and the consequential reassessment of the nature and the very value of remembering (and forgetting) subject to the technologies of and the discourses disseminated by the mass and other media" ("Mediatisation of Memory" 27–28). This "new memory," for Hoskins, radically recalibrates the once mutually exclusive relation between public and private technologies of remembrance: "Whereas the personal writing and production of memory (scrapbooks, diaries, photographic albums, etc.) of the past were intended for limited consumption, mediatisation has delivered a new self-centred (and immediate) public or semi-public and semi-private, documentation and correspondence, in other words a social network memory" ("Mediatisation of Memory" 30). Accordingly, "everyday life," for Hoskins, "is increasingly embedded in the mediascape"; media not only mediate our *consumption* of events, but they actively shape their *production* ("Mediatisation of Memory" 31).

Hoskins's influential account of the full-scale mediatization of memory appears to move from Erll's "plurimedial networks" to a disabling "omnimedial" network that fully absorbs human agency. However, there are good reasons to resist this shift, if only because it threatens to erase a number of tensions and distinctions in a way that impoverishes our account of the mobility of memory. As Aleida Assmann notes in this volume, the networked distribution of memory dispenses with the principle of scarcity that is yet an essential aspect of all memory—without selection, there is no memory, just data. And, as Amanda Lagerkvist underlines in her chapter, human life continues to resist its saturation by media, as its relation to media remains marred by all too human forms of anxiety and insecurity. Most importantly, perhaps, the celebration of the digitization of memory forgets that mediascapes are animated by tensions and overlaps between emergent, residual, and dominant media; indeed, opposing "the strategic amnesia of digital culture" by retrieving obliterated genealogies of media cultures is the explicit aim of the budding field of media archeology (Parikka 13). Thus, a proper account of transmedial memory, we contend, must start from the realization that our lives have become increasingly digitized but that they remain, like all forms of life, marked by regressions, hesitations, tensions, and other hiccups that media memory studies must attend to.

Let us briefly mention three notions that, we believe, manage to factor in the medial constitution of memory while remaining sensitively attuned to differences and difficulties—to what the editors of the important volume *On Media Memory* call media memory's "multichannel outlets, its multiple approaches and research designs, and the various challenges it poses" (Neiger, Meyers, and Zandberg 1). We are thinking, first, of Anna Reading's concept of the "globital memory field," which connects the deterritorializing forces of the global and the digital. For Reading, the concept of the globital makes it possible to study transmedial transfer—between digital and nondigital media but also between different digital media such as smartphones, computers, cameras, and so on—as "a memory assemblage that is dynamic and involves transmedial, globalized, mobile connectivities and mobilizations" (241–42). Second, there is Marita Sturken's notion of "tangled memories," which she coined in the 1990s in a study that underlines the formative role of media in shaping a sense of US national identity—the very sense of identity, that is, that traditional memory theories take for granted. Focusing on the cultural memories of the AIDS epidemic and the Vietnam War, Sturken foregrounds what she calls "technologies of memory ... objects through which memories are shared, produced, and given meaning" (9). These technologies "embody and generate memory" (10), and, as Amanda Lagerkvist emphasizes in her contribution, this materialist perspective makes it possible to read even the body itself as a memory medium. The third notion we want to touch on, Alison Landsberg's aforementioned "prosthetic memory," also routes contemporary memory processes through the mass media and through embodied experience. For Landsberg, the mass media define the context for contemporary practices of remembrance; more specifically, media afford contemporary subjects experiences "through which the person sutures himself or herself into a larger history" (2). Now that memory has entered "the age of technological reproducibility" (14), it is transmitted and disseminated in a fluid and flexible way in which media act as cognitive and affective relays between parents and children and between individuals and communities. Even if Landsberg does not extensively discuss digital memory, her emphasis on the experiential and subjectivity-constituting dimension of memorial transmission makes her work a vital resource for the analysis of memory in a digital age.

The three chapters in this section of the book contribute to our understanding of the medial infrastructures of contemporary memory—of memoryscapes that are undeniably dominated by the digital yet in which power struggles and medial differences continue to matter. José van Dijck's "Connective Memory: How Facebook Takes Charge of Your Past" foregrounds the role that social media have come to play in the ways we remember and see ourselves—both in individual and collective terms. While the Timeline architecture Facebook introduced in 2011 and 2012 invites users to organize their web identities through acts of memorization, van Dijck reveals how the mobility of memory is in fact directed and shaped by the algorithms that power these platforms, which are primarily concerned with monetizing users' data. In an age of social media, van Dijck writes, we have moved from a situation of increased connectedness to almost compulsive *connectivity* in which memory is "transmediated" into a byproduct of algorithms that serve as connectivity engines. If the notion of connectedness refers to horizontal, networked, peer-to-peer communication facilitated by digital platforms, the notion of connectivity, by contrast, underlines that these platforms now *construct* and *exploit* rather than merely *enable* connections between users. Not only have technological developments made it possible for social interactions and cultural production to be thoroughly mediated by digital platforms (what is sometimes called "radical connectivity"), but as these developments have also enabled the transformation of the social value of connectedness into monetary profit, such platforms work to actively *promote* connections through coding technologies (what van Dijck calls "automated connectivity"; van Dijck 13). This means that "connectedness is often invoked as the pretense for generating connectivity, even now that data generation has become a primary objective rather than a by-product of online sociability" (van Dijck 12). This shift toward a "platformed" sociality has altered the very ways in which individuals connect: pressured by invisible algorithms that aim to maximize connections and the data they generate, users are motivated to concern themselves with performances of self-branding and the accumulation of social capital, rather than with self-expression and communication per se.

This condition of almost total absorption by algorithms raises questions about human agency and embodied experience. Amanda Lagerkvist's "Embodiments of Memory: Toward an Existential Approach to the Culture of Connectivity" is an ambitious effort to extend the vocabulary and the conceptual framework for studying the digital memory ecology. Lagerkvist highlights a conspicuous gap in many theories of digital memory, as they fail to account for the seemingly paradoxical fact that we inhabit these ecologies as both fully embodied and totally mediated: what is needed, Lagerkvist argues, is new terms to map the frictions between these two modes of saturation. How, Lagerkvist asks, do media of memory produce performances of memory across the realms of the body, digital media, physical artifacts, and space? By coining the notion of "mediatized performativity," the essay understands embodiment and ubiquitous mediation as coconstitutive. Focusing on four modalities of media embodiment—the performative body, the device body, and the implied and the implicated body—the chapter offers conceptual tools to account for the discontents, the malfunctions, and other generally overlooked existential dimensions of media memory.

The last contribution to this section of the book testifies to the persistence of tensions between digital and nondigital media in the contemporary media ecology. Brian Johnsrud's "Metaphorical Memories of the Medieval Crusades after 9/11" explores the transmedial circulation—as well as the resistance to such circulation—of crusader analogies in the post-9/11 media ecology. Focusing on the movement of key crusader analogies across academic and popular historiography through different venues, media, and platforms to describe the wars in Iraq and Afghanistan, Johnsrud analyzes how the widespread academic condemnation of such comparisons has had the effect of marginalizing them. Eventually, digital media allowed popular voices to establish an alternative historical authority, which, in a surprising twist, created opportunities for conspiratorial claims to migrate to traditional realms of historical authority, such as academic historiography. Johnsrud's chapter responds to the need for a fine-grained and flexible study of media assemblages as theorized in the other chapters in this section. By touching on the question of (challenges to) disciplinary authority, it at the same time anticipates the question of mnemonic mobility and disciplinary identity that takes center stage in the last section of the book.

TRANSDISCIPLINARY MEMORY

As the previous sections of this introduction have amply demonstrated, it is by now a commonplace that memory can be regarded as not just a property of individual minds and brains but as taking place in social interaction, shaped by political circumstances, informed by different cultural traditions, and enabled by evolving media technologies. Hence, an integrative understanding of memory drawing on various disciplines and areas of expertise seems called for. As Astrid Erll points out, over the past three decades, memory has emerged as "a genuinely transdisciplinary phenomenon whose functioning cannot really be understood through examination from one single perspective" (*Memory in Culture* 38). Memory studies is an area of inquiry that spans the humanities, social sciences, and natural sciences, involving such diverse disciplines as history, sociology, psychology, philosophy, literary studies, media studies, the arts, anthropology, architecture, museology, and neuroscience. The contributions to the last section of the book explore to what extent the recent emphasis on the mobility of memory enables a recalibration of the relations between several of these fields and disciplines.

Seeing signs of growing convergence, Erll observes that "the disciplines of memory studies are steadily moving towards one another, and scholars are increasingly interested in the possibilities offered by interdisciplinary exchange" (*Memory in Culture* 38). Landmark moments in this evolution were the launch in 2008 of the journal *Memory Studies,* which offers a platform for cross-disciplinary dialogue and whose contributors invoke a wide variety of traditions and frameworks, and the publication of field-defining collections and surveys such as Jeffrey K. Olick, Vered Vinitzky-Seroussi, and Daniel Levy's *The Collective Memory Reader;* Erll and Ansgar Nünning's *Cultural Memory Studies: An International and Interdisciplinary Handbook;* and Erll's *Memory in Culture.* Other indications of the manifestation of memory studies as a fundamentally interdisciplinary field are the establishment of research initiatives such as the Center for Interdisciplinary Memory Research at the University of Flensburg, Germany, directed by Harald Welzer, and the Interdisciplinary Memory Group at the New School for Social Research, as well as the creation of academic programs such as the Luce Program in Individual and Collective Memory at Washington University in St. Louis, which offers students the opportunity to study with faculty from a wide range of disciplines.

The institutionalization of these multifaceted approaches reflects Andreas Huyssen's contention that "memory is one of those elusive topics we all think we have a handle on. But as soon as we try to define it, it starts slipping and sliding, eluding attempts to grasp it either culturally, sociologically, or scientifically" (*Present Pasts* 3). Accepting that such hermeneutic slipperiness demands the development of adaptive and innovative methodologies, the aforementioned initiatives embrace memory studies' emergence as "a non-paradigmatic, transdisciplinary, centerless enterprise" (Olick and Robbins 105). However, some critics remain more skeptical of the variegated nature of the field. According to Olick, for example, the "interdisciplinary integration of memory studies" envisaged by Erll (*Memory in Culture* 175) largely remains at the level of aspiration rather than reality:

> Interdisciplinarity is a concept that has never really fulfilled its promise, even in this most "trans-disciplinary" field. We all write a lot about how we need to take the work of other disciplines seriously, but rarely does this go beyond reading and citation … Actual cross-disciplinary research, however, has been much rarer than affirmations about its necessity and desirability … We need to think more about genuine interdisciplinary cooperation, cooperation that is beyond the level of mutual referencing. (23–24)

A similar concern is expressed by Adam D. Brown and his colleagues, who question whether scholarly meetings promising interdisciplinary approaches to memory and other such attempts at collaboration across disciplinary lines do not "more often result in multidisciplinarity, rather than interdisciplinarity, in which scholars are exposed to other disciplines' perspectives, but little is transferred from one academic discipline to the next" (118). While these are important caveats, the three chapters in this section go some way, we believe, toward redeeming the unfulfilled promise of genuine interdisciplinarity in memory research. Conceiving of memory studies as a site of both conversation and contestation between disciplines, they show how actor-network theory, ecocritical, and digital humanities approaches and methodologies can inform and enrich memory research.

Frauke Wiegand's essay "The Agency of Memory Objects: Tracing Memories of Soweto at Regina Mundi Church" enriches our conceptual repertoire for thinking about contemporary constellations of memory. It does so in an explicitly transcultural and transmedial context, as it analyzes the acts of memory taking place in the small, almost hidden exhibition space of the Regina Mundi Church in Soweto, South Africa, home to the photographic exhibition "The Story of Soweto." Alongside iconic photographs by well-known apartheid and postapartheid photographers, the exhibition walls are full of personal inscriptions—written messages, tags, and small poems in a range of South African and other languages, signed and dated, overwriting or supplementing each other, and, importantly, constituting a popular motif for visitors' snapshots. The essay maps this complex and ever-changing media assemblage by introducing actor-network theory to the field of memory studies. Developing the idea that objects and images that leave a trace can act as mediators of memory, the chapter sheds light on the different life cycles of memory objects and their multiple mediations.

In "Cultural Memory Studies in the Epoch of the Anthropocene," Richard Crownshaw engages the small but growing body of research on the relationship between oil and culture that has emerged together with the increased attention to the notion of the Anthropocene. The chapter demonstrates that petrofiction studies, in particular, has drawn on postcolonialism, ecocriticism, and the transnational turn in literary studies to map the global and environmental implications of oil production, transit, and consumption, and of energy (in)securities and dependencies. By considering the often surprising ways in which oil can prompt acts of cultural remembrance and forgetting, Crownshaw's chapter aims to draw the field of memory studies into the orbit of these concerns. It explores "petromemory" in the postoil science fiction of James Howard Kunstler. Kunstler's *World Made by Hand* remembers (from the future) oil in its absence, emphasizing the role it played in the ecological catastrophes it projects and constructing a postoil imaginary to explore the possibilities of thinking beyond a melancholic attachment to oil. This case study finds that national or humanist frameworks of memory cannot contain the global or indeed planetary (geopolitical as well as ecological) implications of oil supply and exhaustion. Transdisciplinary engagement thus emerges as one way to begin the daunting task of mapping the novel planetary reality in which an ecologically attuned memory operates.

The globalizing force of the Anthropocene is only one of the developments that have recently expanded the scale of memory; the datafication of human life, which inscribes human behavior in databases that the human mind cannot begin to apprehend, is another one. Jessica K. Young's "'Filled with Words': Modeling the September 11 Digital Archive and the Utility of Digital Methods in the Study of Memory" confronts the possibilities and liabilities digital media pose for the collection, preservation, and dissemination of individual and collective memories. Given the perceived limitations of traditional humanistic methodologies for studying the massive amounts of information collected across digital media, this chapter asks what the tools engineered by the emergent interdisciplinary field of digital humanities can offer the study of a large corpus of testimonies collected in online user-generated archives and specifically what these tools can add to the methodological analysis of a cultural memory of trauma. As a case study, it uses a form of "distant reading" called Latent Dirichlet Allocation (LDA) topic modeling to examine the 12,500 personal stories collected and shared by the September 11 Digital Archive. LDA topic modeling allows memory scholars to examine how certain topics, such as media dissemination, patriotism, and the historicization of the events, capture the imagination of responders at certain points in time, turning the mass of data into a meaningful engagement with cultural memory and decisively enriching the repertoire of memory studies of the future.

Foregrounding the transcultural, transgenerational, transmedial, and transdisciplinary dynamics of memory and tracing numerous intersections and divergences between these vectors of mobility, this volume seeks to provoke closer attention to memory's unbounded properties. At stake in this endeavor, we believe, is the challenge to conceive of memory outside of normative cultural, generational, medial, and disciplinary frameworks without losing sight of the important particularities that attend local and generational articulations of memory and continue to do so even in a globalized and digitized world. Cumulatively, the essays in this book argue for an acknowledgment of the complexity and plurality of mnemonic movement, and they warn against the temptation to elide the role that hegemonic institutions, such as the nation-state, continue to play in contemporary memorative practice, to occlude the ways in which the changing media and technologies of memory shape our understanding of the past, or to neglect the elisions and biases that can arise from oversubscription to particular disciplinary epistemologies. In so doing, *Memory Unbound* argues that memory studies must adapt its methodologies to interrogate and accommodate the changing political, economic, technological, and environmental climate of the global age and the manifold social, political, and ecological challenges that accompany these developments. Moreover, as many of the contributors to this collection propose, this work must remain sensitive to the inequitable distribution of power and resources and the role that memorative discourses may play in ongoing struggles for justice, equality, and varying forms of (political, cultural, or juridical) representation.

This volume has its roots in a series of events on new directions in memory studies that were held in Ghent, Stockholm, London, and Maastricht in recent years: a lecture series for Ghent University's Internationalization@ Home program titled "Memory Unbound" in 2012; the second edition of the summer school organized by the Mnemonics network—an international collaborative initiative for graduate education in the field of memory studies—on the same topic in Ghent in 2013; the third edition of the Mnemonics summer school, which was titled "Media of Memory" and took place in Stockholm the following year; and three linked workshops on "The Natural History of Memory" that were held in London, Ghent, and Maastricht in 2014 and 2015. As the collection has evolved, it has remained important to us to recognize these origins, bringing together many of the leading scholars of memory with emerging voices in the field and exposing established methodologies and models of memory to new perspectives and approaches. Consisting of twelve specially commissioned essays, *Memory Unbound* transforms our current knowledge of the movements of memory across cultures, generations, media, and disciplines and sets an ambitious agenda for the future of memory studies.

Lucy Bond is a lecturer in English literature at the University of Westminster and a member of the London Cultural Memory Consortium. She is the author of *Frames of Memory after 9/11: Culture, Criticism, Politics, and Law* (Palgrave Macmillan, 2015) and a coeditor (with Jessica Rapson) of *The Transcultural Turn: Interrogating Memory between and beyond Borders* (De Gruyter, 2014). Her research examines the biopolitics of contemporary American memorial culture in memorative practice and theory.

Stef Craps is an associate professor of English literature at Ghent University, where he directs the Cultural Memory Studies Initiative. He is the author of *Postcolonial Witnessing: Trauma Out of Bounds* (Palgrave Macmillan, 2013; paperback 2015) and *Trauma and Ethics in the Novels of Graham Swift: No Short-Cuts to Salvation* (Sussex Academic Press, 2005) and has guest edited special issues of *Criticism: A Quarterly for Literature and the Arts* (2011; with Michael Rothberg) and *Studies in the Novel* (2008; with Gert Buelens) on the topics of, respectively, transcultural negotiations of Holocaust memory and postcolonial trauma novels.

Pieter Vermeulen is an assistant professor of American and comparative literature at the University of Leuven. He is the author of *Geoffrey Hartman: Romanticism after the Holocaust* (Continuum/Bloomsbury, 2010; paperback 2012) and *Contemporary Literature and the End of the Novel: Creature, Affect, Form* (Palgrave Macmillan, 2015) and a coeditor of, most recently, *Institutions of World Literature: Writing, Translation, Markets* (Routledge, 2015; with Stefan

Helgesson) and a special issue of the *European Journal of English Studies* (2015; with Virginia Richter) on creatureliness.

WORKS CITED

Anderson, Benedict. *Imagined Communities: Reflections on the Origin and Spread of Nationalism.* London: Verso, 2006.

Assmann, Aleida, and Sebastian Conrad, eds. *Memory in a Global Age: Discourses, Practices, and Trajectories.* Basingstoke: Palgrave Macmillan, 2010.

Assmann, Jan. "Communicative and Cultural Memory." *Cultural Memory Studies: An International and Interdisciplinary Handbook.* Ed. Astrid Erll and Ansgar Nünning. Berlin: De Gruyter, 2008. 109–88.

———. *Cultural Memory and Early Civilization: Writing, Remembrance, and Political Imagination.* Cambridge: Cambridge University Press, 2011.

Bell, Duncan. "Mythscapes: Memory, Mythology, and National Identity." *British Journal of Sociology* 54.1 (2003): 63–81.

Bolter, Jay David, and Richard Grusin, eds. *Remediation: Understanding New Media.* Cambridge: MIT Press, 1999.

Bond, Lucy. *Frames of Memory after 9/11: Culture, Criticism, Politics, and Law.* Basingstoke: Palgrave Macmillan, 2015.

Bond, Lucy, and Jessica Rapson, eds. *The Transcultural Turn: Interrogating Memory between and beyond Borders.* Berlin: De Gruyter, 2014.

Brown, Adam D., et al. "Introduction: Is an Interdisciplinary Field of Memory Studies Possible?" *International Journal of Politics, Culture, and Society* 22 (2009): 117–24.

Butler, Judith. *Precarious Life: The Powers of Mourning and Violence.* London: Verso, 2004.

Craps, Stef. *Postcolonial Witnessing: Trauma Out of Bounds.* Basingstoke: Palgrave Macmillan, 2013.

Craps, Stef, and Michael Rothberg. "Introduction: Transcultural Negotiations of Holocaust Memory." *Criticism: A Quarterly for Literature and the Arts* 53.4 (2011): 517–21.

Crownshaw, Rick, ed. *Transcultural Memory.* New York: Routledge, 2014.

De Cesari, Chiara, and Ann Rigney, eds. *Transnational Memory: Circulation, Articulation, Scales.* Berlin: De Gruyter, 2014.

Erll, Astrid. "Literature, Film, and the Mediality of Cultural Memory." *A Companion to Cultural Memory Studies.* Ed. Astrid Erll and Ansgar Nünning. Berlin: De Gruyter, 2010. 389–98.

———. *Memory in Culture.* Trans. Sara B. Young. Basingstoke: Palgrave Macmillan, 2011.

———. "Travelling Memory." *Parallax* 17.4 (2011): 4–18.

Erll, Astrid, and Ansgar Nünning, eds. *Cultural Memory Studies: An International and Interdisciplinary Handbook.* Berlin: De Gruyter, 2008.

Erll, Astrid, and Ann Rigney. "Introduction: Cultural Memory and Its Dynamics." *Mediation, Remediation, and the Dynamics of Cultural Memory.* Ed. Astrid Erll and Ann Rigney. Berlin: De Gruyter, 2009. 1–11.

Fine, Ellen. "The Absent Memory: The Act of Writing in Post-Holocaust French Literature." *Writing and the Holocaust.* Ed. Berel Lang. New York: Holmes and Meier, 1988. 41–57.

Garde-Hansen, Joanne, Andrew Hoskins, and Anna Reading, eds. *Save as ... Digital Memories.* Basingstoke: Palgrave Macmillan, 2009.

Gilroy, Paul. *The Black Atlantic: Modernity and Double Consciousness.* Cambridge: Harvard University Press, 1997.

Halbwachs, Maurice. *On Collective Memory.* Trans. Lewis A. Coser. Chicago: University of Chicago Press, 1992.

——. *Les Cadres sociaux de la mémoire.* Ed. Gérard Namer. Paris: Albin Michel, 1994.

Hirsch, Marianne. *Family Frames: Photography, Narrative and Postmemory.* Cambridge: Harvard University Press, 1997.

——. "Family Picture: *Maus*, Mourning, and Post-Memory." *Discourse* 15.2 (1992–93): 3–29.

——. *The Generation of Postmemory: Writing and Visual Culture after the Holocaust.* New York: Columbia University Press, 2012.

——. "Projected Memory: Holocaust Photographs in Personal and Public Fantasy." *Acts of Memory: Cultural Recall in the Present.* Ed. Mieke Bal, Jonathan Crewe, and Leo Spitzer. Hanover: University of New England Press, 1999. 3–23.

——. "Surviving Images: Holocaust Photography and the Work of Postmemory." *Yale Journal of Criticism* 12.1 (2001): 5–37.

Hodgkin, Katharine, and Susannah Radstone. "Patterning the National Past." *Memory, History, Nation: Contested Pasts.* Ed. Katharine Hodgkin and Susannah Radstone. New Brunswick: Transaction, 2006. 169–74.

Hoskins, Andrew. "Media, Memory, Metaphor: Remembering and the Connective Turn." *Parallax* 17.4 (2011): 19–31.

——. "The Mediatisation of Memory." *Save as ... Digital Memories.* Ed. Joanne Garde-Hansen, Andrew Hoskins, and Anna Reading. Basingstoke: Palgrave Macmillan, 2009. 27–43.

Hungerford, Amy. *The Holocaust of Texts: Genocide, Literature, and Personification.* Chicago: University of Chicago Press, 2003.

Huyssen, Andreas. *Present Pasts: Urban Palimpsests and the Politics of Memory.* Stanford: Stanford University Press, 2003.

——. *Twilight Memories: Marking Time in a Culture of Amnesia.* New York: Routledge, 1995.

Kansteiner, Wulf. *In Pursuit of German Memory: History, Television, and Politics after Auschwitz.* Athens: University of Ohio Press, 2006.

Klein, Kerwin Lee. "On the Emergence of *Memory* in Historical Discourse." *Representations* 69 (2000): 127–50.

Landsberg, Alison. *Prosthetic Memory: The Transformation of American Remembrance in the Age of Mass Culture.* New York: Columbia University Press, 2004.

Levy, Daniel, and Natan Sznaider. *The Holocaust and Memory in the Global Age.* Philadelphia: Temple University Press, 2005.

McGlothlin, Erin. *Second-Generation Holocaust Literature: Legacies of Survival and Perpetration.* Rochester: Camden House, 2006.

Moses, A. Dirk. "Empire, Colony, Genocide: Keywords and the Philosophy of History." *Empire, Colony, Genocide: Conquest, Occupation, and Subaltern Resistance in World History.* Ed. A. Dirk Moses. New York: Berghahn, 2008. 3–54.

Neiger, Motti, Oren Meyers, and Eyal Zandberg. "On Media Memory: Editors' Introduction." *On Media Memory: Collective Memory in a New Media Age.* Ed. Mottio Neiger, Oren Meyers, and Eyal Zandberg. Basingstoke: Palgrave Macmillan, 2011. 1–24.

Nixon, Rob. *Slow Violence and the Environmentalism of the Poor.* Cambridge: Harvard University Press, 2011.

Nora, Pierre. "Between Memory and History: *Les Lieux de mémoire.*" *Representations* 26 (1989): 7–25.

Olick, Jeffrey K. "'Collective Memory': A Memoir and Prospect." *Memory Studies* 1.1 (2008): 19–25.

Olick, Jeffrey K., and Joyce Robbins. "Social Memory Studies: From 'Collective Memory' to the Historical Sociology of Mnemonic Practices." *Annual Review of Sociology* 24 (1998): 105–40.

Olick, Jeffrey K., Vered Vinitzky-Seroussi, and Daniel Levy, eds. *The Collective Memory Reader.* Oxford: Oxford University Press, 2011.

Parikka, Jussi. *What Is Media Archeology?* Cambridge: Polity, 2012.

Raczymow, Henri. "Memory Shot Through with Holes." Trans. Alan Astro. *Yale French Studies* 85 (1994): 98–106.

Reading, Anna. "Globalisation and Digital Memory: Globital Memory's Six Dynamics." *On Media Memory: Collective Memory in a New Media Age.* Ed. Motti Neiger, Oren Meyers, and Eyal Zandberg. Basingstoke: Palgrave Macmillan, 2011. 241–52.

Rigney, Ann. "The Dynamics of Remembrance: Texts between Monumentality and Morphing." *A Companion to Cultural Memory Studies.* Ed. Astrid Erll and Ansgar Nünning. Berlin: De Gruyter, 2010. 345–53.

Rothberg, Michael. *Multidirectional Memory: Remembering the Holocaust in the Age of Decolonization.* Stanford: Stanford University Press, 2009.

Schwab, Gabriele. *Haunting Legacies: Violent Histories and Transgenerational Trauma.* New York: Columbia University Press, 2010.

Sierp, Aline. *History, Memory, and Trans-European Identity: Unifying Divisions.* New York: Routledge, 2014.

Silverman, Max. *Palimpsestic Memory: The Holocaust and Colonialism in French and Francophone Fiction and Film.* New York: Berghahn, 2013.

Simpson, David. *9/11: The Culture of Commemoration.* Chicago: Chicago University Press, 2006.

Sturken, Marita. *Tangled Memories: The AIDS Epidemic, the Vietnam War, and the Politics of Remembering.* Berkeley: University of California Press, 1997.

Tomsky, Terri. "From Sarajevo to 9/11: Travelling Memory and the Trauma Economy." *Parallax* 17.4 (2011): 49–60.

van Alphen, Ernst. "Second-Generation Testimony, Transmission of Trauma, and Postmemory." *Poetics Today* 27.2 (2006): 473–88.

van Dijck, José. *The Culture of Connectivity: A Critical History of Social Media*. Oxford: Oxford University Press, 2013.

Weissman, Gary. *Fantasies of Witnessing: Postwar Efforts to Experience the Holocaust*. Ithaca: Cornell University Press, 2004.

Part I

Transcultural Memory

Chapter 1

Staging Shared Memory

Je Veux voir and *L'Empreinte de l'ange*

Max Silverman

PREFACE

A man who looks through an open window from outside never sees as much as the same man looking directly at a closed window. There is no object more profound, more mysterious, more fertile, darker yet more dazzling than a window lit by a candle. What we can see in sunlight is always less interesting than what takes place behind the pane. In this dark and luminous hole life lives, dreams and suffers.

Beyond the waves of rooftops I can see an old woman, already wrinkled, poor, permanently hunched over something, who never leaves her room. From her face, her clothes, her manner, from virtually nothing at all I have recreated this woman's story, or rather her legend, and sometimes I weep when I recount it to myself.

If this had been a poor old man, I would have done the same with his life just as easily.

And I go to bed, proud of having lived and suffered in others than myself. Perhaps you will say to me: "Are you sure that this story is true?" What does it matter what outside reality is if it has helped me to live, to feel that I am a living being and to know what this is like.[1]

It might seem perverse to place a text that contains nothing explicit concerning memory in the preface to an essay on that subject. However, I am using the prose poem "Les Fenêtres" (The Windows) by the nineteenth-century French poet Charles Baudelaire for this purpose, as the central premise of the poem—the imaginative and empathetic encounter with the other—is crucial to the work of memory that I wish to discuss in the film *Je Veux voir* (2008, I Want to See), directed by the Lebanese filmmakers Joana Hadjithomas and Khalil Joreige, and the novel *L'Empreinte de l'ange* (1998, The Mark of the Angel) by the Canadian writer Nancy Huston. I have chosen these two works because central to both is an encounter with the other that disperses memory across time, space, the individual, and the collective and reforms it in surprising ways.

I will argue that the transcultural encounters that take place in these works in the present (of filming, of writing)—a process that I will term the "staging" of shared memory—are constitutive of the creative act of memory. I will also suggest that the staging of memory in these two works transforms the initial impulse behind "Les Fenêtres" to create a different ethics of memory. By disrupting the sovereignty of the self through its encounter with the other, this ethics of shared memory is neither voyeuristic nor solipsistic, located neither within the individual nor within the community, but open-ended and ambivalent. In this way, this essay foregrounds the ethics and aesthetics of staging as crucial aspects of transcultural memory processes; it underlines the performative dimension of the articulations that memory studies has come to describe under such rubrics as multidirectional, prosthetic, or, in my own case, palimpsestic memory.

JE VEUX VOIR: IMAGINATION AND ETHICS

The film *Je Veux voir* was made in the aftermath of the war in Lebanon of 2006.[2] Part road movie, part documentary, it pairs the icon of French cinema, Catherine Deneuve, with the Lebanese actor Rabih Mroué. Catherine is in Lebanon for a gala evening in Beirut hosted by the French ambassador. But she expresses a desire to go to the south of Lebanon because, as she says, "Je veux voir" (I want to see). Mroué, who has never met Deneuve before, is both himself (the actor Rabih Mroué) and her driver from Beirut to the frontier with Israel via the village, now destroyed, where his grandmother used to live and where he spent his summers as a young boy. The film finishes at the end of the day of the road trip back in Beirut at the gala.

As in most road movies, the comfort zones of the protagonists are disturbed by the encounter between different lives and, as the film's title suggests, different ways of seeing. We first see Catherine looking out at Beirut through a window, the screen through which the city outside is refracted, while saying "Je veux voir" (see Illustration 1.1). She expresses a desire to break out of the screen to see some other reality of Lebanon behind the

Illustration 1.1. *Je Veux voir.* Screen capture, DVD (Soda Pictures Ltd, 2010).

stereotyped images: "We've only seen images on the television which don't seem real. I want to see" (On n'a vu des images qu'à la télévision et ça semble irréel. J'ai envie de voir.). Yet, as the pair drive through the suburbs of Beirut and then out of the city to the village where Rabih's grandmother used to live, it becomes clear that it is not a question of her view of Lebanon, dependent on TV images (the "unreal"), simply giving way to a more authentic view (the "real") as she begins to see through Rabih's eyes and penetrate "real" Lebanon.

Thankfully, the film refuses to lapse into a stark binary opposition between stereotypes of Lebanon exposed by the "authentic" Lebanese look. When Catherine says "I want to see" Rabih mimics her—"I also want to see" (Moi aussi, j'ai envie de voir), he says—showing that this is as much a journey for him as for her. Rather, there is, for both, an interaction between different stories, perspectives and voices that, by overlaying one with another so that the trace of one is always to be found in the other, denies the singularity of each and, in the process, produces a hybrid and ambivalent vision. In "Les Fenêtres," Baudelaire describes the transformative power for the self of imaginatively placing oneself in the position of the other. In *Je Veux voir,* seeing is, similarly, transformed through the relation between one way of looking and another.

A moving scene in the film centers on Rabih's fascination with Catherine's portrayal of "Belle de Jour" (Séverine Serizy) in Luis Buñuel's famous 1967 film of the same name. Clearly, *Je Veux voir,* like Buñuel's film, wants to situate "seeing" in that hinterland between "the real" and the imagined (or fantasy). Deneuve herself appears both as star (photographed with United Nations soldiers at a checkpoint on the southern border with Israel, observed by men in the street as the car passes, fêted at the gala back in Beirut, with cameras clicking as she enters) and as the "real" Catherine, so that one can never tell how real her fears are (constantly reminding Rabih to put on his seat belt, terrified as Israeli planes break the sound barrier as they fly overhead in southern Lebanon) or how much she is still acting (she is, of course, always aware that the camera is on her).

But Rabih is also an actor, so that what seems to be the authentic anguish he feels searching unsuccessfully through the rubble of his grandmother's village for traces of her former house is again tempered by the fact that it is difficult to disentangle his affective life and memories from the character he is portraying in the film. His relationship with his country and his past (and his own self) is similar, in this sense, to the relationship between Catherine and her film persona, a tension that is dramatized in *Belle de jour* through the play between the real (Séverine) and fantasy (Belle de Jour), the conscious and the unconscious.[3]

The indirectness of the telling of stories and ways of seeing and the transformative nature of the encounter with the other are beautifully dramatized when Rabih recites Séverine's famous monologue in *Belle de jour*, first in French and then in Arabic, so that her persona is doubled by his, her words are spoken by him, and the original French is translated into Arabic. These mediations and translations do not so much ruin the original (lost forever for both of them) as allow it to return in a transformed way (like the traumatic past of war-torn Lebanon).

He asks her whether, in reciting the speech, he should say "mon chéri" or "ma chérie" (in fact, he has said "ma chérie"), to which she replies that if he is speaking her lines as her, then he must say "mon chéri" as the speech in the film is addressed to her husband Pierre. By placing himself in the position of the other (as the Arabic version does to the French), he not only displaces his own subject position but also that of Catherine as she hears her lines spoken in a way that she has never heard before. "It's lovely like that" (Ça semble très joli comme ça), she says when he has spoken her words in Arabic, a language that she does not understand and that is completely strange to her.

If her way of seeing depends on seeing through his eyes, his way of seeing (as I have suggested) similarly depends on seeing through her eyes. He has himself feared going back to his grandmother's village and to his own past, because, with all the destruction in the country, "everyone was there to take pictures" (tout le monde était là pour prendre des images), making him feel like "a tourist in my own country" (un touriste dans mon propre pays).

However, he adds, it will be different now "because of the film" (à cause du film) and because "I will appear with you in the images" (je serai là avec vous pour paraître dans les images). "It will be different with you" (Avec vous, ça sera différent), he says.

As in Alain Resnais's *Hiroshima mon amour* (1959), of which the encounter between Catherine and Rabih is profoundly reminiscent, the presence of the other is a prerequisite to the displacement of subject position central to a transformed vision.[4] In her influential book *Unclaimed Experience,* Cathy Caruth proposes (specifically in relation to Resnais's film) that one traumatic event cannot be told in terms of its singularity and specificity but only indirectly through other stories (27). A "truer" reading of history may therefore be dependent on showing "through other stories" rather than on the "purity" and "authenticity" of firsthand experience.

Yet, it is not simply a question of a more "truthful" testimony (and, as Baudelaire says in "Les Fenêtres," even if truth is attainable, it is not the most important issue at stake here). In his book *Diasporas of the Mind,* Bryan Cheyette reminds us that, in her analysis of Adolf Eichmann at his trial in Jerusalem in 1961, Hannah Arendt "noted Eichmann's inability to 'think from the standpoint of somebody else'" and his "'lack of imagination'" (10). It was this lack of imagination—and hence of affect and empathy—that allowed Eichmann to think of the transport of Jews to the death camps in technical rather than human terms.

The inability to "think from the standpoint of somebody else" and the failure of imagination are therefore, ultimately, human and ethical, rather than merely epistemological, questions. In her monologue in *Belle de jour* recounted by Rabih over a black screen, Séverine explains how close she feels to Pierre ("I have never felt so close to you" [je ne me suis jamais sentie aussi proche de toi]) after having adopted the new persona of "Belle de Jour." This is a closeness "which has nothing to do with pleasure. It's way beyond that" (qui n'a rien à voir avec le plaisir. C'est bien au-delà). Imagination—dulled by the object-driven consumerism of bourgeois society and only accessed through Séverine's fantasy persona locked in her unconscious—is at the heart of the transformative process of empathy with the other.

In *Je Veux voir,* different viewpoints straddle each other to release imagination from the anesthetizing grip of the superficial image. Seated in the car as they drive through Beirut, Catherine and Rabih are filmed through the windshield, but their faces inside the car are sometimes overlaid with reflections of ruined buildings in the streets outside (see Illustration 1.2). At other times, the camera is situated in the back seat of the car so that the shots are rear views of their heads but with the face of Rabih also visible in the rear-view mirror. At the gala back in Beirut at the end of the day, Catherine is

Illustration 1.2. *Je Veux voir.* Screen capture, DVD (Soda Pictures Ltd, 2010).

looking past the assembled official guests, including the French ambassador to Lebanon, searching for Rabih ("I'm waiting for my friend" [J'attends mon ami], she explains) while Rabih is filmed looking out at her in a final encounter between their two looks.

I suggest that the overlaying of one look with another leads to neither the conflation of looks nor the maintenance of their distance one from the other but instead brings them together to create a new vision, displacing the singularity of each vision across different sites, times, and points of view. In this sense, the most personal memory (for example, Rabih's sense of loss and anguish at not being able to locate his grandmother's house amid the rubble) can never be unequivocally related to a specific and singular event or place but is always indirectly implicated in (or contaminated by) other regimes of sense and other ways of seeing (not the least of which is Catherine's anxious looks at him as he searches the devastated site).

More generally, the individual stories of Catherine and Rabih and the collective stories of Europe and the Middle East (not to mention the implicit commentary throughout on the relationship between Beirut and southern Lebanon) are brought together in such a way that the personal and the political, memory and history, and the past and the present are, similarly, denied their own specificity and are caught up in a process that Jean-Michel Frodon has felicitously called the "dynamic of the trace" (dynamique de la trace; 60). The story of the city can be told only through its hidden relationship with the south and "the West" (and, of course, with Israel), and the story of the present can be told only through its buried past—with making visible the loss and destruction that the renovators are quickly covering over—as the traces of one are always in the other. Rabih's question "But Catherine, will you come back?" (Mais Catherine, est-ce que tu reviendras?) is thus a possible indication of his need for Catherine's presence as a means of providing a different way of seeing so as to go beyond the new surface of the reconstructed city.

In a stunning sequence filmed by the sea, where the remains of buildings from the war-torn suburbs of Beirut are being taken in trucks to be destroyed, the camera (hovering between the point of view of the two sets of eyes in the car as it passes and some indeterminate space of its own) pans slowly across mounds of tangled rubble—diggers and bulldozers looking like prehistoric monsters—as Rabih describes, in Arabic, the slow descent of all the remains to the bottom of the sea, to be forgotten, to disappear without trace (see Illustration 1.3). But the film's intervention in this process of disappearance allows the traces to linger and be read through a complex prism of different looks, times, and sites. Film here is a performative act as it stages encounters and reworks memories in the present.[5] *Je Veux voir* does not simply record the relationship between a complex past and the present or the visible and the invisible; it actually stages this process creatively in the "now" of its enunciation.

In the destroyed village of Rabih's grandmother, Rabih cannot even get his bearings amid the rubble. "There was a road here" (Il y avait une route), he says; "The road seems to have disappeared. I don't know where the house is. Everything has changed" (On dirait que la route a disparu. Je ne sais où est la maison. Tout a changé). This is where he spent his childhood, but he

Illustration 1.3. *Je Veux voir.* Screen capture, DVD (Soda Pictures Ltd, 2010).

says, "I don't recognize anything" (Je ne reconnais rien). However, the film has established a way of seeing that seems to transcend Rabih's incredulity (or, at least, add a further layer to it), not to restore his lost past in a sort of Proustian epiphany but as a way of reading inside and outside, the one and the other, presence and absence at one and the same time.[6]

In *Hiroshima mon amour* "lui" famously says to "elle" that she "saw nothing in Hiroshima. Nothing" (tu n'as rien vu à Hiroshima. Rien), to which "elle" replies that she "saw everything. Everything" (J'ai tout vu. Tout). The encounter between the two opens up a new space for seeing for both, one that contains the seeing of both everything and nothing. Similarly, in *Je Veux voir,* "opening one's eyes" means just such an ambivalent encounter with the traces of other stories.

L'EMPREINTE DE L'ANGE: A BENJAMINIAN ENCOUNTER

The action in Nancy Huston's novel *L'Empreinte de l'ange* (translated as *The Mark of the Angel*) takes place between 1957 and 1961 but moves backward and forward in time too. In May 1957, Saffie, a twenty-year-old German woman, arrives in Paris having suffered some sort of traumatic past that has left her in a state of blankness and lack of affectivity. She meets a French flautist, Raphael, whom she marries and with whom she has a child, Emil, while remaining all the while in her state of virtual catatonia. It is only when she starts a passionate affair with Andràs, a Hungarian Jew living in the Marais district of Paris having fled the Russian invasion of his country the year before, that Saffie's wall of blankness breaks down and the past comes flooding back, along with her sexual desire.

She and her mother had been raped by the liberating Russian army at the end of the war. Her mother committed suicide shortly after, her brother then went mad and was committed to an asylum in 1953, and finally, in 1955, she learned of her beloved father's complicity in the Final Solution. Andràs, for his part, lost his father, his two brothers, his uncle, and most of his extended family to the Nazis and is, at present, heavily engaged in pro-FLN (Front de Libération Nationale [National Liberation Front]) activities as part of the Algerian struggle for independence. Although Andràs is more open about his past than the repressed Saffie, the details of their respective traumas are, nevertheless, only revealed gradually and in the intimacy of their relationship. The action traces their affair through the next few years, up to the events of 17 October 1961 (the date of the murder by the French police of at least 120 demonstrating Algerians in Paris) in which Andràs's close friend Rachid, an FLN militant, is killed.

Like Didier Daeninckx's *Meurtres pour mémoire* (1984), *L'Empreinte de l'ange* treats the interconnections between the Holocaust and the Algerian War (and other instances of extreme violence and suffering). In 1999, just a year after the publication of *L'Empreinte de l'ange*, the Franco-Algerian writer Leila Sebbar, close friend and collaborator of Nancy Huston, published *La Seine était rouge* (The Seine Was Red), which deals with a similar imbrication of histories of racialized violence. For Andràs it is imperative to see the connections between one war and another and, hence, to tell the story of one war through another. This is in contrast to the naïve Saffie, who not only has repressed her own traumatic past but is also unaware of continuing violence in the present in the form of the Algerian struggle for independence and who believes that "war" means World War II and is thus over. At one point, Andràs shouts:

> No! The war is not over! ... From '40 to '44 France lets Germany fuck her in the ass and she's ashamed, so in '46 she starts a war in Indochina. In '54 she loses this one too, the Viets fuck her in the ass and she is ashamed, so three months later she starts a war in Algeria. You don't know? (106)

> *C'est pas fini la guerre! ... Entre 1940 et 1944 la France se laisse enculer par l'Allemagne, elle a honte alors en 1946 elle commence la guerre à l'Indochine. En 1954 elle la perd, les Viets l'enculent, elle a honte alors trois mois après elle commence la guerre à l'Algérie. Tu sais pas?* (112)[7]

At times it might appear in the novel as though the connections made between different sites and times of extreme violence demonstrate a cyclical view of history in which the same structure is repeated over and over again. Andràs's direct comparison between camps in the past and the present appears to suggest this understanding of history:

> I know what's going on! Already, near to Paris, there are concentration camps for Muslims! ... *It's still happening!* The people who arrest the Muslims now, they're the same Scheisskopfe that deport the Jews in '42! The French generals who torture in Algeria now, they learn their job here—with the Gestapo! (185–86)

> *Je sais ce qui se passe! Autour de Paris, déjà, les camps de concentration pour les musulmans! ... Ça continue! Les rafles, les ratonnades, c'est les mêmes Scheisskopfe qui les font! Les gens qui torturent à l'Algérie, ils ont appris leur métier ici, avec la Gestapo!* (186–87)

However, despite Andràs's claim, history in the novel is not simply represented as a continual repetition of the same violence. As in *Je Veux voir*, at the heart of *L'Empreinte de l'ange* is the way in which the connection between different times and sites established through the imaginative and affective investment in the story of the other transforms memory and history into a hybrid and ambivalent process. One memory (Saffie's experience in World War II) can only return through another (Andràs's experience in World War II and the Algerian War of Independence), not as simple repetition but as a condensation of traces of different times and places. As Lorraine Day suggests, "Both need to work on past terrors that are associated with the legacy of the other, and that cannot be borne, except perhaps through the capacity to share imaginatively and empathetically in the pain of the other (and of others)" (102).

Connections between different events do not simply result in a bland fusion but open up memory and history to the complex, tense, and unresolved relationship between similarity and difference, sometimes with disturbing effects. So, for example, although the imposition of curfew (for Jews during World War II and Algerians in Paris in October 1961) is presented by Andràs as simple repetition (it is only the victim who is different), it turns out to be a far more complicated process when Saffie's childhood memories in Germany are taken into account. Andràs proclaims:

> "Saffie, do you know what it means, a curfew?" Saffie does know but suspects that her German childhood memories might not be welcome in this context. "A curfew for Muslims. Only twenty years after the curfew for the Jews. Same thing! Same thing! Except 8:30pm for the Muslims and 8pm for the Jews." (184)

> *"Saffie tu sais ce que ça veut dire, un couvre-feu?" Saffie le sait, mais doute que ses souvenirs d'enfance allemande soient les bienvenus dans ce contexte. "Un couvre-feu rien que pour les musulmans. Vingt ans seulement après le couvre-feu pour les juifs. Pareil! Pareil! Sauf que huit heures et demie pour les musulmans et huit heures pour les juifs."* (185)

A similar discordant relationality characterizes the moment when Saffie describes her father's role in the gas chambers while she and Andràs are looking out over the shantytown of Nanterre and at the misery of the Algerians living there (179–181; 180–82). These are disturbing moments of intersection between memories of extreme violence due to the discontinuities and contradictions as well as the similarities between them. Rather than a simple repetition of the same across history, this treatment demonstrates that the stories relating to different characters and their sites of trauma tend to intersect on multiple levels in an indeterminate way.

The significance of the encounter between different temporal and spatial moments of trauma lies not in an understanding of history as cyclical but in the creative and transformative potential that is produced through the narrative staging of the encounter itself. If seeing is a performative act in *Je Veux voir,* then memory in *L'Empreinte de l'ange* is also a dynamic, illuminating, and open-ended process in the present. The treatment of the mark of the angel of the novel's title exemplifies the transformative and ambivalent nature of staging encounters between characters caught up in a history of camps. As Andràs runs his finger lightly down Saffie's face, he murmurs:

> "This is where the angel puts a finger on the baby's lips, just before it's born—*Sshh!* says the angel—and the baby forgets everything. All it learned before, up in paradise—forgotten. So it can come into the world innocent ... Without the angel," Andràs goes on, laughing "*who* wants to get born? Who could agree to come into all this shit? Ha?! Nobody! A lucky thing there's the angel!" (124)

> *"C'est ici ... où l'ange pose un doigt sur les lèvres du bébé, juste avant la naissance – Chut! – et l'enfant oublie tout. Tout ce qu'il a appris là-bas, avant, en paradis. Comme ça, il vient au monde innocent ..." Sinon, poursuit Andràs en riant, "qui veut naître? Qui accepte d'entrer dans cette merde? Ha?! Personne! On a besoin de l'ange!"* (128–29)

As described by Andràs, the mark of the angel is a mark of blissful forgetting—presumably forgetting the perfection of paradise; otherwise everything else would seem imperfect in comparison. However, the angel's mark is itself a trace of the past that has been erased and, as such, can be interpreted by Andràs (and the reader) as designating that absence. In this sense, then, the mark of the angel is ambivalent as a mark of presence and absence, remembering and forgetting, past and present (and future), and perfection (wholeness) and imperfection (catastrophe).

The angel appears one last time, in the epilogue. We have learned that, when Raphael became aware of the affair between Saffie and Andràs, he accidentally killed his son Emil and that Saffie disappeared the day after, never to reappear. In the epilogue we are now in the present, thirty-five years later. Raphael and Andràs, now old men, catch sight of each other by chance in a bar called Terminus nord (North Terminus) at the Gare du Nord. We read:

> You must have noticed this—how elderly people seem to recover an air of innocence. Merciful time comes to rub an eraser across their minds and bodies, blurring their distinctive traits, wiping out their memories—dissolving, one by one, the harsh lessons life has inflicted on them ... One forgets, you know ... Oh yes, one forgets ... We must, after all, recover our innocence before going to meet the angel. Ah yes. All of us are innocent still. (221–22)

> *Tous les vieillards retrouvent un air d'innocence, vous avez dû le remarquer. Le temps miséricordieux vient passer l'éponge sur leurs corps et leur esprit, estompant leurs signes distinctifs, effaçant leurs souvenirs, faisant s'évaporer l'une après l'autre les dures leçons que la vie leur*

a infligées. On oublie, vous savez, on oublie ... Il s'agit de recouvrer l'innocence avant de
partir rejoindre l'ange. Tous, nous sommes encore innocents. (219–20)

Despite the apparent forgetting of the past recounted in this passage and the recovery of lost innocence that comes with age, the whole scene suggests something far more ambivalent than that. The earlier scene involving the angel has been reversed: now the past that must be erased is not that of the perfection of paradise but the imperfections of painful memories. Nevertheless, the angel is once again associated with a split look—turning both back to the past and forward to the future—and the opposing poles of forgetting and remembering. These divergences are fused in the present moment.

The fact that the chance meeting takes place at a station—a site of return as well as departure—metaphorically captures the common point of different trajectories. More significant, however, is the fact that the two men catch sight of each other, not face on but "reflected in the wall of mirrors, so that Raphael sees him [Andràs] simultaneously from the front and from the back" (221) (reflété dans le mur de miroirs, de sorte que Raphael le voit à la fois de face et de dos [219]), hence making their fused look a complex superimposition of different planes and perspectives. At the end of the text (in an image uncannily similar to the final exchange of looks between Catherine and Rabih at the end of *Je Veux voir*), they are held in this position for eternity: "They continue to stare at each other. Sincerely, almost serenely. We don't see them separate" (222) (Dans la glace, leurs regards sont collés l'un à l'autre. Regards francs, Presque sereins. On ne les voit pas se séparer [220]).

And the book concludes, "And that's the end? Oh, no. I promise you it's not. All you have to do is look up—it's going on around you all the time" (222) (Et, c'est la fin? Oh! non. Je vous assure que non. Il suffit d'ouvrir les yeux: partout, autour de vous, cela continue [220]). Just as the mark of the angel seems, paradoxically, to abolish the past while acting as a trace of that past, so the epilogue of the novel leaves us with an image that faces different ways and whose meaning is indeterminate.

In Walter Benjamin's famous commentary on Paul Klee's painting "Angelus Novus" in his ninth "Thesis on the Philosophy of History," the angel is caught in contemplation, looking back at the past while being hurled by the storm of progress toward the future, recognizing the catastrophe of history—the debris of which is piling up at his feet—while dreaming of "making whole." Huston's text leaves us with a similar "dialectical image" (or, as Benjamin says elsewhere, "a constellation saturated with tensions" or "dialectics at a standstill"). Huston also takes from Benjamin the importance of being able *to read* the image as such: as Benjamin says, "The image that is read—which is to say, the image in the now of its recognizability—bears to the highest degree the imprint of the perilous critical moment on which all reading is founded" (463).

The narrator's injunction at the end of *L'Empreinte de l'ange*—"It's a question of opening your eyes"—also suggests that history must be read in the present in dialectical terms, for which purpose the mark must appear, in a flash, as "the imprint of the perilous critical moment."[8] The imprint, or mark, of the angel only becomes recognizable as the site of the dialectical work of history through a reading of its multiple (but invisible) connections, overlays, and intersections. It is here, then, in the staging of encounters through the imprint of history, that memory in *L'Empreinte de l'ange* becomes equated with the performative acts of narration and reading in the present (or, rather, in that instant in which the distinctions between past, present, and future have broken down), and the characters and narrator in the text connect with the readers of it.

This also means that, rather than simply passive victims of events, characters (and readers) become active players in the unfolding of memory and history—not in terms of repeating acts from the past (that is, still locked in a melancholic state inherited from the initial traumas and therefore fated to act out the same forever) but able to recognize the process in which they are caught. This does not provide a resolution (nothing so simple), and there is certainly no redemptive outcome (Emil dies, Saffie disappears, and Andràs grows old without ever seeing her again). It does, however, open up a critical space in which history can be apprehended in the moment and a new ethical relationship with the other can potentially emerge.[9]

Elsewhere, I have used the figure of the palimpsest to define the present staging of the overlapping of traces of the past (Silverman, *Palimpsestic Memory*). Huston's self-conscious narrator dramatizes the dynamic and performative process of writing the past (storytelling) in this way. Opening one's eyes is the spark (of illumination, imagination, and creativity) that makes our reading of the trace the moment of transformation of that mark into a multilayered and interwoven texture composed of individual psyche, collective meaning, and the layering of time.

THE TRANSFORMED LOOK

The "je" in *Je Veux voir* is neither Catherine nor Rabih but a composite of both—of self and other—as one only sees differently through the other. As Joana Hadjithomas and Khalil Joreige say of the encounter, "neither him, nor her but something other, something new" (ni lui, ni elle, mais quelque chose d'autre, de nouveau; Silverman, "Entretien"). The same blurring of

the distinction between one and the other could be said to occur with regard to Saffie and Andràs in *L'Empreinte de l'ange*. Both works end in a fused
but ambivalent look. Both draw from the same impulse behind the creative
act in Baudelaire's "Les Fenêtres": imaginative investment in the other as a
means of transforming self and reshaping reality.

However, they also transform that impulse in their own making. What,
in "Les Fenêtres," appears to be the privileged look of the male (voyeuristic?)
flâneur—a one-way investment in the other that is transformative for he who
sees but not necessarily for the objectified (feminine) other of the look—is,
in the two works discussed here, a mutual encounter. The look in *Je Veux
voir* and *L'Empreinte de l'ange* is deobjectified, degendered, and stripped of
the hierarchical power relations that, it could be said, underpin the look in
Baudelaire's poem.

The staging of a split and hybridized look is central to the depsychol-
ogizing of memory that takes place in both works and its dispersal across
different individuals, sites, and times. In his discussion of the films of Alain
Resnais, Gilles Deleuze talks of the construction of a "memory for two,
memory for several, memory-world, memory-ages of the world" (mémoire
à deux, mémoire à plusieurs, mémoire-monde, mémoire-âges du monde
[119]). This description of a memory that belongs to each person and everyone could also be applied to *Je Veux voir* and *L'Empreinte de l'ange*.[10] In this
sense, memory is not located within distinct and separate cultures but in the
encounters between cultures, times, and sites.

By transforming the Baudelairean mechanics of imagination and empathy, the two works place a different ethical imperative at the heart of shared
memory: the conversion of a (potentially) oppressive system of objectifica-
tion (and dehumanization) of the other into the (potentially) liberating (non-)
system of relationality. It would clearly be rash to celebrate unequivocally
this imaginative and empathetic leap, as the dangers of these processes have
been well documented (in, for instance, Aleida Assmann's contribution to
this volume). These dangers include a banal identification with the other
in which "regarding the pain of others" (in Susan Sontag's words) is little
more than an excuse for superficial hand-wringing—vicarious identification
in which the pain of others is little more than an excuse for self-gratifica-
tion; manipulation and instrumentalization of empathy for political ends;
suffering overload in the age of communication so that the attention span of
empathy with victims is fleeting as the next catastrophe takes its place; the
immersion in illusory worlds so that imaginative investment effaces any critical or political impulse; the immersion in the affective also to the detriment
of a critical or political response; the relativization of subject positions to the
detriment of moral judgments; and so on.

Imaginative shared memories can, of course, also lead to reductive versions of community according to a variety of (sometimes highly dangerous) ethnocultural criteria. However, I would suggest that, in *Je Veux voir* and *L'Empreinte de l'ange*, questions of empathy, ethics, memory, and history are negotiated in subtle, complex, and indeterminate ways so that relationality never collapses into the law of the same and the transformative nature of the encounter is never simply a heroic and uplifting resolution of difference. In these works, staging shared memory takes place in that ambivalent critical and affective space where homogeneity and heterogeneity, and wholeness and fragmentation, are false dichotomies and where there is no ultimate resolution of this Janus-like process.

Max Silverman is a professor of modern French studies at the University of Leeds. He works on post-Holocaust culture, postcolonial theory and cultures, and questions of memory, race, and violence. His most recent monograph, *Palimpsestic Memory: The Holocaust and Colonialism in French and Francophone Fiction and Film* (Berghahn, 2013), considers the connections between the Holocaust and colonialism in the French and Francophone cultural imaginary. He has recently published three coedited books with Griselda Pollock on the theme of the "concentrationary": *Concentrationary Cinema: Aesthetics as Political Resistance in Alain Resnais's "Night and Fog"* (Berghahn, 2011), *Concentrationary Memories: Totalitarian Terror and Cultural Resistance* (IB Tauris, 2014), and *Concentrationary Imaginaries: Tracing Totalitarian Violence in Popular Culture* (IB Tauris, 2015).

NOTES

1. "Celui qui regarde du dehors à travers une fenêtre ouverte, ne voit jamais autant de choses que celui qui regarde une fenêtre fermée. Il n'est pas d'objet plus profond, plus mystérieux, plus fécond, plus ténébreux, plus éblouissant qu'une fenêtre éclairée d'une chandelle. Ce qu'on peut voir au soleil est toujours moins intéressant que ce qui se passe derrière une vitre. Dans ce trou noir ou lumineux vit la vie, rêve la vie, souffre la vie. Par delà des vagues de toits, j'aperçois une femme mûre, ridée déjà, pauvre, toujours penchée sur quelque chose, et qui ne sort jamais. Avec son visage, avec son vêtement, avec son geste, avec presque rien, j'ai refait l'histoire de cette femme, ou plutôt sa légende, et quelquefois je me la raconte à moi-même en pleurant.
Si c'eût été un pauvre vieux homme, j'aurais refait la sienne tout aussi aisément. Et je me couche, fier d'avoir vécu et souffert dans d'autres que moi-même. Peut-être me direz-vous : 'Es-tu sûr que cette légende soit la vraie?' Qu'importe ce que peut être la réalité placée hors de moi, si elle m'a aidé à vivre, à sentir que

je suis et ce que je suis?" (Baudelaire 129). All translations from the French are my own except where otherwise stated.

2. An earlier version of this section on *Je Veux voir* appeared as "The Art of Seeing in *Je Veux voir.*" *War, Memory, Amnesia: Postwar Lebanon.* Spec. issue of *Contemporary French and Francophone Studies* 18.5 (2014): 523–29.

3. Hadjithomas and Joreige are also consciously playing here with Jean-Luc Godard's statement that the Jews are on the side of fiction and the Palestinians are on the side of documentary. The formal interplay is, thus, also a blurring of the frontiers between "opposing" camps (Hadjithomas and Joreige 9–12).

4. This is just one of the many filmic citations in *Je Veux voir.* In an interview I conducted with the directors in June 2014, they said, "Even the title *Je Veux voir* refers to 'you saw nothing,' the sentence that's repeated at the beginning of *Hiroshima.* Of course, because this is also a form of sharing, of meeting after a catastrophe. For us, this reference was certainly in the film" (Même le titre *Je Veux voir* fait référence à 'tu n'as rien vu,' cette phrase répetée au début *de Hiroshima.* Bien sûr parce que c'est aussi une forme de partage, de rencontre après une catastrophe. Pour nous, cette référence est là bien sûr dans le film; Silverman, "Entretien" 534. The influence of Resnais on the work of Hadjithomas and Joreige might well include the blurring of the line between memory and imagination. Resnais, it will be recalled, famously stated that he preferred to talk of his work in terms of imagination rather than memory (Monaco 11).

5. "We work very little on the past or on civil wars per se but rather on the traces and the consequences of these in our present" (Nous travaillons peu sur le passé ou les guerres civiles en elles-mêmes mais plus sur les traces et les conséquences de ces dernières sur notre présent; (Hadjithomas and Joreige, "Une Conversation" 103).

6. Hadjithomas and Joreige talk of displacing the scopic drive to release what they call the "emancipated spectator" (spectateur émancipé; Hadjithomas and Joreige, "Une Conversation" 105).

7. Huston translated the French original into English and I use her translation here. Page numbers from the English and French editions will follow quotations in the text.

8. Hadjithomas and Joreige describe their filmmaking in a similarly Benjaminian way: "We realised that most of our films take place in one day: *A Perfect Day, Cendres (Ashes), Je veux voir, Khiam, Open the Door.* In an almost unconscious way, we are caught in a moment of pure present-ness, as in Kafka's metaphor used by Hannah Arendt in which Man is trapped between an infinite past which pushes him forward and an infinite future which pushes him back. We are prisoners between the two and it's in this breach between one and the other that we attempt to create something in the present" (On s'est rendu compte que la plupart de nos films se déroulaient en une journée: *A Perfect Day, Cendres, Je veux voir, Khiam, Open the door,* d'une façon presque inconsciente on était bloqué dans un moment de pur présent comme dans cette métaphore de Kafka qu'utilise Hannah Arendt où l'homme est coincé entre le passé infini qui le pousse en

avant et le futur infini, qui le pousse en arrière. Nous sommes prisonniers entre les deux et c'est dans cette brèche entre l'un et l'autre que nous tentons de créer quelque chose au présent; Silverman, "Entretien" 538–39.

9. For a discussion of the articulation of storytelling, reading, the imagination, empathy, and ethics in *L'Empreinte de l'ange,* see Holmes 85–92.

10. For further discussion of "secondary," "split," and "shared" memories, see especially Hirsch; Landsberg; Rothberg; Rothberg et al.; Silverman, *Palimpsestic Memory;* and Weissman.

WORKS CITED

Baudelaire, Charles. "Les Fenêtres." *Petits poèmes en prose (le spleen de Paris).* Paris: Garnier-Flammarian, 1967. 129.

Belle de jour. Dir. Luis Buñuel. Paris Film Productions, 1967. Film.

Benjamin, Walter. *The Arcades Project.* Cambridge: Harvard University Press, 1999.

Caruth, Cathy. *Unclaimed Experience: Trauma, Narrative and History.* Baltimore: Johns Hopkins University Press, 1996.

Cheyette, Bryan. *Diasporas of the Mind: Jewish and Postcolonial Writing and the Nightmare of History.* New Haven: Yale University Press, 2013.

Day, Lorraine. "Trauma and the Bilingual Subject in Nancy Huston's *L'Empreinte de l'ange.*" *Dalhousie French Studies* 81 (2007): 95–109.

Deleuze, Gilles. *Cinema 2: The Time-Image.* Trans. Hugh Tomlinson and Robert Galeta. London: Athlone Press, 1989.

Frodon, Jean-Michel. "Des films au cinéma, entrer dans la vie des traces." *Joana Hadjithomas et Khalil Joreige.* Ed. Clément Dirié and Michèle Thériault. Zurich: JRP/Ringier, 2013. 59–63.

Hadjithomas, Joana, and Khalil Joreige. *Aida, Save Me! (Aida, sauve-moi!).* London: Gasworks, 2009.

———. "Une Conversation avec Dominique Abensour, Etel Adnan, Rabih Mroué, Jacques Rancière, Michèle Thériault, Jalal Toufic, Anton Vidokle." *Joana Hadjithomas et Khalil Joreige.* Ed. Clément Dirié and Michèle Thériault. Zurich: JRP/Ringier, 2013. 97–112.

Hiroshima mon amour. Dir. Alain Resnais. Argos Films, 1959. Film.

Hirsch, Marianne. *Family Frames: Photography, Narrative and Postmemory.* Cambridge: Harvard University Press, 1997.

Holmes, Diana. "To Write Is a Transitive Verb: Nancy Huston and the Ethics of the Novel." *Contemporary French and Francophone Studies* 14.1 (2010): 85–92.

Huston, Nancy. *L'Empreinte de l'ange.* Arles: Actes Sud, 1998.

———. *The Mark of the Angel.* New York: Vintage International, 1999.

Je Veux voir. Dir. Joana Hadjithomas and Khalil Joreige. Mille et une productions, 2008. Film.

Landsberg, Alison. *Prosthetic Memory: The Transformation of American Remembrance in the Age of Mass Culture.* New York: Columbia University Press, 2004.

Monaco, James. *Alain Resnais.* Oxford: Oxford University Press, 1979.

Rothberg, Michael. *Multidirectional Memory: Remembering the Holocaust in the Age of Decolonization.* Stanford: Stanford University Press, 2009.

Rothberg, Michael, Debarati Sanyal, and Max Silverman, eds. *Noeuds de mémoire: Multidirectional Memory in Postwar French and Francophone Culture.* Spec. issue of *Yale French Studies* 118–119 (2010).

Silverman, Max. *Palimpsestic Memory: The Holocaust and Colonialism in French and Francophone Fiction and Film.* New York: Berghahn, 2013.

——. "Entretien: Joana Hadjithomas et Khalil Joreige." *Contemporary French and Francophone Studies* 18.5 (2014): 530–41.

Weissman, Gary. *Fantasies of Witnessing: Postwar Efforts to Experience the Holocaust.* Ithaca: Cornell University Press, 2004.

Chapter 2

Remembering the Indonesian Killings

The Act of Killing and the Global Memory Imperative

Rosanne Kennedy

INTRODUCTION

In this chapter, I take Joshua Oppenheimer's documentary film *The Act of Killing* as a case study for analyzing the discourses and networks that enable the memory of a "forgotten genocide" (Oppenheimer, "*Democracy Now* Interview") to travel transnationally and to become a "prosthetic memory" (Landsberg) for viewers distant from the events. A transnational collaboration between a Jewish American man and an anonymous Indonesian co-director and crew, *The Act of Killing* remembers the mass killings of half a million or more suspected communists in Indonesia in 1965–1966. With its controversial methods of capturing on film and conveying to national and global publics a perpetrator memory of the killings, this visually spectacular but disturbing film raises issues that have been at the forefront of the study of history, memory, and trauma over the past twenty-five years.[1]

Cosmopolitan tropes, discourses, and languages enable films from "foreign" contexts and about unfamiliar events to travel transnationally. The most visually explicit cosmopolitan language in *The Act of Killing* is that of Hollywood cinema, which helps render the film intelligible to distant audiences. Many scenes feature TV screens, a figure of global visual and media culture but also of witnessing. What have received less notice, however, are the explicit and implicit ways in which cosmopolitan Holocaust memory practices inform the film's act of remembering the Indonesian mass killings. In his interviews and cinematic methods, Oppenheimer repeatedly draws on the Holocaust, with its idiom of witnessing and testimony, as a paradigm for conveying the legacy of the Indonesian genocide in the present. Indeed, the film assemblage—which includes not only the film but also interviews with the filmmaker, film publicity, and a "Say Sorry for '65" campaign— exemplifies the core features of the global memory imperative. It also reveals some of the transcultural limitations in this theory of how Holocaust memory mobilizes publics and moves human rights norms and interventions across national borders.

The global memory imperative, a concept coined by sociologists Daniel Levy and Natan Sznaider (*Human Rights and Memory*), is primarily a conceptual model. They propose that a shared memory of the Holocaust acts as an ethical prod to agents—national governments, international bodies such as nongovernmental organizations and the United Nations, and global civil society—to intervene in ongoing genocides and, increasingly, to seek redress for past genocides. Well over a decade ago, Andreas Huyssen cautioned that while comparisons with the Holocaust may energize memories of other genocides, the analogy could also obscure their specificity or trivialize them.[2] By contrast, for Levy and Sznaider it is precisely the status of the Holocaust as a deterritorialized icon, emptied of specific historical content, that enables it to function as a "global symbol" and, therefore, as the foundation for a shared cosmopolitan memory, which in turn facilitates a global human rights culture (*Holocaust and Memory; Human Rights and Memory*). Since the 1990s, "[t]he Holocaust has evolved from a European concern into a universal cipher primarily via the related legal codification of crimes against humanity. It is frequently tapped to comment on injustices and human rights abuses as such (in both the legal and commemorative discourses)" (Levy 18). The value of Holocaust memory today, in a global memory culture, does not stem from any specific lessons to be learned by studying the events in their historical particularity but rather from the attention it directs to human rights abuses and to the potential redress and resolutions offered by the human rights regime. In sum, their model is not simply a *description* of the spread of human rights culture in a transnational world; it *advocates* a global human rights culture as a triumph of transnational solidarity over national intransigence in the face of national human rights abuses.

Levy and Sznaider contend that the global human rights regime, fueled by the imperative to act on memories of genocide, is constraining national sovereignty by bringing international scrutiny to bear on the human rights violations of offending nations (*Human Rights and Memory*). Their optimistic claims for human rights as a global phenomenon rest to a significant degree, however, on the status of the Holocaust as a shared collective memory for the European Union, which is constituted through officially sanctioned commemorative rituals such as an International Holocaust Remembrance Day. At this juncture in memory studies—after the transnational turn and the emergence of the concept of global memory (Assmann and Conrad)—it is worth asking just how "global" the global memory imperative is. How widely and with what effects do the norms and values associated with Holocaust memory travel outside of Europe? In Asia? In Indonesia, a predominantly Muslim nation?[3] What kind of commemorative and countermemory work do they legitimate? What resistance do they encounter?

Within theorizations of global and traveling memory, film has been granted a privileged position as a kind of prosthesis that can facilitate a mediated form of distant memory for viewers outside of the local or national collective that has an experiential or historic relation to the memory of an event (Landsberg). Levy and Sznaider assign global media, especially film, a formative role in producing a shared "cosmopolitan memory" of the Holocaust ("Memory Unbound"). They are quick to point out that this mediated form of memory is not "homogenizing," since transcultural carriers such as film will accrue different meanings and affects in local contexts. As Aleida Assmann argues, however, in models of transnational memory that attribute change in the scale and reach of memory practices primarily to global media technologies there is little room to consider human agency or transnational networks. She contends, "It is not only the connectivity of digital technologies and the media itself, but also the work of new transnational actors and institutional networks that are reshaping the global world from above and below" (548). It is precisely this combination—of global media and transnational actors and institutions—that constitutes the assemblage surrounding *The Act of Killing*. Transnational human rights organizations publicize the film and simultaneously invite audiences to pressure Indonesia to acknowledge past crimes, investigate perpetrators, and provide redress to victims.

Within memory studies, discussion about the travels of memory across borders has faltered on conceptual terminology and frameworks, particularly the "transcultural" and the "transnational." These terms have particular relevance in relation to the global memory imperative, which works on the seam at which the transcultural and the transnational mesh. While transculturality acknowledges the challenges presented by borders, it has mainly been applied "to the study of mobility and flows rather than the social and political factors, as well as cultural ones, that may impede them" (De Cesari and Rigney 4). In a recent volume on *Transnational Memory*, Chiara De Cesari and Ann Rigney aim to correct this bias by analyzing both the cultural and the sociopolitical factors that shape the ease with which mediated memories travel and the obstacles they encounter. They argue that the combination of the concept of the "transnational," which recognizes the legal boundaries of nation-states, together with "memory" invites analysis of "the interplay ... between state-operated institutions of memory and the flow of mediated narratives within and across state borders" (3). *The Act of Killing*, which draws on a range of cultural tropes and visual languages to give meaning to a little-known genocide, provides a fruitful site for consideration of the interactions between the transcultural and transnational dimensions of traveling memory.

FRAMING MEMORY: HOLOCAUST,
HUMAN RIGHTS, HOLLYWOOD

In Indonesia, the killings have been the subject of myth and propaganda, and as such have been mythologized rather than simply forgotten or silenced. When Suharto came to power in 1968, his administration rewrote history textbooks, erected monuments, and inaugurated annual commemorations, thereby crafting an official narrative of the bloody events that preceded his rise and legitimated his regime.[4] In part due to the control of his regime over information flow, there has been widespread obfuscation around the events that led to the mass killings. Since Suharto's resignation in 1998, the official narrative has come under fire as "debate about the events of the 1965 killings and the aftermath has gained unprecedented liveliness and breadth in Indonesia" (Schreiner 262). Human rights activists, anthropologists, historians, writers, and artists have all been engaged in initiatives to solicit memories and testimonies from long-silenced victims and their families as a ground for constructing a countermemory of the genocide and securing justice for survivors and victims' families (Brauchler; Kammen and McGregor; Zurbuchen). A lot of this material is published in Indonesian and so has not made its way into transnational circuits of distribution.

It is in the opening created by the challenges to the nationalist narrative that *The Act of Killing* hopes to produce a countermemory that will achieve impact within Indonesia. Grace Leksana proposes that film will provide an important vehicle for reconstructing "the nation's social memory ... since film had such a major contribution to constructing the existing social memory" (183). Globally, however, the film travels as a memory of a "forgotten genocide" and is valued perhaps more for its innovations in capturing and conveying perpetrator memory than for exposing the impunity that still protects killers within Indonesia. One of the key dangers of the film is that it presents Medan, where gangsters enjoy privilege and notoriety, as a synecdoche for Indonesia.

The making of *The Act of Killing* involved transnational collaboration from the outset. Oppenheimer was in Sumatra filming a documentary about exploited plantation workers in the oil plantation belt of northern Sumatra, near Medan, when he learned they were afraid to form a union. Their fear stemmed from memories of the anticommunist purges of 1965–1966, in which at least 500,000 Indonesians were violently killed (Cribb, "Indonesian Massacres"). The plantation workers asked Oppenheimer, an outsider with a camera, whether he could find out what had happened to their relatives during the purges and how they died, and told him that the perpetrators— who had never been brought to justice—were living in the area. Oppenheimer interviewed forty perpetrators before he met Anwar Congo, a charismatic man who boasted of having killed hundreds in the purges. In 1965, Anwar was a "movie theater gangster" who scalped tickets to Hollywood films; the gangsters had a vengeance against communists because they wanted to ban American films. Oppenheimer provided Anwar and Hermann—a younger man who did not participate in the killings but is a protégé of the film's featured paramilitary, Pemuda Pancasila—with the resources to make a film in which they reenact the killings. One wonders whether they realized their confessions and testimonies would reach a global public or whether they had any idea of how that public would judge them.

The film follows Anwar and Hermann and their circle of gangsters over five years as they discuss and perform scenes in which they reenact the executions through the mediation of Hollywood genres such as gangster, Western, noir, and musical, thereby translating gangster culture and mass killing into a global vernacular. Only about a quarter of the scenes are reenactments; other scenes show Pancasila Youth rallies, in which anticommunism is espoused as an ideology and gangsters are celebrated as "free men"—represented by the pop song "Born Free"—who live by their criminal wits and are an asset to the state. Some scenes feature Oppenheimer (whose face we never see) in conversation with publishers, journalists, a member of parliament, and other civic "leaders," in which they freely discuss their role in the killings and their support for "gangster culture." Interspersed throughout are spectacular and surreal scenes in which Anwar and Hermann, in lavish costumes, give free rein to their fantasies. Their willingness to discuss and reenact their crimes, and fantasies of crimes, on film delivers the film's initial shock to audiences.

Through numerous interviews, panels, and presentations, Oppenheimer has tirelessly prepared the ground for the reception of *The Act of Killing*. In interviews for American and European media (available to a global public via the Internet), he has repeatedly invoked the Holocaust to legitimate his project, including the associated apparatus of testimony and the language of trauma, thereby providing a familiar discursive framework for the interpretation and reception of the film into transnational markets. For instance, in an interview for *Democracy Now,* he draws an analogy between Nazi Germany and Medan, the third largest city in Indonesia, where perpetrators live freely and still wield power in the community:

> It's as though I'm in Nazi Germany 40 years after the end of the Holocaust, and it's still the Third Reich, the Nazis are still in power. So the official history says nothing about the killings. But, and yet, the aging SS officers have been allowed to boast about what they've done ... so that they've become these kind of feared proxies of the state in their communities, in their regions ... And I realized at that point that this was a reality so grave, so important, that I would give it whatever it took of my life ... So I felt entrusted by the survivors and the human rights community to film every single person I could find.

Interesting here, although Oppenheimer does not mention it, is that the group instigating the mass killings at the time itself drew an analogy between its actions and those of the Nazis, using the word "GESTAPU," spelled with U rather than O (Roosa). The analogy tells us little of relevance about Medan today, but it morally legitimates the project of filming perpetrators to reveal the impunity they enjoy in the present. For an American audience, Oppenheimer's discourse appeals to a ubiquitous and troubling dichotomy of good versus evil and the supposedly universal value of human rights. It risks, however, repeating the discourse of an earlier era—the white man's civilizing mission—in which transnational activists "rescue" Indonesia from its own authoritarian rulers.

Gathering testimony from perpetrators was a key part of the national publicity strategy for *The Act of Killing.* Oppenheimer hoped the film would "open" a national conversation within Indonesia on the relationship between "genocide, terror, corruption, and thuggery" in the past and present (Interview by Amy Goodman). To publicize the release of the film in Indonesia, he worked with the editor of *Tempo Magazine,* who published a special double edition that featured seventy-five pages of "boastful testimony" by perpetrators and twenty-five pages on the film. Reflecting on this publication, Oppenheimer invokes the Holocaust as a universal trope:

> Indonesians were astonished that this holocaust that everybody knew had happened was suddenly filling the pages of the most important news publication after having never appeared in the media before. The film has come to Indonesia like the emperor's new clothes, just as the survivors and the human

rights community hoped that it would. It has opened a space to talk about the relationship between genocide, terror, corruption, and thuggery. (Interview by Amy Goodman)

Although his claims may exaggerate the film's impact in Indonesia, they reveal his conception of the film as "coming to Indonesia" from the outside world—even though it was filmed in Indonesia, features Indonesians, and is about events that took place in Indonesia.

What comes from outside, what is foreign in the Indonesian context, is the framing discourse of the Holocaust and all that it connotes: the international human rights regime, justice for survivors, redress. Indeed, Holocaust remembrance is a "foreign" import to Indonesia, a predominantly Muslim nation at a considerable geographic and cultural distance from Europe—revealing the cultural, religious, and national borders that impede the travels of Holocaust memory and bring into question its global reach. For instance, in January 2015, the American Cultural Center in Jakarta, rather than an Indonesian organization, promoted International Holocaust Remembrance Day, hosting a panel discussion ("International Day"). The Turkish Embassy in Jakarta also released a statement discussing the global significance of Holocaust remembrance and its role in providing refuge for Jews fleeing Nazi oppression (Turkish Foreign Ministry). Given the outsider status of these cultural institutions in Indonesia, there is little indication that the Holocaust has become a prosthetic memory for many Indonesians.

Oppenheimer does not simply invoke the Holocaust trope in discursively framing the film for international audiences. He also adopts and adapts the testimonial methods through which Holocaust memory has been transmitted to a global public. Like Claude Lanzmann, he favors testimony over archival images as a means of making a "film for today." Discussing Lanzmann's film *Shoah,* Oppenheimer observes that "the now of the film" is the time of Lanzmann's shooting in the early 1980s, and "he's witnessing people going through trauma as they remember what they did" ("BYOD Interview"). The ritualistic presentation of testimony and witnessing in *The Act of Killing,* even presented as it is through reenactments in the style of Hollywood B-grade films, positions the film in a tradition of Holocaust memory. By recording and documenting perpetrators and the various performative modes in which they testify, the film captures the impunity and culture of boasting that is still protected in Indonesia by the military today. The payoff is that the film gains political purchase in the present, in the *political now* of Indonesia.

In a post-Holocaust memory culture, testimony is regarded as an exemplary, belated mode for reckoning with one's moral implication in traumatic events. In Holocaust circles, the testimonial practice of seeking survivor testimony and transmitting it to a receptive public carries with it expectations of listening and empathy. Whereas most of the interviews in *Shoah* are with survivors and bystanders, who are positioned as morally deserving of empathy, *The Act of Killing* solicits perpetrator testimony ("BYOD Interview"). Through extending a testimonial method to the perpetrators, the film invites viewers to expand their circle of humanity by identifying with Anwar's pain. The narrative trajectory of the film builds to a putative climax in which viewers are led to believe that Anwar, taken to the rooftops where he routinely executed innocent people, belatedly recognizes his moral responsibility for his past deeds. While the camera lingers on Anwar's pain at the memory of what he has done, several troubling scenes reveal the exploitative use of children who show signs of distress when performing in violent scenes. The children, neighbors, and even victims and witnesses to the genocide are not, however, positioned as subjects for our empathy. We are asked to accept these ethically troubling scenes, in which a kind of violence is enacted in the present, as the cost of producing perpetrator testimony.

The Act of Killing is a case in which Holocaust memory productively generates the memory of another genocide, albeit one that occurred under very different historical circumstances and used different means. Huyssen contends that the Holocaust trope can "block insight into specific local histories" and flatten out historical complexity (14), and *The Act of Killing* has been criticized for providing little historical insight into the killings (Cribb, "*The Act of Killing*"; Fraser). Oppenheimer is on record as stating that, in contrast to Lanzmann, he is keen to explore the "why" of the genocide, but in fact, *The Act of Killing,* like Lanzmann's *Shoah,* provides insight into the "how" but little insight into the "why." Instead, through re-enactment and testimony, the film remembers the methods through which a genocide was carried out, framed within a culture of gangsterism that still celebrates, protects, and normalizes the killers today.

THE AESTHETICS OF TESTIMONY:
GENOCIDE, PERFORMANCE, SPECTACLE

In both human rights activism and aesthetic genres such as literature, memoir, and film, one of the legacies of the Holocaust has been the idiom of witness testimony. Survivor testimony is a familiar, even anticipated, feature of documentary films that seek to capture and transmit memories of violence and genocide and their effects in the present (Sarkar and Walker; Wieviorka). In this context, perpetrator testimony is becoming even more common (Morag). Testimony is also used in humanitarian contexts to advocate emergency interventions (Fassin and Rechtman). Testimony is not a universal idiom; there are significant differences between the paradigm of testimony emerging from the Holocaust and grounded in trauma theory, and humanitarian testimony, which emerges in contexts of immediate crises and seeks international intervention. In *The Act of Killing,* however, both of these paradigms shape the methods and presentation of testimony. Indeed, the publicity for the film measures its innovations precisely in its deviation from normative expectations regarding testimony:

> When approached to make a film about their role in the genocide, Anwar and his friends eagerly comply—but their idea of being in a movie is not to provide reflective testimony. Instead, they re-create their real-life killings as they dance their way through musical sequences, twist arms in film noir gangster scenes, and gallop across prairies as Western cowboys. (*The Act of Killing*)

Striking here is the clash between the register of "reflective testimony" associated with the Holocaust and human rights, and that of Hollywood cinema, with its values of entertainment and commerce. Huyssen's adage that, in an era of global media, critics must think of "traumatic memory and entertainment memory together, as sharing the same public space" applies to *The Act of Killing* (19).

In one of his interviews, Oppenheimer returns to the distinction between testimony and performance. When filming perpetrators, he says, "I wasn't getting the kinds of sober testimony you expect from crimes against humanity ... I was getting something much closer to performance. Performance is always for an audience ... Who was their imagined audience? If I could answer that question, we could understand the whole system of corruption that's in place here" ("BYOD Interview"). One answer to that question comes from a scene set in a TV studio in Medan, in which the audience for Anwar and Hermann's performance is their circle of gangsters. The TV show's glib hostess, who praises them for having developed "a more humane method of killing," is a parody of the banality of mass culture.

Sober testimony, however, is also performative in the sense that it is directed to an audience. As Shoshana Felman has argued, in testifying "before an audience of readers or spectators ... memory is conjured ... to address another, to impress upon a listener, to appeal to a community" (Felman and Laub 204).[5] The sticking point, then, is not that *Shoah* is sober testimony while *The Act of Killing* is performance or reenactment. It is rather the aesthetics of the performances—the tone, mood, affect—and the associated connotations that distinguish the sober testimony of the former from the reenactments of the latter. Reenactment is often measured by its verisimilitude to an event, but the reenactments in *The Act of Killing* are as much a performance of fantasy as they are of actual events. The film's camp aesthetic—its confronting fusion of the gravitas of genocide, Hollywood spectacle, and Indonesian vernacular codes, conventions, and references—flouts moral and aesthetic norms and expectations for remembering genocide. This combination of a camp aesthetic and genocide can make the film disorienting, if not simply offensive, to Global North audiences who have been schooled in the protocols of post-Holocaust testimony, memory, and justice—thereby revealing cultural norms and cultural legibility as a limit of traveling memory.

Documentary film has been described as "a discourse of sobriety" that seeks rhetorically to advance a truth or make a case (Nichols). As Bill Nichols has observed, "The pleasure and appeal of documentary film lies in its ability to make us see timely issues in need of attention ... [It] contributes to the formation of popular memory. It proposes perspectives and interpretations of historic issues, processes, and events" (ix). *The Act of Killing*, which is concerned with how the past shapes the present, uneasily fuses two traditions of testimony—Holocaust and humanitarian. In the context of the Holocaust, testimony is a technology of memory, particularly traumatic memory. In the humanitarian tradition, testimony is a means of compelling an empathic response with the aim of legitimating a "humanitarian" intervention in the present.

I have argued above that the film invites audiences to identify with Anwar's pain and trauma. To demonstrate how *The Act of Killing* rhetorically supports the case for human rights intervention in Indonesia, I consider a powerful sequence of scenes that revolves around the reenactment of an execution. This sequence occurs midway through the film and marks a turning point. Just prior to this sequence, Adi, a fellow executioner with Anwar, is shown at the airport arriving from Jakarta, the plane a figure of "travelling memory" (Erll). In contrast to Anwar's provincialism and naïveté, Adi introduces a cosmopolitan and knowing perspective and recognizes the implications of Oppenheimer's film project for national(ist) memory.

The scene that opens the sequence is the only one that involves a direct engagement between the perpetrators and a survivor, Suryono, a neighbor of Anwar. Apparently spontaneously, Suryono tells the assembled killers a "true story" of his personal memory of the killings. In this scene, the perpetrators are unexpectedly confronted with the effects of the anticommunist killing, as Suryono relives his painful childhood memory. This scene is in many ways a familiar one of posttraumatic testimony. Suryono describes what happened, and as he narrates his story, he becomes visibly affected and his bodily movements and behaviors convey the lingering trauma. For instance, he laughs when telling the story, but at the same time, he laments,

"I was so young. Afterwards, all the Chinese were moved to a shantytown. That's why I didn't go to school." (One feels that Lanzmann would nose in here, questioning the victim about why he is laughing when his story is tragic.) This scene has the hallmarks of a *Shoah* moment: the child survivor, who clearly has traumatic memories of the events and their effects on his life, smiles as he tells the story. (In *Shoah,* a man smiles wryly while telling Lanzmann about the time he found his wife and children in a mass grave he was forced to dig up. Lanzmann asks him why he is smiling, and he responds: "What do you want me to do, cry? It is better to live.") The neighbor smiles in an effort to retain control. In this case, the smile goes unquestioned, contributing to the perversity of the scene.

When delivered in humanitarian contexts, victim or survivor testimony calls for an empathic response—acknowledgment of wrongdoing or at the very least respect for suffering. Instead, after telling his harrowing story, Suryono deferentially apologizes to the perpetrators for the possible offence caused by sharing his painful memory. At the risk of annoying the gangsters, however, he pleads for his story to be included in the film on the grounds that it is true. This exchange between victim and perpetrators illustrates what Dori Laub identifies, in the context of Nazism, as the "very explicit Nazi attempt to erase the experience of the victim and to inscribe it with a myth, which became history for them" (Laub and Finchelstein 60). This same dynamic, in which silence is imposed on victims, who are expected to accept that silence as reality, occurs in the perpetrators' responses to Suryono's testimony. One by one they chime in with justifications for why Suryono's story cannot be included in their film—thereby imposing a silence on the victim. Their responses, as well as their demeanors (close-ups show them fidgeting and avoiding eye contact), reveal that they are neither inclined nor morally capable of taking on the role of the witness—of actively listening and responding to Suryono's testimony.[6] The scene demonstrates the perverse response to victim testimony in a culture of impunity. It reveals that as long as a culture of impunity prevails in Indonesia, and the perpetrators are still "free men," victims will not be heard and will not receive justice. In the act of including Suryono's testimony in his film, however, Oppenheimer performs the role of humanitarian witnessing that the perpetrators refuse.

Two scenes later, still on the same set, Suryono "plays" the role of the victim. About to be executed, he begs to be able to give a note to his family. His "play-acting" appears to have triggered the real terror associated with memories of the past, and the camera lingers on his face as he quivers and screws up his muscles, struggling to control emotion. It is impossible for the viewer to distinguish his reaction to this traumatic memory in the present from "play-acting" at being killed. In a countershot, the camera zooms in on the faces of Anwar and then Adi, both of whom witness a mock execution that is eerily "true." Adi says to Anwar, "It's sadistic." The undecidability of the referent of this phrase—does it refer to the sadism of past executions or the sadism of putting Suryono through this traumatic reenactment in the present?—heightens its ironic effect.

Afterward, the perpetrators and gangsters discuss the implications of including the scene for how the past will be remembered. Adi, the voice of instrumental rationality, declares that the film will change the way the genocide is remembered in Indonesia. Viewers—and here he has in mind a *national* public—will remember the anticommunist killers rather than the communists as "the cruel ones." If the film succeeds, it will undermine the nationalist myth of communist evil as well as the culture of impunity and the ideology of gangsterism. Adi exits the film at this point, and afterward the camera turns its gaze on Anwar's nightmares, inviting audience speculation that he is suffering for his crimes.

Adi belligerently defends nationalist memory in the face of international judgment. On the way to the airport, when Oppenheimer confronts him with the possibility of being brought to The Hague and thus being subjected to an *international* public rather than a *national* one, Adi counters, "History is written by winners." Unseen but heard from the back of the car— a ghostly presence—Oppenheimer, speaking in the voice of international justice, admonishes Adi: "Truth is good for the victims." (Although he speaks in Indonesian, Oppenheimer's American accent positions English-speaking viewers in a position of identification with him.) Adi responds aggressively, saying that one day the Geneva conventions will be replaced by the Jakarta conventions. Deploying comparative memory as a rhetorical defense, Adi further retorts that the United States has not dealt with its own genocide against native peoples. In this exchange, Adi defends Indonesian sovereignty against the imputed "imperialism" of the international human rights regime and reveals the cultural and political limits of the global memory imperative. In terms of the film's formal structure, this scene repeats the rampant denialism of the earlier scene in which the gangsters dismiss Suryono's testimony. Considered from a rhetorical perspective, however, these scenes endorse the global human rights agenda and legitimate the kind of transnational human rights intervention that is a characteristic feature of the global memory imperative.

It is important to note, however, that Adi's belligerent (if misdirected) authoritarian nationalism may be heard differently by sectors of the Indonesian population, which is extremely diverse, and by audiences in the West and elsewhere—for instance in nations that have had their own strug-

gles with the regime of international human rights and transitional justice mechanisms. Adi's defiant rejection of internationalism and the West
as determining the standards by which Indonesia should be judged may
appeal to some Indonesian viewers. Indonesia achieved its independence
from the Netherlands only in 1949 and has a strong military and authoritarian ideology that is frequently at loggerheads with its Western neighbors, particularly Australia. The scenes of Suryono's testimony, in which
he reveals a deep embodied pain that he has not been allowed to express,
may also be *felt* very differently by national audiences and by transnational
ones.

CONCLUSION: TRAVELING MEMORY AND HUMAN RIGHTS

The Act of Killing travels globally as a memory of a forgotten genocide, in
part due to its innovative aesthetic but also due to widespread fascination
with representations of extreme violence. The film's fusion of an Indonesian
vernacular, Hollywood spectacle, and cinematic methods associated with
Holocaust memory provides an example of "rooted cosmopolitanism": a
global paradigm that is localized in specific nations, producing a novel local
memory (Beck). "Rooted cosmopolitanism" refers to processes that take
place within national societies but are framed by global concerns, values,
and discourses. In this case, a cosmopolitan post-Holocaust memory culture
provides both a moral imperative and practical strategies for remembering
the Indonesian anticommunist killings. The filming, however, takes place
in Indonesia, with Indonesians involved in filming, acting, and production.
This "rooted cosmopolitanism"—a spectacular blend of flamboyance, transgression, violence, and perhaps remorse—can be disorienting, but it also produces a new vision.

The film's cross-border travels, I have argued, are facilitated by filmic
strategies associated with post-Holocaust memory culture and human rights.
The global memory imperative holds that Holocaust memory, articulated
through global media such as film, can provide the means for spreading
human rights globally. On this theory, human rights activists, both domestic and international, pressure a nation-state to conform to human rights
norms. This model, I have argued, elucidates *The Act of Killing*'s combination
of a Holocaust memory paradigm and the discourse of human rights, which
is most evident in the scenes involving Adi.

This synthesis of global memory and human rights is also evident in the
publicity for the film. While analogies with the Holocaust do not illuminate
the specificity of the history of the Indonesian genocide, they do lend the

film legitimacy and authorize it as a cultural memory of genocide. According to the global memory imperative, the memory of genocide produces a moral imperative to intervene, which Oppenheimer facilitates through his activist human rights networks. A tireless campaigner both for *The Act of Killing* and for the human rights message it carries, he has embedded the film in a human rights campaign aiming to pressure the Indonesian government to apologize to the anticommunist victims and their families. The official website for the film includes a link to the "Say Sorry for '65" campaign, which connects transnational publicity for human rights in Indonesia with publicity for the film.[7] For instance, the film website offers visitors to the site the opportunity to watch the trailer, purchase the DVD, sign a petition supporting the campaign, and donate to human rights organizations supporting justice in East Timor, West Papua, and Indonesia.

The "Say Sorry for '65" campaign is an example of how a film about a "forgotten genocide" travels on transnational human rights discourses and networks, and how these legitimate a human rights campaign that takes as its addressee a national government. What merits attention is the directionality of these discourses and campaigns. Through the film, European models of post-Holocaust memory and human rights are used to give meaning to an Indonesian genocide. Audiences are solicited through a transnational human rights campaign that invites them to pressure the Indonesian government to apologize. These transnational initiatives are undertaken in the interest of producing a countermemory of the genocide in Indonesia, and securing a belated acknowledgment for victims and their families from the government. The "Say Sorry for '65" focus on Indonesian accountability would seem, then, to support Huyssen's observation that, regardless of the transnational tropes that are used in producing and giving meaning to the past, the political impact of memory is still primarily national rather than transnational.

For national audiences the film brings into memory a sequestered past and, with it, the opportunity to ask questions that have been silenced. In Indonesia today, however, it appears unlikely that there is the political will, at the state level, to address the violence of '65. A Truth and Reconciliation Commission was legislated in 2004 but was struck down by the constitutional court on the grounds that its stipulation that victims would only receive reparations if they agreed to amnesty for perpetrators was unconstitutional. Progress has since stalled, and victims' rights groups have voiced concerns about the lack of a concrete strategy to ensure truth, justice, and reparations for victims. In a 2012 statement marking the International Day for the Right to the Truth Concerning Gross Human Rights Violations and for the Dignity of Victims, Amnesty International called for the minister responsible to make a National Truth and Reconciliation Commission a priority.

The resistance to a state-mandated reconciliation process raises the issue—both practical and ethical—of raking up memories of the past where justice will not be forthcoming. Indonesian film critics have noted how painful it is for survivors to watch the film, while anthropologist Elizabeth Drexler, who has conducted fieldwork on the aftermath of violence in Aceh, argues against publicly remembering traumatic events when it is unlikely justice will be delivered. There is also the question of support for an apology among ordinary Indonesian citizens. One of the few times in which audiences see an Indonesian reaction to Anwar and his cronies discussing their murderous exploits is in the bemused reactions of Indonesian professionals working in a TV studio who are watching Anwar being interviewed about the film they are making. Their confusion about how many people were killed during the anti-communist massacres, and their surprise at seeing the gangsters alive, let alone on TV, conveys that the massacres have been obscured in Indonesian history and public memory.

It is worth noting, however, that the transnational travels of memory, and of human rights, may have unanticipated effects. Although I have focused here on cosmopolitan discourses emerging in the Global North, and how they have shaped the film's acts of memory, transnationalism is itself multidirectional. Commenting on the "shrill calls" by some Chinese bloggers for Indonesia to apologize to China for the massacres—on the grounds that Indonesians of Chinese descent were especially targeted—historian Robert Cribb argues that this call distorts the historical facts. He contends that in fact a miniscule percentage of the half a million or more massacred—about 2,000—were of Chinese descent, and he applauds Indonesia as having admirably accommodated a wide range of ethnicities with little ongoing violence ("Comment"). The case of the Chinese bloggers is a timely reminder that transnationalism not only involves relations between Indonesia and the West but also includes Asian and other transnationalisms. In the longer term, the film may provoke other unanticipated reactions from citizens of authoritarian regimes in Asia and elsewhere.

Rosanne Kennedy is an associate professor of English literature and gender, sexuality, and culture at the Australian National University. Her work brings together memory studies, human rights, and feminist/queer theory to analyze the textual transmission and transnational circulation of memories of violence and displacement, with a focus on settler colonial and postcolonial texts and contexts. She has coedited special issues of the *Australian Humanities Review* on "scales of memory" (2016; with Maria Nugent), *Memory*

Studies (2013; with Susannah Radstone), and *Australian Feminist Studies* (2011; with Gillian Whitlock) as well as *World Memory: Personal Trajectories in Global Time* (Palgrave Macmillan, 2003; with Jill Bennett). She is currently working on a monograph with the working title *Moving Testimonies: Art, Advocacy and Transnational Publics.*

NOTES

1. For a representative range of responses to the film, see the essays collected in *Film Quarterly* 67.2 (2013) and *Critical Asian Studies* 46.1 (2014).
2. Every year, new books are published that invoke the Holocaust as a moral frame for their acts of remembering a forgotten genocide. For a critical analysis of one such case, see De Mul.
3. According to the 2011 census, Indonesia has nearly 203 million Muslims (87.2% of the population), which is the largest Muslim population of any nation.
4. Many of these histories, monuments, and ceremonies center on Lubang Buaya, the site at which six generals were killed; this act was pinned on communists and used to justify the killings (Leksana; Schreiner).
5. Michael Rothberg describes *Shoah*, a paradigm of "sober testimony," as a "performative reenactment" (qtd. in Vice 84).
6. On the significance of the role of the listener to testimony, see Laub and Finchelstein.
7. See the "Say Sorry for '65" campaign publicity on the *The Act of Killing* website: http://www.actofkilling.com/#action. This page has a hyperlink to an online petition hosted by Change.org: https://www.change.org/p/president-sby-say-so rry-for-65.

WORKS CITED

Assmann, Aleida. "Transnational Memories." *European Review* 22.4 (2014): 546–56.

Assmann, Aleida, and Sebastian Conrad, eds. *Memory in a Global Age: Discourses, Practices and Trajectories.* Basingstoke: Palgrave Macmillan, 2010.

Beck, Ulrich. "The Cosmopolitan Society and Its Enemies." *Theory, Culture, & Society* 19 (2002): 17–29.

Brauchler, Birgit, ed. *Reconciling Indonesia: Grassroots Agency for Peace.* London: Routledge, 2009.

Cribb, Robert. "*The Act of Killing.*" *Critical Asian Studies* 46.1 (2014): 147–49.

——. "Comment: Analysing the Act of Killing." *SBS.com.au* 4 Mar. 2014. Web. 26 June 2015.

——. "The Indonesian Massacres." *Century of Genocide: Eyewitness Accounts and Critical Views.* Ed. Samuel Totten, William S. Parsons, and Israel W. Charny. 2nd ed. New York: Routledge, 2004. 233–60.

De Cesari, Chiara, and Ann Rigney. "Introduction." *Transnational Memory: Circulation, Articulation, Scales.* Ed. Chiara De Cesari and Ann Rigney. Berlin: De Gruyter, 2014. 1–25.

De Mul, Sarah. "The Holocaust as a Paradigm for the Congo Atrocities: Adam Hochschild's *King Leopold's Ghost.*" *Criticism: A Quarterly for Literature and the Arts* 53.4 (2011): 587–606.

Drexler, Elizabeth F. *Aceh, Indonesia: Securing the Insecure State.* Philadelphia: University of Pennsylvania Press, 2008.

Erll, Astrid. "Travelling Memory." *Parallax* 17.4 (2011): 4–18.

Fassin, Didier, and Richard Rechtman. *The Empire of Trauma: An Inquiry into the Condition of Victimhood.* Trans. Rachel Gomme. Princeton: University of Princeton Press, 2009.

Felman, Shoshana, and Dori Laub. *Testimony: Crises of Witnessing in Literature, Psychoanalysis, and History.* New York: Routledge, 1992.

Fraser, Nick. "We Love Impunity: The Case of *The Act of Killing.*" *Film Quarterly* 67.2 (2013): 21–24.

Huyssen, Andreas. *Present Pasts: Urban Palimpsests and the Politics of Memory.* Stanford: Stanford University Press, 2003.

"Indonesia: Victims Still Waiting for Truth and Justice for Past Human Rights Violations." *Amnesty.org.* Amnesty International 24 Mar. 2012. Web. 26 June 2015.

"International Day of Holocaust Remembrance." *@America* n.d. Web. 26 June 2015.

Kammen, Douglas, and Katharine McGregor. *The Contours of Mass Violence in Indonesia, 1965–68.* Honolulu: Asian Studies Association of Australia in association with University of Hawaii Press, 2012.

Landsberg, Alison. *Prosthetic Memory: The Transformation of American Remembrance in the Age of Mass Culture.* New York: Columbia University Press, 2004.

Laub, Dori, and Federico Finchelstein. "Memory and History from Past to Future: A Dialogue with Dori Laub on Trauma and Testimony." *Memory and the Future: Transnational Politics, Ethics and Society.* Ed. Yifat Gutman, Adam D. Brown, and Amy Sodaro. Basingstoke: Palgrave Macmillan, 2010. 50–65.

Leksana, Grace. "Reconciliation through History Education: Reconstructing the Social Memory of the 1965–66 Violence in Indonesia." *Reconciling Indonesia: Grassroots Agency for Peace.* Ed. Birgit Brauchler. London: Routledge, 2009. 175–91.

Levy, Daniel. "Changing Temporalities and the Internationalization of Memory Culture." *Memory and the Future: Transnational Politics, Ethics and Society.* Ed. Yifat Gutman, Adam D. Brown, and Amy Sodaro. Basingstoke: Palgrave Macmillan, 2010. 15–30.

Levy, Daniel, and Natan Sznaider. *The Holocaust and Memory in the Global Age.* Philadelphia: Temple University Press, 2006.

——. *Human Rights and Memory.* University Park: Pennsylvania State University Press, 2010.

——. "Memory Unbound: The Holocaust and the Formation of Cosmopolitan Memory." *European Journal of Social Theory* 5.1 (2002): 87–106.

McLagan, Meg. "Human Rights, Testimony, and Transnational Publicity." *Nongov-ernmental Politics*. Ed. Michel Feher, Gaëlle Krikorian, and Yates McKee. New York: Zone Books, 2007. 304–17.

Morag, Raya. "Perpetrator Trauma and Current Israeli Documentary Cinema." *Camera Obscura* 27.2 (2012): 92–133.

Nichols, Bill. *Representing Reality: Issues and Concepts in Documentary*. Bloomington: Indiana University Press, 1991.

Oppenheimer, Joshua. "BYOD Interview with Joshua Oppenheimer." Interview by Ondi Timoner. *TheLip.tv* 7 Nov. 2013. Web. 3 Feb. 2014.

———. Interview by Amy Goodman. *Democracy Now* 19 July 2013. Web. 4 Feb. 2014.

Roosa, John. *Pretext for Mass Murder: The September 30th Movement and Suharto's Coup D'état in Indonesia*. Madison: University of Wisconsin Press, 2006.

Sarkar, Bhaskar, and Janet Walker, eds. *Documentary Testimonies: Global Archives of Suffering*. New York: Routledge, 2010.

Schreiner, Klaus H. "Lubang Buaya: Histories of Trauma and Sites of Memory." *Beginning to Remember: The Past in the Indonesian Present*. Ed. Mary S. Zurbuchen. Seattle: University of Washington Press, 2005. 261–77.

The Act of Killing. VHX n.d. Web. 26 June 2015.

Turkish Foreign Ministry. "Press Release Regarding the International Holocaust Remembrance Day, 27.01.2015." Turkish Embassy in Jakarta 27 Jan. 2015. Web. 26 June 2015.

Vice, Sue. *Shoah*. Basingstoke: Palgrave Macmillan on behalf of the British Film Institute, 2011.

Wieviorka, Annette. *The Era of the Witness*. Trans. Jared Stark. Ithaca: Cornell University Press, 2006.

Zurbuchen, Mary S. "Historical Memory in Contemporary Indonesia." *Beginning to Remember: The Past in the Indonesian Present*. Ed. Mary S. Zurbuchen. Seattle: University of Washington Press, 2005. 3–32.

Chapter 3

Transnational Memory and the Construction of History through Mass Media

Aleida Assmann

⤐◈⤏

THE TRANSNATIONAL TURN

Over the last five years or so, we have witnessed the remarkable career of the term "transnational," which has rapidly replaced previous terms such as "postcolonial" and "multicultural" in our academic discourse. While due to historical changes and disappointing developments these latter terms have lost much of their glamor, the new term seems to encapsulate a vision of a better world to which cultural studies can help contribute with its new terminology. Hence, a "transnational turn" has been announced by historians and theorists in various subfields of cultural studies such as literary studies, media studies, migration studies, and memory studies. Looking beyond the borders of nations is certainly not a totally new enterprise; indeed, more inclusive perspectives and comparative methodologies have for a long time been implemented in imperial, international, and global history. The new focus on the transnational, however, is more specific. In the words of Micol Seigel:

> [It] examines units that spill over and seep through national borders, units both greater and smaller than the nation-state ... Transnational history does not simply cover more ground; it is not equivalent to world history ... Perhaps the core of transnational history is the challenge it poses to the hermeneutic preemi-

nence of nations. Without losing sight of the "potent forces" nations have become, it understands them as "fragile, constructed, imagined." Transnational history treats the nation as one among a range of social phenomena to be studied, rather than the frame of the study itself. (63)

We can pause to reflect on the term "transnational" and try to sort out some of its meanings. I single out four of these. The term can refer, first of all, to non–state actors that operate in different countries. Among these are so-called TNCs, the transnational corporations of global capital (for instance ITT, General Motors, and Royal Dutch Shell) and other representatives of power in a global arena. The term can also be applied, second, to geopolitical units comprising different nations such as the European Union with its twenty-eight member states or the Gulf Cooperation Council with its six member states. These states have voluntarily given up some of their sovereignty in favor of common economic and political interests, profiting from mutual exchange and support, common measures, and joint action. A third important dimension of the meaning of the term points to the impact of media. These channels of communication and distribution have created networks of communication that are providing individuals all over the world with new possibilities to think, to express themselves, and to act beyond their local and national frameworks. And finally, the term relates to individuals and groups that move in space either voluntarily or under political or social pressure, while retaining or reconstructing within and among themselves a diasporic connection to their former homelands.

When analyzing the term "transnational" more closely, we soon detect that it is deployed not only as a descriptive tool but also as a prescriptive term that carries a set of normative implications. Its success clearly relies heavily on this inherent value dimension that endows it with a new perspective and vision. This normative stance is often underpinned by a cosmopolitan ethos that implies a general dissatisfaction with the dated nineteenth-century ideal of the autonomous, free, coherent, and bounded nation and the desire to move forward toward a new political imaginary that dissolves the nation in ongoing local and global reconfigurations. The general challenge of the "trans-" is to go beyond national identifications, investments, and interests and to explore new forms of belonging, participation, and cultural identification in a world characterized by dispersed and displaced populations with different historical experiences and trajectories.

In this context, as Donald Pease emphasizes, the transnational can also "call forth different representations of the past. It does not negate the past, but it does foster a rethinking of the national in the light of newly invented spatial and temporal coordinates" (5). "Trans-" can stand for "transit," emphasizing movement in space across national borders, but it can also stand for "transfer," "translation," and "transmission," the cultural work of reconfiguring established national themes, references, representations, images, and concepts. Nations are not elided in this transnational perspective, but they are symbolically and politically recast; they are imagined differently as inherently and externally relational, embedded, and contextualized, always implicated in and partaking of larger processes and changes.

The interpretive framework of the transnational turn also carries a promising potential for memory studies as it stimulates new perspectives on the larger political and cultural contexts in which memories are selected, constructed, and contested. In what follows, I will leave the abstract and somewhat hyperbolic rhetoric of the "trans-" behind and focus on specific contexts in which the term has been or can be applied.

TRANSNATIONAL MEMORIES AND THE ROLE OF THE MEDIA

In the introduction to a volume I edited with Sebastian Conrad, we glossed the altered relations between memory and the global as follows:

> Until recently, the dynamics of memory production unfolded primarily within the bounds of the nation-state; coming to terms with the past was largely a national project. Under the impact of global mobility and movements, this has changed fundamentally. Global conditions have powerfully impacted on memory debates, and, at the same time, memory has entered the global stage and global discourse. Today, memory and the global have to be studied together, as it has become impossible to understand the trajectories of memory outside a global frame of reference. (2)

With this volume, we draw attention to the shift toward transnational memory and try to reassess the discursive framing of this new development. Memories are indeed more and more leaking or breaking out of the "container of the nation-state" (Levy and Sznaider 2) due to the formation of a global arena that rests mainly on two pillars: first, the connectivity of digital technologies and media, which construct, enable, and exploit connections between people, as explained in the introduction to this volume, and, second, new transnational actors and corporate networks that are reshaping the global world from above and below.

In an article with the programmatic title "Travelling Memory," Astrid Erll argues against what has come to be termed "methodological nationalism" in the study of cultural memory and advocates looking at forms in which memories are generated and circulated outside the national frame. Her concept of "travelling memory" is geared to a world of communication flows and great migrant mobility. As media and people are incessantly on the move, Ann Rigney notes, new possibilities arise "for shaping post-national citizenship and for creating new lines of solidarity within the global arena" (618).

In their influential book *The Holocaust and Memory in the Global Age* (2006), Daniel Levy and Natan Sznaider argue along similar lines, describing a global scenario in which the constraints of ethnic nationalism and particularism give way to a universal and cosmopolitan memory for postnational citizens of the world. For these scholars, new communication technologies, the media, and heightened forms of mobility are crucial agents of change. Yet, as Max Silverman demonstrates in his contribution to this volume, such heightened connectedness is not only to be celebrated. In addition, change cannot be attributed to technological structures alone evolving according to a self-propelling process of modernization that is going global. Such a conceptual framework emphasizes technological determinism and leaves little room for *human* agency. Indeed, memory is taken all too easily beyond all boundaries if we focus directly on a cosmopolitan community that is composed of none other and nothing less than humanity itself. Although this is a very optimistic and attractive vision, moving directly from nationalism to the global sphere of media circulation is a problematic step, as it covers up many concrete problems that are challenging and vexing not only scholars in memory studies but also, for instance, international political actors.

Within the realm of the transnational, in other words, we need to acknowledge some borders that continue to exist and are even resurrected by new memory communities. Rigney, for instance, has observed that in the discussion of transnational memory there is a "striking lack of attention to Europe." Her point is that Europe stands for a different form of the transnational that "represents neither the national nor the global," which is what makes it "theoretically so fascinating" (618). To account for this intermediate state of the transnational, one would have to introduce a concept of transnational identity that is *not* global.

We may thus distinguish between two approaches to transnational memory that are by no means mutually exclusive: an actor-shaped approach to transnational memory underlining the crucial role of human agency, including individuals, politicians, nongovernmental organizations, and institutional networks, on the one hand, and a media-shaped approach focusing on digital technologies and their global transformative effects, on the other. How such an approach works can best be analyzed with the help of a concrete example. I will therefore present and discuss a challenging new per-spective that has emerged under the label of the "connective turn."

THE CONNECTIVE TURN (ANDREW HOSKINS)

Over the last two decades a growing body of work in media and communi-cation studies has emerged that investigates the general mediatization of life and memory. These studies are built on a firm theoretical consensus that there is no human life to be lived outside of media—a situation that generates a number of conceptual challenges that are explored extensively in Amanda Lagerkvist's chapter in this book. In line with this consensus, Mark Deuze has advocated a "media life" perspective "to recognize how the uses and appropriations of media penetrate all aspects of contemporary life" (137). Roger Silverstone, for his part, has shown how "Media ... define a space that is increasingly mutually referential and reinforcive, and increa-singly integrated into the fabric of everyday life" (Orgad 34).

In German memory studies, the intricate interrelation between mem-ory and media has also been the object of much research. An early study was published by the research group of Vittoria Borsò, Gerd Krumeich, and Bernd Witte of the University of Düsseldorf titled "European Mem-ory: Alterity and National Historiography. Old and New Cultural Archives." Their book *Medialität und Gedächtnis* (2001) was based on the media theory of Niklas Luhmann. The next generation of media research in memory studies is represented by Erll and Rigney, who published their influential book *Medi-ation, Remediation, and the Dynamics of Cultural Memory* in 2009. This collection of essays was based on the media theory of Siegfried J. Schmidt and Rich-ard Grusin. I want to focus here on the work of Andrew Hoskins, a vocal proponent of the connective turn who has based his research exclusively on electronic media.

With the introduction of digital technologies, the relation between memory and media has been profoundly reconfigured, which calls for new approaches and new methodologies. In this process, we are confronted with new "turns" and visions. Hoskins, the founding editor in chief of the suc-cessful journal *Memory Studies,* is an energetic and influential figure in the field of digital memory studies. In this field, the interrelation between mem-ory and media has already become an undisputed truism: "Media life is also memory life. Memory is lived through a media ecology wherein abundance, pervasiveness and accessibility of communication networks, nodes, and dig-ital media content, scale pasts anew" (Hoskins 29).

Theoretically speaking, this tight coupling of media and memory is not without pitfalls. There is no doubt that media have always shaped memory and that digital technology today has a growing impact on individual and collective images of the past. Media, indeed, are the environment in which all acts of remembering are embedded, supplying props and patterns that shape, consolidate, and support our memories. Hoskins, however, goes one step further. His description of the "connective turn" stresses the *total* fusion of memory and media (what is also called "radical connectivity"). With the "'outsourcing' of memory on or to the Internet," he argues, mediated memory has become shapeless and diffuse: it is now "pervasive, accessible, disposable, distributed, promiscuous" (19)—and, we may add, pernicious, as the Internet, it turns out, has acquired an inexorable memory that retains everything and gives away freely what we would rather forget and have others forget.

There is obviously a price to be paid for the outsourcing of human memory to the Internet: humans are in danger of losing control over their private data and memories. What Hoskins emphasizes, however, is a new collapsing of the terms "memory" and "media." At this point it is important to abandon the enthusiastic rhetoric of the "connective turn" for a moment in order to recover some important conceptual distinctions between the two leading terms. "Media" are considered insatiable; their storage capacity is continuously enlarged. Their job is to package, multiply, and distribute information and circulate it ever more rapidly in ever wider circles. In doing so, they aim to connect more and more people. Indeed, electronic media have an inbuilt tendency to disregard borders and boundaries: they traverse, transgress, transcend.

"Memory," on the other hand—in spite of the title of this book—was always considered to be bounded. It has its limits, wherever these might be drawn, negotiated, and redrawn. There is no meaningful concept of memory that can totally dispense with the notion of scarcity and the necessity for selection, which it entails due to its links to particular identities and embodied perspectives. If we dismiss forgetting altogether, which is an inbuilt energy and organizing principle working within memory, we profoundly change the meaning of the term. In a "postscarcity culture" of what José van Dijck calls "automated connectivity" (13), we are perhaps no longer dealing with memory but with data, information, or knowledge—in other words, with concepts that lack the notion of boundedness, constraints, and contours and share the endless extensibility of media.

While it is the purpose, propensity, and function of media to connect and to create ever more links, to transcend, and to globally expand, it has so far been the purpose and function of memory to *distinguish,* creating horizons and perspectives that back up distinct individual and collective identities. A universal or global memory of mankind—if it exists at all—would be the exception rather than the rule. It is true that the connective structure of media evolves beyond groups, nations, and cultures, mixing everything. If we collapse media and memory, however, we negate the fact that memory is shot through with forgetting, premised on scarcity, and bound to identities. We may of course stress the cognitive function at the expense of the identity function, but then we no longer speak of memory but of information, collective consciousness, the "extended mind," or the "digital archive."

Hoskins's claim is that after the connective turn, memory has lost its moorings in identity and has become totally fluid and free floating. He perceives the link between identity and memory as an obsolete relic of the pre-digital past that has been superseded by the availability of digital archives. With the arrival of digital archives, memory has been dissolved and disappeared, which means that we all may now easily move from the national to the transnational; in the words of Arjun Appadurai, quoted by Hoskins: "Instead of presenting itself as the accidental repository of default communities (like the nation), the archive returns to its more general status of being a deliberate site for the production of anticipated memories by international communities" (Appadurai qtd. in Hoskins 25).

In his rhetoric of the connective turn, Hoskins describes the displacement of a memory culture premised on scarcity by a media culture premised on plenitude. The world of the new digital media has become a postscarcity culture in which the hold on memory has been changed fundamentally. Scarcity, for Hoskins, is a matter of the past: today everything is within instant reach, as more and more information is effortlessly storable, accessible, and transmittable. New forms of connectedness through social media have, since the invention of Facebook in 2004, led to an enormous multiplication and communication of messages, a development that has thoroughly changed our world. While traditional mass media catered information and entertainment to the recipient and consumer, the Internet now provides huge databases with open access to self-serving users who are able not only to "tweet" back but also to encode their own messages and circulate their media products across global networks.

While the print media and TV came to the reader and viewer, the users of the Internet instantly provide themselves with what they need. This transformation, which has also been analyzed by experts in other fields (such as John Tomlinson and José van Dijck), has strongly affected the dimensions of space and time and profoundly changed the structure of the public: whatever is being communicated is also deterritorialized, disembedded; it is disrupted from its point of origin and disconnected from the time regime of scheduled events to be reconnected in an ongoing "broad present" (Gumbrecht). Owing to ever smaller and smarter handheld devices, the new media culture constructs the "HereNow" of a cyberworld structured by its own spatiality and temporality.

Against this background, Hoskins proclaims the triumph of the media and the dissolution of collective memory. As a digital native, he feels estranged by older epistemologies and claims a new view of experience and the world. The "media generation" can no longer discern a distinction between the world and the media or imagine a life outside the media: media have "become vastly important conceptual and experiential categories, the stakes from which we pitch our tents of knowledge" (Dominic Boyer qtd. in Hoskins 19).

The question is this: has the structure of individual and collective memory as we knew it come to an end in the brave new world after the connective turn? Are we dealing here with an empirical description or instead with a dramatization proleptically elaborating the conceptual framework of a new disciplinary paradigm? Hoskins does not seem quite decided himself: "The shifts in media-memorial cultures refract a tension between those who embrace a vision of memory as always already transformed—mediatized—and those who resist and condemn the metaphorical and the medial expansion of memory. Perhaps this is an overstatement" (29).

We are indeed dealing with a sea change in the structure of the archive, but how are we to theorize and describe it? Hoskins creates a polarization between two irreconcilable paradigms. He uses the standard linear narrative of modernity, proclaiming abrupt endings and new beginnings. This is what the "turn" in "connective turn" really means: exit the old model, enter the new one. We know that especially in the academic world, our cognitive frames have their exits and their entrances, some of them being rather short-lived. But this narrative, I would contend, is a huge simplification, assuming the automatic disappearance of the old with the advent of the new. Perhaps we can conceptualize change in more complex ways as an evolutionary process in which new developments coexist and interact with previous systems in challenging ways.

There is certainly something absolutely new about the connective turn and that has to do with a new differentiation, a new complexity, new variations, and new distinctive values attached to henceforth coexisting media and to new configurations of media and memory. Yet our notions of media and memory do not absorb and efface each other. Is the Internet really creating a global archive that is dissolving the contours of memories and deconstructing identities? Rather than focusing only on media and dropping the concept of memory altogether, I suggest that we need both terms to describe the new fractions, tensions, and reactions that are arising between the two. Instead of a narrative of turns and replacements, we need a narrative of *shifts* of media regimes focusing on new constellations of media and memory and thus on changing perspectives on the past, the present, and the future.

BETWEEN NATIONAL AND EUROPEAN HISTORY: THE GERMAN TV MINISERIES *GENERATION WAR*

We should not forget that while the Internet is in the process of creating a global archive that is accessible to users all over the world, older mass media are still around. Many of them function within a national framework, cultivating the self-image of "teachers of the nation" recreating perspectives on national memory for succeeding generations and large audiences. In the last section of this essay, I focus on a recent example of the visual reconstruction and reception of history on German TV. It is obvious that the further historical events recede into the past, the more dependent succeeding generations will be on mediated reconstructions of this past. Among them, high-budget visual narratives produced by mass media, such as films and TV series, attract large audiences.

The example I want to look at in more detail in order to map the interaction of these different dynamics is the miniseries *Unsere Mütter, unsere Väter.* Produced by Nico Hofmann (born in 1959) for the ZDF, a German public television broadcaster, and released internationally as *Generation War,* it was televised in Germany in March 2013. It marked a new beginning after the era of Guido Knopp, the former chief designer of popular history on German television. It also marked the borderline dividing personal embodied memories characterized by cognitive limits and emotional charge from succeeding generations who are exclusively relying on mediated forms of "postmemory," based on hindsight knowledge and retrospective reconstructions of history. The ZDF epic discards the voice of historical witnesses, choosing instead the genre of a feature film with six fictional characters and a dramatic plotline placed in a carefully documented historical setting of World War II.

The series received heavy media coverage and reached seven million German viewers. It had been praised in advance in *Der Spiegel* as "a new milestone in German memory culture" (Von Leick). The producer and his team pursued a twofold aim: to uncover a hitherto unacknowledged view of the events of World War II and to do so by adapting to the established visual style and sound design of high-tech filmmaking.[1] Instead of choosing high-profile historical characters such as Albert Speer or Erwin Rommel, the series features ordinary, private, and individual experiences of the war.

The protagonists of the series are "our mothers and fathers," thus rendering German history as family history.

Three of the six fictive characters do in fact have biographical models, as they are based on none other than the parents of producer Nico Hofmann himself: the two soldiers Wilhelm and Friedhelm are versions of his father, while Charlotte, the BDM (Bund Deutscher Mädel [League of German Girls]) nurse (a member of the girls' wing of the Nazi Party youth movement), is inspired by his mother. What the producer and his team intended was not just another history lesson but a restaging of family stories that had remained largely untold.

By introducing his personal backstory, Hofmann offered the viewers a version of German family history that they could also accept as their own. The fictive plot was to mirror real personal experiences and stimulate memories, discussions, and storytelling in the family. The series is emphatically not based, like so many Guido Knopp docudramas, on material from the historical archive but is staged as a unique chance to belatedly witness—through the keyhole, as it were—seminal events in our parents' and grandparents' life stories. The focus is thus not only on the historical facts but also on the family memory, including its emotional charge.

This series was made by members of the second and third generations for the young third generation, while at the same time it confronted the first generation with their own disavowed experiences. The memories of the parents' generation have changed ownership, so to speak, as they have moved into the custody and authority of the next generation: it is now the children who are telling their parents what they have experienced (and never been able to admit) and how they are to evaluate it. The later generation claims to finally break the silence of the older generation by telling us the parents' story truthfully, "as it really happened." The most important historical source of the work is thus its producer's family memory.

With his series, he instructs not only the succeeding generations but also his own parents about World War II, confronting them with their hidden secrets. As Hofmann notes, "My father is now 88, and for the first time he is able to speak about the war years with an exactness which I had never expected." He adds, "I believe that it was good for him that he saw the series. And for me it was important." His mother confirms this assessment; he notes that it was the first depiction of World War II of which she could say: "It was exactly like that!" (Kühn and Brauck).[2] In an interview with *Der Spiegel,* the producer further confesses, "For me, this film is the end of 30 years of family strife." The laconic comment of the interviewer was "This therapy cost the ZDF fourteen million Euros!" (Kühn and Brauck). As therapy for a single individual this is quite a price, but as therapy for a whole nation it would be a real bargain.

Critical voices differed considerably from this self-description, pointing out that not only does the ZDF film show

> what in Germany can now be discussed. It also shows what is still silenced ... This concerns the fact that Hitler was liked and accepted. It is never mentioned in this popular film that the political support of the NS regime was a general consensus. There are many Nazis in the film, but they are always the others. The film therefore reproduces exactly the blind spots of German family memory. (Kamann 10)

No matter how shocking and brutal the war scenes, German family memory still remains under the constraints of particular taboos.

History textbooks used to be "weapons of mass instruction," to use Charles Ingrao's phrase. Today, they are being replaced more and more by iconic films. Generations of American youngsters have learned the history of World War II by watching Spielberg's *Saving Private Ryan* (1998) and of the Holocaust by watching *Schindler's List* (1993). Hollywood and Spielberg have entered into an effective pedagogical alliance in their project of consolidating public knowledge about historical events of paramount importance. Technically and aesthetically sophisticated films endowed with huge budgets are now forming the gripping narratives and coining the indelible images through which history is not only learned and remembered but also sensually encountered and vicariously "witnessed."

These media events have a double effect: they work as important memory triggers, stimulating public interest, attention, empathy, and critical discussion, on the one hand, while, on the other, they create a screen memory in the double sense of the term, both as a visual projection in the public sphere and as a covering up of sore spots in the unruly complexity of historical reality. This double function of arousal and closure seems to be a general feature of the presentation of history in the mass media. It generates a dynamic that is decidedly more complex than the picture of general connectedness that research on media and memory often presents.

The ZDF film epic is made for a young generation that is no longer the object of extended Holocaust pedagogy but is very well trained in the visual language of violence as elaborated by Hollywood studios. What do these young people actually retain from such a film, which most of them view as exciting entertainment? I am not engaging here with the issue of possible historical errors; we heard the standard justification of the filmmakers: that all the data were professionally authorized.

My concern is not with historiographical veracity but with the more general question of historical understanding, awareness, and sensibility. On this level, the film is rather disappointing, not only because it reinforces older stereotypes but also because it is misleading and counterproductive in a European perspective. The work that claims to fill in gaps of family memory and national memory inadvertently contributes to reinforcing such gaps on the transnational level. While members of the young generation have in the meantime absorbed certain knowledge about Jewish victims in the context of an international memory and media culture, they as yet know very little about Polish and Russian victims of German warfare.

The exhibition "Verbrechen der Wehrmacht" (1994), on the crimes of the German armed forces, for instance, started its presentation only with the war against Russia in June 1941, which confirms a deeply entrenched caesura that the ZDF film once more subscribes to. The violent invasion of Poland is again dropped from attention and memory, a negligence that deeply irritates Polish audiences. In his review of the film, Konrad Schuller reminds his German readers of a blind spot in their national memory: "Poland was Hitler's first victim; six million Poles died in consequence of the German occupation, half of them Jewish. No other country has had a greater loss in relation to its population. Only in Israel might the nightmares about 'our mothers, our fathers' be even more pressing" (Schuller, "Sie schonen sich nicht").

In addition, the ZDF epic contains extended passages in Polish that present the gross anti-Semitism of Polish partisans. It is a historical fact that there were anti-Semites among the members of Poland's Home Army (the AK), but this is hardly a justification for the film to vilify this stronghold of Polish resistance, which is a hallowed Polish "*lieu de mémoire.*"[3] This is not just a matter of negligence or ignorance but a problematic form of "externalizing" a German problem by simply shuffling it across the border. This presentation of the AK is all the more counterproductive in a country that is in the process of self-critically confronting its past.[4] It also prolongs nasty German stereotypes against Poles, which in Germany itself usually go unnoticed and enjoy considerable popularity among different segments of society. What is hardly known and acknowledged in Germany, however, is that Poles—in spite of Jedwabne and widespread anti-Semitism—constructed an extended support network for hiding and helping Jews under Nazi occupation; 6,394 Polish "Righteous among the Nations" are registered in Yad Vashem compared with 525 German ones.

A total of 3.7 million Poles saw the film on a Polish TV channel. In spite of its scandalous passages, it also met with a number of positive responses. In Russia, where the ZDF miniseries also stimulated hot debates, the reception was much more resentful. Here, many of the critics defended the honor of the Red Army and the heroic suffering of the Russian nation as the collective victim of Nazi terror. One critic, the nationalist-conservative Maksim Shevchenko, argued that the film failed to show the Germans as invaders slaughtering 27 million Russians: "This was the greatest genocide in the history of mankind: the murder of Soviet civilians. But everybody talks only about the Holocaust, nobody acknowledges this massive massacre" (Franke). National mass media events, as we can see here, are received today in an increasingly European and transnational perspective. This, however, does not necessarily mean that national frames are automatically disappearing on the way to more inclusive transnational and global perspectives.

CONCLUSION

There is no doubt that we have entered an era in which TV program directors and film teams have a growing role in mediating history and reshaping national memories. In the digital era of hypervisualization we are in the process of technically creating—literally—new images of the past. Several Central and Eastern European countries are currently engaged in restaging the history of World War II in television series and films, stimulating heated debates in a transnational public arena of keen mutual observation across national borders. But, as Rosanne Kennedy also demonstrates in her contribution to this section, while the media travel, the memories often stay within certain cultural and political bounds.

This is a new challenge and, as I would like to argue, an important research area for teachers and historians as well as scholars of media and cultural studies. This is not a time for professional arrogance, drawing a safe and comfortable dividing line between *them,* the producers of mass images on the one hand, and *us,* the critical and informed audience on the other, since most of these productions are permeated with scholarly expertise and guided by the professional advice of historians.[5] Given the large budget, high technical quality, and enormous impact of this segment of mass culture, it is no longer appropriate to cultivate an attitude of indifference and turn one's back on this topic. We had better watch closely how this trend will evolve—whether it will stimulate and heighten collective animosities and nationalistic narcissism or whether these products will eventually become more sensitive and dialogic, reimagining national pasts in a more comprehensive European framework.

In the mean time we have learned that our rhetoric of the "trans" was perhaps a bit too euphoric. What is celebrated in one perspective is feared from another point of view. We have experienced a shift in our framework from a positive to a negative view of globalization, which ceases to be celebrated when the movement is no longer directed towards extension but is reversed and perceived as invasion. With the historic flow of migrants, globalization is forced upon Europe in utterly new ways and it will be important for our theory to live up to this reality and to face its complexity.

Aleida Assmann was a professor of English literature and literary theory at the University of Konstanz from 1993 to 2014. She received an honorary degree from the University of Oslo (2008) and the Max Planck Research Award (2009). Her main areas of research are historical anthropology, history of media, history and theory of reading and writing, and cultural memory, with special emphasis on the Holocaust and trauma. Publications in English include *Memory in a Global Age: Discourses, Practices and Trajectories* (Palgrave Macmillan, 2010; with Sebastian Conrad), *Cultural Memory and Western Civilization: Functions, Media, Archives* (Cambridge University Press, 2012), *Memory and Political Change* (Palgrave Macmillan, 2012; with Linda Shortt), *Empathy and Its Limits* (Palgrave Macmillan, 2015; with Ines Detmers), and *Shadows of Trauma: Memory and the Politics of Postwar Identity* (Fordham University Press, 2016).

NOTES

1. Christoph Classen offers a detailed description of the visual aesthetics of the film. Classen writes about the specific genre of docudrama, which creates a mix between historical research and popular drama. This style, competently reproduced by Hofmann's teamWorx, was invented and developed in Hollywood and has become the benchmark in high-quality war films, combining an emotionally charged fictional plot with a claim to historical authenticity. Signature elements of this style of filming are a gripping dramaturgy evolving in short clips, fast cuts, graphic scenes of violence, slow-motion effects, and the use of close-ups.
2. All translations from the German are my own.
3. Jerzy Marganski, the Polish ambassador in Berlin, made this point quite clearly. He emphasized that the Poles are being informed by historians about anti-Semitic excesses in the AK, yet to represent this feature of the organization as the whole truth was creating justified discontent. See "ZDF weist polnische Vorwürfe."
4. In 2001, President Aleksander Kwasniewski publicly apologized for the Polish pogrom against Jewish "neighbors" in Jedwabne. The Poles, writes Konrad

Schuller, have increasingly taken responsibility for their atrocities against Germans after World War II: "They look very closely when Germans are involved, trying to arrive at more differentiated judgements" (Schuller, "Über Widerstand und Antisemitismus").

5. Historian Norbert Frei differs from many of his colleagues in his thoroughly positive judgment of the film. A reason for this may lie in the fact that he was appointed as historical advisor for the film, which has incorporated various insights drawn from his historical research.

WORKS CITED

Assmann, Aleida, and Sebastian Conrad. "Introduction." *Memory in a Global Age: Discourses, Practices, and Trajectories.* Ed. Aleida Assmann and Sebastian Conrad. Basingstoke: Palgrave Macmillan, 2010. 1–16.

Borsò, Vittoria, Gerd Krumeich, and Bernd Witte, eds. *Medialität und Gedächtnis: Interdisziplinäre Beiträge zur kulturellen Verarbeitung europäischer Krisen.* Stuttgart: Metzler, 2001.

Classen, Christoph. "Unsere Nazis, unser Fernsehen." *Zeitgeschichte-online* Apr. 2013. Web. 19 Feb. 2015.

Deuze, Mark. "Media life." *Media, Culture, and Society* 33.1 (2011): 137–48.

Erll, Astrid. "Travelling Memory." *Parallax* 17.4 (2011): 4–18.

Erll, Astrid, and Ann Rigney, eds. *Mediation, Remediation, and the Dynamics of Cultural Memory.* Berlin: De Gruyter, 2009.

Franke, Thomas. "Verkürzte Wahrheit, verfälschte Geschichte." *Deutschlandfunk* 5 May 2013. Web. 19 Feb. 2015.

Gumbrecht, Hans Ulrich. *Unsere breite Gegenwart.* Frankfurt a. M.: Suhrkamp, 2010.

Hoskins, Andrew. "Media, Memory, Metaphor: Remembering and the Connective Turn." *Parallax* 17.4 (2011): 19–31.

Kamann, Matthias. "Grenzen der Erinnerung." *Welt am Sonntag* 24 Mar. 2013. Web. 19 Feb. 2015.

Kühn, Alexander, and Markus Brauck. "Töten oder getötet werden." *Der Spiegel* 11 Mar. 2013. Web. 19 Feb. 2015.

Levy, Daniel, and Natan Sznaider. *The Holocaust and Memory in the Global Age.* Philadelphia: Temple University Press, 2006.

Orgad, Shani. "The Internet as a Moral Space: The Legacy of Roger Silverstone." *New Media and Society* 9.1 (2007): 33–41.

Pease, Donald E. "Introduction: Re-mapping the Transnational Turn." *Re-framing the Transnational Turn in American Studies.* Ed. Winfried Fluck, Donald E. Pease, and John Carlos Rowe. Hanover: Dartmouth College Press, 2011. 1–46.

Rigney, Ann. "Transforming Memory and the European Project." *New Literary History* 43.4 (2012): 607–28.

Schuller, Konrad. "Sie schonen sich nicht: Polen debattiert *Unsere Mütter, unsere Väter.*" *Frankfurter Allgemeine Zeitung* 23 June 2013. Web. 19 Feb. 2015.

——. "Über Widerstand und Antisemitismus: Diskussion in Polen." *Frankfurter Allgemeine Zeitung* 9 Apr. 2013. Web. 19 Feb. 2015.

Seigel, Micol. "Beyond Compare: Comparative Method after the Transnational Turn." *Radical History Review* 91 (2005): 62–90.

Tomlinson, John. *The Culture of Speed: The Coming of Immediacy.* London: Sage, 2007.

Van Dijck, José. *The Culture of Connectivity: A Critical History of Social Media.* Oxford: Oxford University Press, 2013.

Von Leick, Romain. "Die Wunde der Vergangenheit." *Der Spiegel* 25 Mar. 2013. Web. 19 Feb. 2015.

"ZDF weist polnische Vorwürfe gegen Kriegsepos zurück." *Spiegel Online* 28 Mar. 2013. Web. 19 Feb. 2015.

Part II

Transgenerational Memory

Chapter 4

Small Acts of Repair

The Unclaimed Legacy
of the Romanian Holocaust

Marianne Hirsch and Leo Spitzer

⊂⊱◊⊰⊃

UNCLAIMED LEGACIES

Several years ago we were scheduled to speak at the Wiener Library in London about Czernowitz—a sizeable Eastern European city that had been the capital of a province of the Austrian Habsburg Empire and that had once contained a large German-speaking and highly assimilated Jewish population. We had recently coauthored a book about the afterlife of this city in Jewish memory (Hirsch and Spitzer, *Ghosts of Home*). Some weeks before the talk, we had received a package from a Dr. Harry Jarvis from Bournemouth, England, who was planning to attend. It contained a small sampling of articles he had written about Czernowitz for a Jewish genealogical magazine. Then in his late eighties, Dr. Jarvis was quite eager to speak with us: he was reading our book, he wrote us, and wanted to show us a few things that were important to him.

When we subsequently met Dr. Jarvis and heard his account of the frustrations he had experienced when he tried to convey his family's wartime story to various individuals and institutions, we began to understand his eagerness to find willing listeners. Dr. Jarvis (whose original name had been Jaslowitz) was born and grew up in Cernăuți (as Czernowitz was renamed when it came under Romanian rule) but left in the 1930s during a high point of Romanian anti-Semitic activity and went to study medicine in England. His parents and ten-year-old sister Sonja stayed behind (see Illustration 4.1).

Illustration 4.1. Sonja Jaslowitz with her parents in Cernăuți, c. 1938. Courtesy Dr. Harry Jarvis.

In the course of massive campaigns of "ethnic cleansing" of Jews carried out by fascist Romanian authorities, his father, mother, and sister Sonja were deported eastward in 1942 to a region that came to be known as Transnistria. Fortuitously, however, the three did manage to survive Transnistria's brutal ghettos and concentration camps, and, after being liberated by the Soviet army in 1944, they were repatriated to the Romanian capital, Bucharest. There, not long afterward, Harry's father died from tuberculosis he had contracted in a Transnistrian concentration camp, and Sonja was killed—ironically, a "collateral damage" victim of shrapnel from Allied bombs intended for a German-controlled oil installation near the Romanian capital. She had just turned seventeen.

After the war ended, Jarvis's distressed mother joined her son in London. She brought along a number of family documents she had managed to safeguard, including a folder of poems written by her young daughter while in Transnistria. Some were illustrated with drawings that Sonja had made shortly before her death. Perceiving the testimonial and historical importance of these writings, as well as their potential literary and artistic interest, Harry Jarvis traveled to Israel in the early 1950s to donate them to the newly established Holocaust Museum, Yad Vashem. He hoped that this museum might make these materials public so that Sonja Jaslowitz would be acknowledged and memorialized, her legacy ensured. More generally, he had also wanted his donation to help broaden and factually enhance the then scant knowledge about Transnistria and the Romanian genocide of Jews.

Neither of these things happened. Although his bequest was accepted, Sonja Jaslowitz's Transnistria writings received no noticeable attention by Yad Vashem officials and, even today, cannot be found among the holdings the museum lists on its website index. Frustrated by this inattention, Harry Jarvis nonetheless did not give up and, until his recent death, continued to donate documents, articles, and books related to Czernowitz and Transnistria and the experience of Jews there that he had collected over the years to other institutional archives, many equally uninformed about this distinctive history of genocide and survival.

It was in this spirit that Jarvis approached us, anxious about what would happen to the weighty legacy that had been transmitted to him—a legacy, he worried, he would only be able to sustain for a brief time longer. Raised in Britain, far removed from this family history, his children had little interest in this past, and he thus felt the need to reach us as representatives of a postgeneration who might be interested in receiving, understanding, and transmitting a history that, he feared, might die with him. He especially wanted someone with a background in literature to have Sonja's poems—to "do with them as you wish." Even if they were never published, he hoped they would at least be properly read.

Harry Jarvis's gift of Sonja Jaslowitz's poems to us, and his directive to do with them "as you wish"—a charge that, of course, also indicated that he wanted us to do *something*—left us both excited but also with some amount of unease. Those of us in the postgenerations who are descendants of traumatic genocidal histories often inherit such testimonial objects—small or large, ordinary or remarkable—and we have to decide how to respond to their demands (Hirsch and Spitzer, "Testimonial Objects"). The thin folder Harry Jarvis gave us contained only a small corpus of works produced by a very young girl. But they are quite remarkable. Written in German, Romanian, and French and composed in the ghettos and camps of Transnistria (and then, no doubt, typed and illustrated in Bucharest after her liberation), they evoke the daily life of Jewish deportees and slave laborers in graphic detail. But some are also marked by humor and irony, and they reflect a deep longing for home, all without losing a persistent sense of hope in the future.

Admittedly, the poetic form in which this testimony came to us generated a fantasy on our part, both of "discovering" a talented unknown poet and her small oeuvre and of being able to call attention to improbable acts of creative resistance by someone whose life was so violently cut short. Sonja

Jaslowitz, we thought, might be another Selma Meerbaum-Eisinger. A remarkable young poet and a distant cousin of Paul Celan, Meerbaum-Eisinger died of typhus at the age of eighteen in Mikhailowka, the German forced labor camp near the east bank of the Bug River to which she had been moved from Transnistria.

A volume of fifty-seven poems, written by Meerbaum-Eisinger before her deportation from Cernăuți, has now been published both in German, their original language, and in English translation. Her poetic creations, broadly anthologized in recent years, have received praise as works of a "second Anne Frank" (Meerbaum-Eisinger, *Harvest of Blossoms; Ich bin in Sehnsucht*). Indeed, after decades in obscurity, Selma Meerbaum-Eisinger has become an international icon: a plaque was installed in 2004 on her former house; her poems have been set to music and recorded by the World Quintet; her life has been the subject of three plays in Germany; a German youth literary prize has been named after her; many poems have been written to her by German schoolchildren as part of an ongoing curricular "Project Selma"; and, of course, as a clear instance of the kind of processes that the next section of this book analyzes as transmedial dynamics, she has a Facebook page and numerous Facebook friends.[1]

Is this what we might wish for Sonja Jaslowitz, we wondered? The hyperbolic attention that Selma Meerbaum-Eisinger and her poetry now receive is not unusual in postmemorial generations, but would such attention be an appropriate response to Sonja Jaslowitz's poems in the context of the tragic curtailment of her life story and to the anonymity to which she had been relegated for so long? What postmemorial response might do justice to the vulnerable lives and imaginative production of young artists like Sonja and Selma—or, indeed, of anyone who, like them, experienced circumstances of such traumatic extremity?

The affects, anxieties, and needs that Harry Jarvis transmitted to us, along with the folder of his sister's poems, were undoubtedly compounded by the vast geopolitical changes that have taken place in the many years since the end of World War II. How could Sonja Jaslowitz's history and poetry become intelligible in a context in which memorial transmission is short-circuited by the shifts in national borders; the realignment of political orientation; and the contestation, erasure, and forgetting of particular histories, like Transnistria's? How can postgenerations even begin to think about calibrating the search for acknowledgment and memorialization of people like Jarvis, who incurred the immeasurable loss of loved ones in the killing fields and wakes of the Holocaust, against the very limited possibilities of redress and reparation that exist after decades of neglect and oblivion?

REPARATIVE APPROACHES

In its most common usage, reparation is an ethicopolitical and legal concept—a public acknowledgment of injury by a state or state-connected institution and a compensatory settlement that often, but not always, involves a
monetary award (Torpey, *Making Whole, Politics and the Past*). But reparation
(or repair) is also a key concept in psychoanalysis, particularly in object relations theory, which was inspired by Melanie Klein's revisions of Freud and
her pioneering practical and theoretical work in infant and child psychology.
In Klein's early writings in the 1920s, she brought both these dimensions of
reparation to light, referring to the massive damage done and the economic
needs created by World War I. By the mid-1930s, however, on the basis of
her extensive psychological analysis of infants, she employed the term "reparation" primarily to describe an intrapsychic process of restoration enabling
both a healthy infant (and, by extension, adult) intellectual and psychological development and a secure grasp of reality (Klein, "Love, Guilt, and Reparation").[2] It specifically derives from the infant's ambivalent relationship
to the mother: from her sense of the mother as nurturing love object *and*
as the not always present or available hostile object, tormenting the infant
with hunger and privation, thus eliciting bouts of mistrust, indignant rage,
and fantasies of aggression and injury. Reparation, in the aftermath of these
destructive and hateful fantasized impulses, enables the infant to restore the
mother to a loved, wholesome, and nourishing state. It reflects, in Klein's
words, "a profound urge to make sacrifices, in order to help and to put right
loved people who in fantasy have been harmed or destroyed" ("Love, Guilt,
and Reparation" 311).

This reparative script, Klein further argued, is fundamentally connected to a second intrapsychic process—mourning—one enabling the infant "to work over in its mind a sense of loss entailed in the mother's actual
imperfections" (Likierman 107). Indeed, mourning is in itself reparative—a
means of attempting to recover or restore the object (*wiederherstellen*) and
to make it good again (*wiedergutmachen*). It is a process that *must* be undertaken, Klein argues, even though it can never be adequate to the injury
or the loss. The fantasy of repairing a lost or damaged object is thus complicated by messy, complex, uncontrollable, and contradictory feelings: by
guilt, inadequacy, and frustration; by anger, aggression, and projection;
and, most troublingly, by ambivalence and the inability to tolerate it. In
psychoanalytic terms, mourning and repair are thus not only processes of
working through: they inevitably also involve some amount of acting out
(Klein, "Mourning").

Clearly, Klein's suggestive formulations about injury and the psychological need for repair and mourning have significantly inflected political and legal claims for reparation. Since World War II, for example, as historian Lynn Hunt has argued, human rights discourses have presented such claims on the basis of "emotional appeal(s)" stemming from psychic reparative needs at least as often as those buttressed by "reason"—her abbreviated characterization of more conventionally employed evidentiary formulations (26).

But Kleinian developmental psychology also allows us to appreciate the psychic complexities of what it means to survive or to inherit, however indirectly, traumatic events that fail to be recognized and worked through in a *longue durée* of many decades—what it means, in other words, to live with the dead. What if there is no official body—neither a state nor other national or transnational institution—to recognize or be accountable for political and legal claims? What if denial and obliviousness continue? How can postgenerations mourn? And without the possibility of mourning, how can they even begin to seek repair?

The legal scholar Martha Minow provides one suggestive response. In her book *Between Vengeance and Forgiveness,* she argues that direct victims and survivors of mass violence and historical trauma may be able to begin to address their personal reparative needs by being provided with, first, a venue to "tell [their] story and be heard without interruption of skepticism," and, second, a "commitment to produce a coherent, if complex, narrative about the entire nation's trauma, and the multiple sources and expressions of its violence" (58). In combination, these two reinforce one another: each individual story helps to shape a larger history by providing it with detail, depth, and nuance, and, in turn, each story is enhanced and given broader meaning through its contextualization within a larger historical matrix. Postgenerations haunted by stories that have not been worked through still find that they owe the victims this act of attentive listening, as well as this work of historical repair.

In the spirit of such a modest act of historical and, in this case also literary, redress, the fragmentary story of Sonja Jaslowitz and the little-known history of Transnistria's camps and ghettos need to be told together—along with a reading, translation, and publication of Sonja's poems as well as a reflection on what permitted them to be created. Certainly, a fuller historical account of the conditions in which they were created might influence and, perhaps, enhance how we read them: their testimonial value trumping their literary shortcomings. But it is important to keep in mind that Sonja Jaslowitz's poems are the output of a very young girl whose formal schooling ended at age twelve or thirteen. They are part of a genre of adolescent writing produced, like the writings and drawings of other children and adolescents in ghettos and camps, under extreme duress. Had Sonja lived and gone on to write more poetry, she might have been embarrassed to be identified with what would then have been her juvenilia.

The psychic complexities of the work of reparation, suggested by Melanie Klein, should enjoin those of us in the postgeneration to examine our own motives and stakes, our own needs and desires as we attempt to tell this history and claim an unclaimed legacy. They should warn about the temptation to project our fears and fantasies of vulnerability and our needs for testimonial sincerity and authenticity on children's expressions.[3] They should warn, especially, about the pitfalls that confront any attempted act of historical and literary repair in places and areas where political and legal acknowledgment and reckoning is largely absent.

And yet such an approach to repair—through small acts attuned to small claims—offers a different set of openings in memory studies: it can respond to the vulnerability of personal and familial archives that come to light in chance encounters such as our brief meeting with Harry Jarvis. And it can mobilize these archives to enliven and personalize forgotten histories of places like Transnistria. It might thus take us out of the national and even the transnational frames in which cultural memory has been studied, focusing on local histories and their movement and import, their connections to other small stories, across space and time.

THE FORGOTTEN CEMETERY

The belatedness of the "discovery" of Selma Meerbaum-Eisinger and Harry Jarvis's repeated efforts to gain recognition for his sister Sonja's poetry—each fueled by powerful emotional needs—can, in part, be accounted for circumstantially by the peculiarities associated with the Romanian displacement and genocide of the Jews (Carp).[4] It can be explained by the fact that this history remains largely unincorporated within the paradigm of deportation, ghettoization, and extermination that has shaped Holocaust studies. Some of the reasons for Romania's virtual omission from this transnational master narrative have to do with the predominant conceptualizations of the Holocaust—impressions that for the most part have been shaped by a focus on crimes associated with German Nazism and on Nazi German–established ghettos and concentration/extermination camps in Central Europe and in occupied Poland. Auschwitz, Treblinka, and the Lódz and Warsaw ghettos were—and still largely remain—the principal defining shadows of genocidal evil.

This broad understanding influenced even officials of major Holocaust memorial and research institutions. An example: before the United States Holocaust Memorial Museum belatedly, in 1998, agreed to recognize Transnistria as one of the killing fields on the wall of its Hall of Remembrance, the museum's director, Walter Reich, rationalized previous museum refusals to do this by saying, "We cannot put up the name of every little *shtetl*" (Gold, "How Transnistria"). His erroneous categorization of Transnistria as a shtetl (a small town or village) reflects the widespread public and academic ignorance about this large Romanian-administered region where, over a period of three years, nearly 300,000 Jews and Roma perished.[5]

But events within Romania during the final months of World War II and in the ensuing Cold War era under communism also explain its absence from larger Holocaust histories. Fascist Romania had been Nazi Germany's staunchest ally at the outbreak of World War II and during the first three years of Germany's invasion of the Soviet Union. Hundreds of thousands of Romanian soldiers fought alongside German troops—more men than the total number of troops sent into battle by all other German allies combined. Romanians, however, also suffered extensive military and economic casualties in this alliance: some 370,000 Romanian soldiers were killed in battle or were missing in action; tens of thousands were wounded.

Many in the country became increasingly angry and disillusioned with their leaders, and opponents of the ruling fascists became more daring. In late August 1944, eight months before the end of World War II in Europe, a coup headed by Romania's King Michael and supported by communists and disaffected military officers overthrew the regime headed by Marshal Ion Antonescu and switched Romania's support from the Axis to the Allied-Soviet side (Axworthy, Scafes, and Craciunoiu).

When the war ended, Romanian rule swung increasingly to the Left. Two Romanian People's Tribunals (in Bucharest and Cluj) were established to try suspected war criminals and perpetrators of atrocities. During the Bucharest tribunals, prosecutorial documents were presented on the deportation of Jews to Transnistria, and transcripts of oral testimonies from the accused—though not from surviving victims—were also collected. But, unlike the postwar International Military Tribunals at Nuremberg or the SS trials that were held subsequent to the Nazi defeat, these testimonial materials were not widely disseminated and were largely withdrawn from access.[6]

Indeed, as was argued in the 2005 *Final Report of the International Commission on the Holocaust in Romania*—a commission established nearly sixty years after the conclusion of World War II—the People's Tribunals reflected a bitter end-of-war power struggle within Romania "between the so-called nationalist camp and [a] communist camp supported by the Soviet army" (ICHR

319).[7] Many in Romania "saw the trials as an anti-national act, an attempt by foreigners and their local aides to take their revenge against Romanians." By highlighting "outsiders" and "retribution" as elements influencing their procedures, Romanian nationalists thus delegitimized the tribunals, and the nature, extent, and intensity of fascist era crimes committed by Romanians were not incorporated into Romania's collective self-awareness (ICHR 314–15, 319).

A majority of sentences pronounced by the Tribunals were commuted to lesser punishments within a short time, and almost all convicted perpetrators were released under amnesty offerings in the 1950s and early 1960s. Most importantly, after the war, Transnistria itself ceased to exist as a discrete Romanian-ruled political entity with defined boundaries, and the region was, once again, submerged into the Ukrainian part of the Soviet Union. Since it was no longer part of Romania, the issue of responsibility for what had happened there in the early 1940s faded from the consciousness of non-victimized Romanians. Nonetheless, for many of the Jewish and non-Jewish survivors of Romanian displacement and horrific violence, as well as for their relatives and descendants, the sufferings of the war years remained open wounds. The combined unwillingness of Romanians to bring the fuller story of Transnistria to light and the minimizing of punishment for convicted perpetrators were bitter signals to them that neither historical accounting nor justice had in any sense been served.

What is more, the sites of the camps and ghettos in the area of the former Transnistria itself have remained largely unacknowledged and unmarked in present-day Ukraine. Apart from larger towns like Moghilev and Bershad, Jewish cemeteries were and continue to be neglected, mass graves remain unidentified, and commemorative signs are few. As a result, present-day local inhabitants are remarkably ignorant of the region's violent and murderous history, and returnee survivors and their descendants rarely find the sites of camps and ghettos or the mass graves they come there to seek. All of these omissions magnify affect and need, even as they minimize the possibilities of political and legal reparation at such a vast temporal remove.

To be sure, some information about the Romanian Holocaust did emerge briefly in the aftermath of the war from unofficial accounts by witnesses and survivors. In 1963, for example, informed by some of these testimonies, Hannah Arendt, in *Eichmann in Jerusalem,* singled out the Romanian Holocaust for its "sheer butchery" (Arendt 191–92). But the bulk of archived documentary information about the Holocaust in Romania became publicly accessible only after December 1989 and the subsequent opening of East European archives, following the collapse of the Soviet Union. The possibility of accessing these archival resources has enabled a corrective broadening of the long-existing perception of the German-Polish–centered core boundaries and reach of the Holocaust.

A new multivolume encyclopedia being published by the United States Holocaust Memorial Museum is incorporating materials from previously closed Soviet and East German archives that vastly expand the number of Nazi and Fascist camps and ghettos during the war to 42,500 (including hundreds in Greater Romania)—an immense enlargement of the map of perpetration that will certainly bring about an important shift in public consciousness.[8] But even within this expanded Holocaust history, Transnistria's role is still very much in development.[9]

TRANSNISTRIA: THE DUMPING GROUND

In late August of 1941, as a reward for Romania's material support and military alliance with Nazi Germany in the war against the Soviet Union, Adolf Hitler signed an agreement with his counterpart Führer, the *conducător* Marshal Ion Antonescu, that gave Romania control of a territory of nearly 65,000 square kilometers between the Dniester and the Bug River west to east, and the Black Sea and Lyadova River, south to north. Being "across the Dniester [trans Nistru]" lent the territory its name: Transnistria (Ancel, *Transnistria* I.17–20; see Illustration 4.2).[10]

The Tighina Agreement permitted the German military to set up naval and air bases in this territory and to continue to be allowed to enter it "to perform special jobs"—this, in the aftermath of the wave of genocidal "cleansing" operations in which nearly one third of the area's native Jewish population of approximately 300,000 were murdered by the Einsatzgruppe D, an SS mobile death squad, and by members of the German Eleventh and Romanian Third and Fourth Armies during the initial weeks following Germany's invasion of the Soviet Union (Ancel, *Transnistria* I.20, 50–52).

The agreement left unstated that some of the "special jobs" performed by the German military would eventually be undertaken in conjunction with the privately owned Todt and August Dohrman strategic road and bridge construction companies: periodic raids across the Bug River from German-occupied Ukraine to "recruit" surviving Jews for forced labor. But Romanian officials were clearly unfazed by these German intrusions into Transnistria—indeed, they welcomed them—because they fit well into Marshal Antonescu's vision for the future of this territory: to keep it for the long term and incorporate it as a new province of a Greater Romanian Empire into which ethnic Romanians would be introduced as permanent settlers after the Axis powers defeated the Soviet Union and removed all Jewish

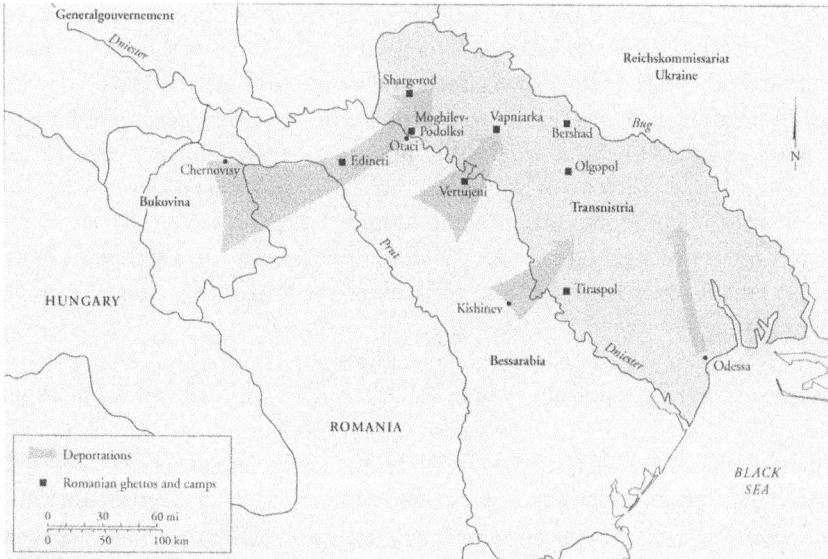

Illustration 4.2. Romania with Transnistria, 1941–1942. Based on maps from the United States Holocaust Memorial Museum.

and Roma inhabitants from the region (Ancel, "Romanian Way" 187–23; *Transnistria* I.20).

In practice, however, these German military raids, while certainly effective in their deadly intent, were not frequent or large enough to eliminate *all* Jews from the province, especially after the decision on the part of Romanian authorities to send hundreds of thousands of *new* Jewish deportees to Transnistria from the country's newly reacquired provinces, Bessarabia and the Northern Bukowina (Ancel, *Transnistria* I.17–19). Initially, underlying these large-scale deportations was the assumption that Jews surviving their brutal displacements would eventually be transferred out of Romanian territory altogether, across the Bug River into German-controlled Ukraine, where they would be subjected to "special treatment," the Nazi euphemism for annihilation.[11] Transnistria, in this plan, was to be nothing more than a large-scale temporary "holding" or "containment" place for deported Jews—a "dumping ground."

To await the mass transfer of Jews across the Bug River—an event that, according to the Tighina Agreement, could take place only "following the completion of military operations"—Romanian authorities established dozens of makeshift ghettos and scores of small concentration camps throughout Transnistria. Guarded by Romanian gendarmes and Ukrainian auxiliaries, and generally fenced in with barbed wire, the camps were set up in abandoned and derelict buildings, barns, stables, and pigsties on the outskirts of villages and kolkhozes (collective farms), while the ghettos were marked off in designated town streets and neighborhoods. All suffered from overcrowding, lack of sanitation, and the immense deprivation of food and potable water. They were exposed to bitterly cold temperatures–the winter of 1941–1942 being one of the coldest on record in Eastern Europe–and to illnesses and epidemics that resulted in mass fatalities.[12]

Unlike the Nazi camps in Germany, Austria, Latvia, Lithuania, occupied Poland, and near the eastern bank of the Bug in occupied Ukraine, which were organized and were generally operated as part of a centralized network and planned system, the Romanian camps were, for the most part, set up in a very improvisatory manner. Although identified with terms similar to those used in the Nazi network–"detention," "internment," "political," "labor," and even "death" camps–the camps were launched and administered haphazardly. They lacked a strategic blueprint, so that the distinctions between the camps themselves were often greater than differences between them and some of the more restrictive Transninstrian ghettos like Shpikov and Tulchin (Golbert 218–21).

Killing methods also differed greatly from Nazi practices of extermination in Poland. Even the worst Transnistrian camps had no gas vans, gas chambers, or ovens. But their decentralized ways, for all their informality, were remarkably brutal. They included mass starvation, deprivation of water, forced marches and relocations, poisoning with food known to be toxic to humans, lack of shelter, and exposure to freezing temperatures and epidemic diseases as well as mass shootings and incinerations (Carmelly; Shachan; USC Shoah Foundation).

Cariera de Piatră, the small concentration/labor camp in which Sonja Jaslowitz and her parents were imprisoned before their transfer to the Tiraspol ghetto and end-of-war repatriation to Bucharest, was located some fifteen kilometers north of the Ladijin ghetto, on an elevated plateau a short ascent from the banks of the Bug. It had once been an active granite rock quarry that the Soviets, before the war, had turned into a punitive camp for criminals. After the Romanians acquired Cariera de Piatră, they initially used the ruins of that camp to literally dump hundreds of Jewish inmates who had been deported from Cernăuți's asylum for the mentally ill in the summer of 1942.

Those among these unfortunate inmates who managed to remain alive did so by finding shelter in wrecked old guard and storage sheds that had partially been built into the rock and by scrounging for whatever edibles they could find. They were joined on the upper plateau level of the Cariera by some 4,000 Jewish deportees from Bessarabia and Bukowina, including the Jaslowitzs, the mother and father of the poet Paul Celan, Selma Meerbaum-Eisinger with her parents, and the future psychoanalyst and co-founder of the Fortunoff Video Archive for Holocaust Testimonies at Yale, Dori Laub, together with his mother. The inmates were told that this camp was a transit camp from which they would be transferred to work destinations elsewhere ("Klara and Dori L. Holocaust Testimony"; Schultz and Timms 188, 194; Weissglas 31–39).

Although many of the Jews sent to Cariera de Piatră died there or in its vicinity—the remaining physically impaired and mentally disturbed inmates from the Cernăuți asylum were shot in late August 1942 by Ukrainian guards working for the Romanians—the camp did indeed serve as a transit point. The deportees were dispersed, for the most part, to places like Michailowka, on the eastern side of the Bug River, that were run as slave labor supply camps by Nazi authorities for the strategic road companies that built roads and bridges for the German military.

We only have sparse information about Sonja and her parents from this period of internment. We have no account of their everyday lives—of how they managed to shelter and feed themselves and survive. We do know that most of the prisoners were regularly marched down for forced agricultural work from the Cariera de Piatră plateau. Unlike many Cariera inmates, Sonja and her parents managed to avoid being selected for forced labor in German-controlled territory. Sonja's poem "Heimweh" (Longing) conveys the intensity of her yearning for home and the darkness of her outlook at the time—a pessimism that she tried to dispel in her concluding lines.[13]

In dieser steinern Natur	In this rocky landscape
wird mein Herz zu Stein	My heart turns to stone
Ich bin eine Verbannte nur	I am the banished one
verurteilt zu Qual und Pein	Condemned to hurt and pain
In meinem Herzen ist eine Bucht	In my heart a canyon
so tief und breit	So deep and wide
Es ist eine grosse Sehnsucht	An endless longing
Und die Heimat ist so weit	For my distant home
Wenn ich an meine Heimat denke	When I think of home
fühle ich heisse Tränen fliessen	Hot tears begin to flow
In mir tobt und zehrt das Heimweh	Longing rages within me
Und mein Herzblut will vergiessen	Draining my heart's blood
Verjagt von seiner Heimatsstätte	Chased from our homestead
Von seinen Lieben, Hab und Gut	From all we knew and loved
Mich drückt die schwere Verbannungskette	Heavy chains of exile
Geknechtet ist mein Lebensmut	Drag me down
	And yoke my courage to live

Wenn mein Blick die Ferne streift dann sehe ich alles	When my eyes gaze to the distance I see it all
Grau und schwer und ach—wie mich die Angst ergreift	So heavy and gray And oh—how fear does grip me
Mein Herz erstirbt—wird tot und lehr	My heart expires—empty and dead
Doch weit in dieser grauen Ferne—	But far away in this gray distance—
uns die Erlösung flammend winkt—	A flickering redemption waves
es leuchtet auf ein Hoffnungsfeuer!	A flame of hope lights up
Das zu neuer Kraft uns zwingt;	Compelling us to strength
Und dieses spricht mit starker Stimme:	And with a powerful
Ertraget euer schweres Sein,	Voice, it calls
denn nach jedem Sturmgewitter—	Endure your cruel lot,
kommt doch wieder Sonnenschein.	The darkest hour Always precedes the dawn.[14]

Certainly, the fact that in spite of the horrors suffered, a sizeable minority of Jews, including the Jaslowitzes, managed to survive the Transnistrian ghettos and camps highlights the interstices that existed in the Romanian treatment of Jews during these years. The very qualities that defined the Romanians as disorganized, unsystematic, improvisatory, haphazard, and venal in contrast to the Germans also provided Jewish deportees and camp inmates some small possibilities to barter for food, to bribe for a favor, to communicate, and even to organize in order to resist and continue to live. This was especially true in the aftermath of the German defeat in Stalingrad in February 1943, the massive Romanian military casualties on the eastern front, and the growing Romanian loss of confidence in Germany's invincibility.

Some Romanian officials began to hedge their bets on the outcome of the war and, not wanting to be punished as war criminals if the Allies won, began to ease up somewhat in their treatment of Jews. By the spring of 1943, it became easier for Jews in Transnistria to barter for food, to bribe for a favor, to communicate, and to organize. It even became possible for some to note events and feelings in journals, to write poetry, to compose camp songs, and to produce drawings and engravings—an art of witness that, though of greatly varying quality, survived to testify to their experience (Gall). These remarkable works provide an expanded context in which to think about Sonja Jaslowitz and her poetic production.

The best-known visual artist working in Transnistria was Arnold Daghani, who later produced an important body of work in England. Daghani survived two years of internment in the deadly Michailowka camp by working as an artist for Nazi officers, but, secretly, he was also able to create a number of testimonial drawings and watercolors in Michailowka and in the Bershad ghetto, to which he and his wife eventually managed to escape not long before the Germans killed off all Jewish slave labor workers on their side of the Bug River. These images bear witness to conditions in the camp and ghetto and to individual prisoners (see Illustrations 4.3, 4.4, and 4.5).

In Vapniarka, a concentration camp the Romanians set up for alleged political "undesirables" (the majority of them Jewish), prisoners participated in multiple cultural activities, among them a rich set of drawings and watercolors testifying to the disease that killed a great number of the camp's inmate population. Romanian authorities in Vapniarka fed the prisoners a daily meal of soup containing toxic chickling peas, *lathyrus sativus,* that attacked the central nervous system, leading to paralysis, kidney failure, and an eventual agonizing death (Hirsch and Spitzer, *Ghosts of Home* 198–231). Vapniarka's artists have left an invaluable visual record of the progress of this disease, the toll it took, and the longing for survival that motivated the prisoners (see Illustrations 4.6 and 4.7). Like Sonja Jaslowitz, they often calibrated horror with small gestures of hope.

Illustration 4.3. Arnold Daghani, Mikhaelowka, 1942. Collection of the Yad Vashem Art Museum, Jerusalem, Arnold Daghani Trust.

Illustration 4.4. Arnold Daghani, Bershad ghetto, 1943. Collection of the Yad Vashem Art Museum, Jerusalem, Arnold Daghani Trust.

Illustration 4.5. In a pencil drawing, Daghani depicts the death of Selma Meerbaum-Eisinger in Michailowka from typhus in 1943. Collection of the Yad Vashem Art Museum, Jerusalem, Arnold Daghani Trust.

Illustration 4.6. Drawings of Vapniarka by Moshe Leibel and Ilie, 1942–1943. Courtesy of the Kessler Archive.

Illustration 4.7. The Little Vapniarka Artists Book (1943), made in honor of Dr. Arthur Kessler, an inmate who exposed the toxic Lathyrus sativus in the soup fed to the prisoners. Courtesy of the Kessler Archive.

SMALL ACTS

The artistic works that were produced in Transnistria—most of them still absent from the canon of Holocaust art and literature—invite us to think about how historical narratives inflected by artistic accounts can become modes of repair. The visual art works, the surviving fragments of memoirs jotted down on site, the poems and writings composed in camps and ghettos—all these call for particular practices of reading, looking, and listening. They invite approaches that resist heroization or redemption: small readings, performed in a minor key and in a spirit of solidarity. And they ask for forms of attunement that constitute expanded notions of responsibility—responsibility not as accountability but, simply, indicative of the ability and willingness to respond (Minow, *Between Vengeance and Forgiveness* 118–47, "Surviving Victim Talk" 1442–45).

The question, therefore, is: how, at a generational remove and great geographic distance, can we bring such a responsive approach and spirit to Sonja Jaslowitz's poems? We can, of course, show and publish them as we are doing here in our effort to connect small, individual stories to a larger group and national history. We can try to enliven the stories of young artists like Sonja Jaslowitz against the backdrop of a history composed of shocking numbers and inassimilable details. We can try to preserve some of the texture of her life, the timbre of her voice, and the sharpness of her humor on the basis of what remains—some photos and drawings, a few lines of her verse. But what more can we do? Should we try to fill in the blanks, imagine what we cannot know, or shall we call attention to the gaps, underscoring the incommensurability of the desire for redress and the impossibility of achieving it? Eve Kosofsky Sedgwick's notion of "reparative reading" might be helpful in an attempt to "claim" legacies such as Sonja Jaslowitz's. As opposed to what she called "paranoid reading," which anticipates an ending that is already predetermined, reparative reading is open to surprises, contingencies, alternative views. Through this perspective, one might, in Sedgwick's terms, entertain the possibility that "the past ... could have happened differently from the way it actually did" (146). How would a reparative reading of Sonja Yaslowitz's poems permit us such a possibility?

All of Sonja Jaslowitz's surviving poems were composed during her internment in Transnistria, first in Cariera de Piatră and later in the Tiraspol ghetto. Sonja may have written poems before she was deported, but none of them have been found. The multiple languages and registers she used (albeit with unequal mastery)—German, Romanian, and French (or "Franco-Romanian")—tell us a great deal about the rich multicultural landscape of her upbringing and incarceration among Czernowitz Jews. They reflect one of the ways she attempted to perpetuate that landscape, even as it and its inhabitants were being destroyed. But their multicultural and multilinguistic makeup, and their failure to fit a continuous national literary tradition, also make it more difficult for poems like hers to be published and recognized.

It is significant that, so far, we have succeeded in placing some of her poems in French translation in a special issue of the *Revue de l'histoire de la Shoah* devoted to Transnistria ("Le Horreur oubliée"). Several of her German poems and a German translation of several Romanian ones have just appeared in an Austrian publication tellingly named *Zwischenwelt* (Ausleitner and Windsperger). Given Romania's continuing reluctance to take responsibility for the murders committed in Transnistria, her Romanian-language poems, particularly, are not likely to find a ready readership and ready publication opportunities in that country today, although we are beginning to develop some leads there as well.

Jaslowitz's poems are mostly rhymed, reflecting the forms typical of the poetry popular and produced in interwar Cernăuți, poetry she would have heard at home and learned in school.[15] But the linguistic differences in them are significant. A few of them, nostalgic ones that reveal her strong longing for home as well as her more allusive, less explicitly referential creations, are in German, as we saw in her poem "Heimweh" (Longing). But most of Jaslowitz's testimonial poems documenting camp and ghetto existence are written in Romanian. Romanian was the official language of Transnistria's camp and ghetto system, and, for Sonja Jaslowitz, it seems to have been the more unambiguous language of witness and communication with fellow prisoners.

While the German poems describe a natural landscape suffused with the effects of oppression and dehumanization, the Romanian ones draw portraits of inmates and guards, complain about punishments, and finely observe and enact small moments of optimism and of despair. A reading that preserves these multilingual resonances would also preclude publication in any one language.

"Cântecul plecării"	"Song of Departure"
Termină cu visarea da da da	Stop your dreaming, yeah yeah yeah
Scoateți din cap plecarea	Get leaving out of your head
Degeaba ai sprat, te-ai zbuciumat te-ai frământat	You hoped, you suffered, you agonized
Și totul ai împachetat	You packed everything up—in vain
Să-ți iei haine groase da da da	Take some warm clothes, yeah yeah yeah
Să-ți dregi pe cele roase	Stitch the torn ones
Și să întorci pe dos tot ce-ai mai gros	Fix them up
Că-i timp ploios și veșnic nu va fi frumos	It will rain it will be bleak
Și să te rogi ca de crăciun	And you should pray that at Christmastime
Să fie Kestorul mai bun	The guard will be well-inclined
Să-ți dea concediua în ajun	And will free you
Vreo două zile	For two days or so
De altfel nici să te gândești	In other ways don't even think
Tiraspol c'ai să părăsești	That you'll ever leave Tiraspol
Căci plecările's povești	Because departure is no more
Pentru copile	Than a tale
	For children

Given the circumstances of their composition, Jaslowitz's poems can be viewed as improbable acts of resistance, defiance, and witness in poetic form. With each line of verse, with each rhyme, she seems to face down oppression and thus perhaps to help others do so as well. But is it not too large a burden on her and on the poems to read them in this way?

"Marşul Transnistriei"	"Transnistria March"
Cânta Transnistria	Sing Transnistria
Şi cântecul tău	And your song
O să răsune	Will resound
Prin munţi şi prin văi	Through mountains and valleys
Cânta Transnistria	Sing Transnistria
Un cântec de foc	A song of fire
Cin'te aude	Whoever hears you
Să mişte din loc	Will move along
Prin voioşieţ	With a light heart
Vom fi fericiţi	We will be joyous
Cu toate că suntem	Even though we are
Rău prigoniţi	Severely tormented
Parola noastră e	Our password is
Fi optimist	Be optimistic
Mereu vessel	Always gay
Si nicicând trist	And never sad
Cântecul nostrum	Our song
Norii va străpunge	Will pierce the clouds
Păn'la fraţii noştrii	Until it reaches
El va ajunge	Our distant brothers
Suferinţa mare	The great suffering
Prin care am trecut	That we had to endure
Mai mândrii şi tare	It will make us
Pe noi n-ea fâcut	Prouder and tougher
Cu sperinţa'n suflet	With hope in our souls
Noi vom birui	We will win
Soarele draptâţii	The sun of justice
Din nou va străluci	Beloved liberty
Libertatea dragă	Will smile on us anew
Ne va surăde iar	It's thus that we will cross
Astfel vom trece	The borders of Transnistria
Al Transnitiei hotar	

Some of the poems, like "Song of Departure," are marked by biting sarcasm and irony. Remarkably, however, some also describe small pleasures that endure even in circumstances of dire suffering. And, like many expressions by children and adolescents, most end in overarching messages of hopefulness and gesture toward a future freedom, toward life. Amid the disappointments occasioned by repeated false rumors of impending liberation that Sonja describes in cruel detail, it must have been hard to continue to hope.

We are, of course, tempted to admire and to celebrate that hopeful-ness, but, doing so, are we not repeating well-worn clichés about children's and adolescent's testimonies and their unmediated sincerity and optimism? Should we not also wonder about the costs of hope in Transnistria? Was Sonja the dutiful daughter who wanted to cheer her parents? Or are her re-petitive assertions of hope gestures imposed on the prisoners, to be read with suspicion? Are they symptoms of ironic resignation, or are we to read them as a young girl's refusal to succumb to despair—a refusal perhaps shared and supported by fellow inmates? Was she temperamentally optimistic, forward looking, and would that make her absurd and meaningless death even more poignant?

For New Year's in 1943, Sonja wrote "Cântecul Revelionului" (The Song of New Year's Eve):

Revelionul noi îl serbâm	We celebrate the New Year
Şi cu toţi ne bucurăm	And together we are glad
C-am trait	We lived
Am izbutit	We managed
Viaţa grea am biruit	We defeated difficulty
Sâ fim veseli, câci de acum	Let's be happy, since from now
Anul ne va aduce ceva mai bun	The year will bring us something better
Încurajare, eliberare	Encouragement, freedom
Şi plecare acasâ	And a way home
Paharul âsta s-îl ridicăm	We raise our glass
Şi într'un glas noi sâ ne urăm	And wish each other
Fraternitate, sânâtate	Friendship, health,
Şi veşnica libertate	And freedom, always.

Revelion in Romanian means "awakening, a new dawn." Given Sonja Jaslo-witz's absurd death, it is difficult for us, now, to return to the end of 1943 and the beginning of 1944 and to imagine the future she was trying to an-ticipate with her song. But perhaps this is the best we could do for her: to attempt to imagine the spirit in which she wrote her poems, rather than reading them under the shadow of finality.

In the absence of a public national or transnational reckoning with the murderous crimes that Sonja endured, the most we can do is perform a reading of her poems that is neither critical, nor analytic, nor apologetic, nor redemptive, but that is, indeed, reparative. We might thus see Sonja's very belief in a future as a modest gesture that stitches together remnants of confidence and expectation for herself and for others. For our postregen-eration, to claim her legacy would then be our way to recognize and call attention to her creative effort: not to great literature and not to heroism but to her intimation of a future in a potential, or virtual, or, one might say, subjunctive mode—from her perspective, what might yet be, and, from ours, what might have been.

The past's future, brought into the present, widens that present, enlarges it with a hopefulness that pierces through layers of darkness. In this spirit, the poems place Sonja Jaslowitz not on the threshold of the catastrophe that was awaiting her but on the threshold of possibility she herself managed to conjure with her words. And, in attempting this manner of reparative reading, perhaps we could leave her there in the poems and their own anachronistic temporality rather than in the catastrophic teleology that was to be hers.

Marianne Hirsch is William Peterfield Trent Professor of English and Comparative Literature at Columbia University and the director of the Institute for Research on Women, Gender, and Sexuality. She is a past president of the Modern Language Association of America. Hirsch's work combines memory studies with feminist theory, particularly the transmission of violent histories across generations. Her recent books include *Family Frames: Photography, Narrative and Postmemory* (Harvard University Press, 1997), *The Generation of Postmemory: Writing and Visual Culture after the Holocaust* (Columbia University Press, 2012), and *Ghosts of Home: The Afterlife of Czernowitz in Jewish Memory* (University of California Press, 2011; with Leo Spitzer). Hirsch is one of the founders of Columbia's Center for the Study of Social Difference.

Leo Spitzer is Vernon Professor of History Emeritus and University Research Professor at Dartmouth College. He writes on responses to colonialism, marginality, and subordination and on Jewish refugee memory and its transmission. His recent books include *Lives in Between: The Experience of Marginality in a Century of Emancipation* (Hill & Wang, 1999), *Hotel Bolivia: The Culture of Memory in a Refuge from Nazism* (Hill & Wang, 1998), and *Ghosts of Home: The Afterlife of Czernowitz in Jewish Memory* (University of California Press, 2011; with Marianne Hirsch). He is currently working on an autohistory, *The Americanization of Poldi,* and, with Marianne Hirsch, on a book on school photographs.

NOTES

We are grateful to Dr. Harry Jarvis, who died in 2014, for giving us his sister's poems and for his confidence in us. Thanks to Roxana Verona and Ivy Schweitzer for their help in translating the poems into French and English. Thanks to Marianne Windsperger for publishing some of the poems in *Zwischenwelt* and to Florence Heymann and Alexandra Laignel-Lavastine for including them in their special issue of the *Revue d'histoire de la Shoah* on the Romanian Holocaust. Audiences at ACLA, the University of Illinois, Ghent University, the University of Cambridge, the USC Shoah Foundation, the University of Amsterdam, the University of Chicago, the "Creation and Postmemory" conference at Columbia University, the École des Hautes Études en Sciences Sociales, and the University of Vienna have provided invaluable suggestions on earlier versions of this argument. This essay appeared in a special double issue on "Figurations of Postmemory" of the *Journal of Literature and Trauma Studies* (4.1–2 (Spring/Fall 2015)) and is reprinted by permission.

1. See https://www.facebook.com/selma.meerbaumeisinger and https://www.facebook.com/pages/Selma-Meerbaum-Eisinger/103150629725186.
2. "Love, Guilt, and Reparation" was first presented as a public lecture in London in March 1936 under the auspices of the Institute of Psycho-Analysis and was subsequently published in 1937. But Klein had begun to develop her ideas about reparation in the 1920s. See Likierman 80.
3. On children's writing during the Holocaust, see especially Borwicz; Coquio and Kalinsky.
4. Republished in a critical edition in French with an excellent introduction and annotations by Alexandra Laignel-Lavastine.
5. Ironically, ten years later, in 2008, Transnistria only merited a brief two-column entry in the then new three-volume *YIVO Encyclopedia of Jews in Eastern Europe.*
6. For his pioneering book on the Romanian Holocaust, *Cartea Neagră,* Matatias Carp managed to acquire documents and photographs (through purchase, friendship, and discreet collaboration) from the Filderman Archives of the Bucharest Jewish Community Federation, the Romanian Ministry of the Interior, and a Wehrmacht officer with access to materials.
7. Some 1,400 cases were prosecuted, but only 668 were delivered, many in absentia.
8. Seven volumes are planned. As of today, volumes I and II are available.
9. Subsequent to Carp's *Cartea Neagră* and the opening of the Soviet and other East European archives, the scholarly contributions of the late Jean Ancel have been outstanding. See Ancel, "German-Romanian Relations."
10. For a summary of the terms of what became known as the Tighina Agreement between Hitler and Antonescu, see Ancel, *Transnistria* I.547; for the full Romanian version of the document, see Ancel, *Transnistria* II.41–42.
11. In his pretrial interrogation by Israeli police, Adolf Eichmann admitted that *Sonderbehandlung* (special treatment) always meant killing.
12. Both historical and survivor accounts from many of the Transnistrian camps and ghettos can be found in Carmelly and Shachan. Also see Gold, *Ruth's Journey*. The most extensive testimony collection about Transnistria's camps and ghettos (more than 400 accounts in several languages) can be found in the University of Southern California Shoah Foundation's *Visual History Archive.*
13. In another version, this poem is named "Transnistria am Steinbruch: Kariera de piatra." It is dated 25 July 1942 (shortly after the family's arrival there).

14. All translations of Jaslowitz's poetry are our own.

15. Borwicz, among others, points out that the extraordinary experiences of the ghettos and camp rarely led to an innovative literary form in children's verse, rather they would tend to fall back on verse forms learned in school. See Coquio and Kalinsky LLX.

WORKS CITED

Ancel, Jean. "The German-Romanian Relations and the Final Solution." *Holocaust and Genocide Studies* 19.2 (2005): 252–75.

——. "The Romanian Way of Solving the 'Jewish Problem' in Bessarabia and Bukovina, June–July 1941." *Yad Vashem Studies* 19 (1988): 187–232.

——. *Transnistria, 1941–1942: The Romanian Mass Murder Campaigns.* 3 vols. Trans. R. Garfinkel and Karen Gold. Tel Aviv: Goldstein-Goren Diaspora Research Center, 2003.

Arendt, Hannah. *Eichmann in Jerusalem: A Report on the Banality of Evil.* New York: Penguin, 1992.

Ausleitner, Judith, and Marianne Windsperger. "Weiterleben in den Gedichten: Die Poesie der Sonja Jaslowitz." *Zwischenwelt: Zeitschrift für Kultur des Exils und des Widerstands* 30.3–4 (2013): 13–17.

Axworthy, Mark, Coronel Scafes, and Cristian Craciunoiu, eds. *Third Axis, Fourth Ally: Romanian Armed Forces in the European War, 1941–1945.* London: Arms & Armour Press, 1995.

Borwicz, Michel. *Ecrits des condamnés à mort sous l'occupation nazie (1939–1945).* 1952. Paris: Gallimard, 1996.

Carmelly, Felicia Steigman, ed. *Shattered! 50 Years of Silence: History and Voices of the Tragedy in Romania and Transnistria.* Scarborough, Ontario: Abbeyfield, 1997.

Carp, Matatias. *Cartea Neagră: Fapte și documente. Suferințele evereilor din România 1940–1944.* Bucharest: Teliere Grafice SOCE, 1946.

Coquio, Catherine, and Aurélia Kalinsky. *L'Enfant et le génocide: Témoignages sur l'enfance pendant la Shoah.* Paris: Robert Laffont, 2007.

Documents Concerning the Fate of Romanian Jewry during the Holocaust. 12 vols. New York: The Beate Klarsfeld Foundation, 1986.

Gall, Matei. *Finsternis: Durch Gefängnisse, KZ Wapniarka, Massaker, und Kommunismus. Ein Lebenslauf in Rumänien, 1920–1990.* Konstanz: Hartung-Gorre Verlag, 1999.

Golbert, Rebecca L. "Holocaust Sites in Ukraine: Pechora and the Politics of Memorialization." *Holocaust and Genocide Studies* 18.2 (2004): 205–33.

Gold, Ruth Glasberg. "How Transnistria Was Added to the Map of Concentration Camps at the U.S. Holocaust Museum in Washington, D.C." *Czernowitz.ephes.com.* 2011. Web. 27 Mar. 2015.

——. *Ruth's Journey: A Survivor's Memoir.* Gainesville: University of Florida Press, 1996.

Hirsch, Marianne, and Leo Spitzer. "Testimonial Objects." *The Generation of Postmemory: Writing and Visual Culture after the Holocaust.* Marianne Hirsch. New York: Columbia University Press, 2012. 177–99.

———. *Ghosts of Home: The Afterlife of Czernowitz in Jewish Memory.* Berkeley: University of California Press, 2010.

Hunt, Lynn. *Inventing Human Rights: A History.* New York: Norton, 2007.

Independent Commission for Human Rights [ICHR]. "Trial of the War Criminals." *International Commission on the Holocaust in Romania: Final Report.* Iași: Polirom, 2005. 313–31.

"Klara and Dori L. Holocaust Testimony." Videorecording HVT 777. Fortunoff Video Archive for Holocaust Testimonies. Yale University, 1986.

Klein, Melanie. "Love, Guilt, and Reparation." *Love, Guilt, and Reparation and Other Works, 1921–1945.* Melanie Klein. New York: Delacorte Press, 1975. 306–43.

———. "Mourning and Its Relation to Manic-Depressive States." *Love, Guilt and Reparation and Other Works, 1921–1945.* Melanie Klein. New York: Delacorte Press, 1975. 344–69.

Laignel-Lavastine, Alexandra, ed. *Cartea Neagra: Le Livre noir de la destruction des Juifs de Roumanie, 1940–1944.* Trans. Alexandra Laignel-Lavastine. Paris: Denoël, 2009.

"Le Horreur oubliée: La Shoah roumaine." Spec. issue of *Revue d'Histoire de la Shoah* 194 (2011).

Likierman, Meira. *Melanie Klein: Her Work in Context.* London: Continuum, 2001.

Meerbaum-Eisinger, Selma. *Harvest of Blossoms: Poems from a Life Cut Short.* Trans. Jerry Glenn and Florian Birkmayer. Evanston: Northwestern University Press, 2008.

———. *Ich bin in Sehnsucht eingehüllt: Gedichte.* Ed. Jürgen Selle. Hamburg: Hoffmann & Campe, 2005.

Minow, Martha. *Between Vengeance and Forgiveness: Facing History after Genocide and Mass Violence.* Boston: Beacon, 1999.

———. "Surviving Victim Talk." *UCLA Law Review* 40 (1992): 1442–45.

Schultz, Deborah, and Edward Timms, eds. *Arnold Daghani's Memories of Mikhailowka: The Illustrated Diary of a Slave Labour Camp Survivor.* London: Vallentine Mitchell, 2009.

Sedgwick, Eve Kosofsky. *Touching Feeling: Affect, Pedagogy, Performativity.* Durham: Duke University Press, 2003.

Shachan, Avigdor. *Burning Ice: The Ghettos of Transnistria.* Boulder: Eastern European Monographs, 1996.

Torpey, John. *Making Whole What Has Been Smashed: On Reparations Politics.* Cambridge, MA: Harvard University Press, 2006.

———, ed. *Politics and the Past: On Repairing Historical Injustices.* New York: Rowman and Littlefield, 2003.

United States Holocaust Memorial Museum (USHMM). *Encyclopedia of Camps and Ghettos, 1933–1945.* Bloomington: Indiana University Press, 2013.

USC Shoah Foundation. *Visual History Archive.* The Institute for Visual History and Education n.d. Web. 27 Mar. 2015.

Weissglas, Isak. *Steinbruch am Bug: Bericht einer Deportation nach Transnistrien.* Berlin: Literaturhaus, 1995.

Yad Vashem. "Romanian-German Relations before and during the Holocaust." *Yadvashem.org* n.d. Web. 27 Mar. 2015.

Chapter 5

Fictions of Generational Memory

Caryl Phillips's *In the Falling Snow* and Black British Writing in Times of Mnemonic Transition

Astrid Erll

GENERATION, MEMORY, AND "BLACK" WRITING IN BRITAIN TODAY

In the opening chapter of Caryl Phillips's novel *In the Falling Snow* (2009), we see the black, forty-seven-year-old protagonist Keith riding the London underground, contemplating a group of teenagers sitting opposite him:

> He can see that, like his son Laurie, all three kids are partly white, but it is clear from their baggy dress sense, and from the way they slouch and speak, that they identify themselves as black ... today's teenagers no longer respect any boundaries. Black youths, white youths, mixed race youths, to them all he is just a middle-aged man in a jacket and tie who looks like he doesn't know shit about nothing. He lowers his gaze and tries to figure out the genders of the gang of three, whose faces remain shrouded beneath oversized hoods. (15)

What Keith realizes here is that some of his tried-and-true concepts of difference in British society have become outdated, in fact "unbound." Racial divides seem to have been displaced by a generational divide. Keith experiences a gap between himself and the young people he sees, and he understands that he cannot rely any longer on his generation's categories (concerning race as well as gender) in order to make sense of the group of youngsters before him.

To be sure, racism has not disappeared in Phillips's novel, but it is shown to play out very differently along generational lines.[1] One of the questions the novel asks is what "being black" means to a middle-aged (and middle-class) man today. Another question is how to gain a sense of genealogy in families and cultural formations disrupted by experiences of migration and diaspora. With these preoccupations, *In the Falling Snow* is a striking example of the heightened reflectiveness on issues of generation and memory that can be found in wide sections of contemporary literature—a feature that defines what I seek to describe in this essay as "fictions of generational memory."

More specifically, I will trace in this essay some of the literary interventions into issues of generation as we find them in black writing in Britain today.[2] I use the term "black writing in Britain" in the sense proposed by John McLeod in his essay "Extra Dimensions, New Routines." McLeod wishes "to retain the political understanding of 'black'" as it emerged in Great Britain in the 1970s and 1980s, but he also makes "a distinction between an older, dominant sphere of literary endeavour and an emergent one that is indebted to, but not overdetermined by, previous contexts and achievements, the political and aesthetic goals of which might be somewhat different, especially as regards writing the nation" (46).

The following discussion moves along the lines of McLeod's argument and shows that there are indeed "extra dimensions, new routines" emerging in contemporary black writing in Britain. Focusing on novels written by authors of (partly) Caribbean descent, which articulate (partly) Caribbean issues, I seek to highlight as one of their new (or at least significantly transformed) themes that of "generation and memory."

It is roughly since the turn of the millennium that questions related to "generation"—those of generationality, genealogy, and genetics—have become an ever-growing concern of black writing in Britain. Thinking about generation is a way of locating people in time (however difficult that may be in postcolonial and diasporic settings), and thus a practice—or a "symbolic form" (Weigel, "Generation")—of cultural memory. A significant number of recent black works in Britain can in fact be viewed as fictions of generational memory.[3] It seems that the heightened presence of memory issues in public discourses on immigration in the past two decades informs these novels (Korte and Pirker) and that at the same time they present invaluable interventions into our thinking about generation and memory, specifically in postcolonial and immigrant societies.

Reading contemporary black writing in Britain as fictions of generational memory, this chapter offers an in-depth interpretation of Caryl Phillips's *In the Falling Snow,* and it looks more briefly at Andrea Levy's *Small Island* and Zadie Smith's *White Teeth.* I am interested in how these novels negotiate what I call the "double logic of *generatio*"—the intersections of generationality and genealogy and their different roads into the memories of a postcolonial and immigrant society (Erll, "Generation"). What I propose is to read these instances of black writing in Britain through the lens not only of memory studies but also of research on generation (from Karl Mannheim's sociology of generations to more recent concepts developed in historiography and cultural studies), thus bringing into view the significant role that memory, generationality, and genealogy play in structuring contemporary literature.

With these questions, my chapter aims at a more nuanced understanding of "transgenerational memory" as one of the key dimensions of "memory unbound." I think it is time to broaden the conceptual repertoire of memory studies' preoccupation with the idea of generation. So far, the field has had a strong focus on the transgenerational transmission of traumatic memory—an area in which Marianne Hirsch's "postmemory" has arguably proved the most influential and fertile concept. But of the memories that travel between generations, traumatic ones constitute surely (and luckily) just a small part.

It therefore seems promising to open up the field's discourse on generation for the many other possible types of memory emerging between and across generations—for those that are "optimistic," "future oriented," and "productive" and for those that are "pessimistic," "inhibiting," and "unproductive." In this process, it may appear necessary to further conceptually fine-tune our understanding of transgenerational memory. To break ground, I propose the conceptual pair of "generationality and genealogy." In this chapter, I look at the complex constellations of generationality and genealogy that emerge in the diaspora, thus combining the transgenerational with the transcultural dimension of memory unbound.

ENTANGLED GENEALOGIES AND GENERATIONALITIES IN *WHITE TEETH* AND *SMALL ISLAND*

"Generation" is derived from the Greek *genesis* and the Latin *generatio* (origin, arise, [pro]creation). Traditionally, the term combined the meaning of both these terms: vertically, the production and reproduction of a species from one generation to the other and, horizontally, members of the species that have the same age. Synchronic generations describe forms of contemporaneity, while diachronic genealogy is essentially about transmission across time.[4] This double logic of *generatio*—contemporaneity and transmission—unfolds in the ways that intra- and intergenerational aspects are connected and intersect.

The problem of generation as familial genealogy has traditionally characterized the "black British *bildungsroman*" (Stein). In his study of black British literature, Mark Stein asserts, "The conflict of generations is part and parcel of the novel of transformation, and it is of particular importance in that different generations correspond to different cultural and social affiliations" (25). Conflicts between what in *White Teeth* Zadie Smith calls "*fathersons, oldyoung, borntherebornhere*" (219) imply a sense of genealogical transmission disrupted by migration. At the same time, many novels of the 1980s and 1990s that operated according to the black bildungsroman pattern bore witness to the emerging collective identity of a "second generation" of immigrants, thus unfolding the double logic of *generatio*.

Since the turn of the millennium, a widening of the range of generational concerns has been noticeable in black writing in Britain. Novels in this field are characterized by the fact that they present what one might call radically transcultural approaches to generation, in both its diachronic and its synchronic sense. To exemplify these dynamics, I will briefly draw on two of the best-known British novels of the new millennium: Zadie Smith's *White Teeth* (2000) and Andrea Levy's *Small Island* (2004).

Zadie Smith's now classic novel *White Teeth* is, among many other things, an intervention in the thinking about the complexities of genealogy and cultural memory in immigrant societies. In an important book on what she calls "genea-logic," Sigrid Weigel has shown in detail how the concept of genealogy intricately combines nature and culture: the very idea of genealogy traditionally revolves around the bodily, material, *and* cultural continuum of a species. Genealogy thus points to inheritance as well as to heritage; to biological continuity, that is, as well as to social continuity (Weigel, *Genea-logik*). *White Teeth* addresses these ambivalences in the discourse on genealogy.

It shows, specifically, how ideas of transmission along the lines of nature and culture play out in migrant settings. In its "Root Canals" chapters, *White Teeth* traces the genealogies of its London-based characters back to the Caribbean and to South Asia, to colonialism, the Indian Mutiny, and World War II. Many of these "roots" are familial genealogies based on biological procreation. But more importantly, some are also genealogies of "interracial" friendship, such as that between Samad and Archie, the Bangladeshi and the Englishman at the heart of the novel's story. And it is these genealogies of human attachment—affiliative genealogies, as it were, to use Edward Said's term—that are seen to prevail in the end.

White Teeth sets such histories of interaction and friendship in stark contrast to that other way of establishing roots: genetics. The "Future-Mouse" subplot about genetic engineering involves a Nazi doctor and thus reminds readers of the very genealogy of genetics, namely its implication in racism and eugenics. With its focus on genetics, *White Teeth* also appears as a pre-scient comment on genealogical practices in today's multicultural Britain. Channel 4's recent TV format *Empire's Children,* for instance, addresses the legacies of the British Empire through the family histories of British celebri-ties, while the 2003 BBC documentary *Motherland: A Genetic Journey* uses DNA testing to unravel the African roots of British descendants of Caribbean immigrants. It seems that the British Empire itself has become a terrain for genealogical thinking and DNA testing a major medium for negotiating cultural remembrance.[5]

Genealogical "purity" as it is represented in the Chalfens' family tree in the novel—at least in the young, mixed-race protagonist Irie's eyes—is cast aside as an impossible endeavor. Instead, what Irie, and by extension post-colonial Britain, have to face is coming to terms with their "chaotic, random flesh" (*White Teeth,* 342), with genealogies that are more often than not based on "rumour, folk-tale and myth" (338). As Irie thinks about her Caribbean ancestry, *White Teeth* pictures her family tree and, in the novel's typical mock scientific way, gives this a highly ironic twist by providing the following key to it:

Key
& = copulated with
% = paternity unsure
? = child's name unknown
G = brought up by grandmother (338)

The family tree as an age-old metaphor and mode of representing (usually genteel) genealogy (Weigel, *Genea-logik*) is thus adapted to the realities of the ordinary people populating today's postcolonial and multicultural societies.

While *White Teeth* teases out the multicultural complexities of genera-tion as diachronic genealogy, Andrea Levy's *Small Island* is more concerned with the dynamics of synchronic generation—that is, with generationality. *Small Island* explores the generational fundaments of multicultural Britain by drawing on the myth of the Empire Windrush: the Empire Windrush generation, the wave of British Caribbean people who migrated to Britain after World War II, was reinvigorated and publicly commemorated in Great Britain in 1998 on the occasion of the fiftieth anniversary of the eponymous ship bringing West Indian immigrants to Britain.

Those Caribbean (and South Asian) citizens of the British Common-wealth who came to the "motherland" (one of the many colonial metaphors of generation) after World War II were asked to give testimony in oral his-tory projects; their voices were collected in Mike Phillips and Trevor Phil-lips's *Windrush: The Irresistible Rise of Multi-racial Britain* and their histories visualized in the BBC 2 series *Windrush.* The postwar immigrants were thus turned into a broadly identifiable, highly mediatized generation, Britain's alleged "first generation of black immigrants" (Brunow).

In his classic "The Problem of Generations," first published in 1928, Karl Mannheim theorized generation in this synchronic sense. He distinguishes between three aspects of generation: first, generation in the broadest sense as a social "location" (in the way that class is a social location); second, the "generation as actuality," which is characterized by the shared experience of sociopolitical events; and third, the—even smaller—"generational unit," whose members respond in a similar way to these events. Mannheim, and the sociological research that has followed him (Eyerman and Turner; Schuman and Scott), emphasizes that generations are *not* cohorts in the strict biological sense but social phenomena based on shared experience, a sense of temporal rootedness and collective memory. More recently, social historians have introduced the concept of "generationality" in order to highlight questions of identity and processes of identification in the social production of generations:

> The term "generationality" ... has a twofold meaning. On the one hand, it refers to characteristics resulting from shared experiences that either individuals or larger "generational units" collectively claim for themselves. On the other hand, it can also mean the bundle of characteristics resulting from shared experiences that are ascribed to such units from the outside, with which members of other age groups—and often also public opinion as expressed in the media—attempt, in the interest of establishing demarcations and reducing complexity, to identify presumed generations as well as the progression of generations. (Reulecke 119)

When we look at the Empire Windrush generation from the angle of generation theory, it becomes clear that as a historical fact, it refers certainly not to *a* generation. Instead, mass immigration to Britain after World War II extended over a period of more than twenty years, and it involved people of very different age groups and identitarian alignments. Neither is it exactly the *first* generation of black immigrants, as there is a much longer history of black presence in Britain. It is, however, clearly, a generationality. "Empire Windrush" refers to the public memories of mass immigration to Britain; it is produced by collective, mediatized commemoration; it is an occasion for self-identification, and for the identification of others, *as a* generation.

Small Island intervenes into this collective production of a generationality by extending Empire Windrush's boundaries: the novel paints a vivid picture of postwar London in 1948, where the newly arrived immigrants from the Caribbean, Hortense and Gilbert, interact with the white Londoners Queenie and Bernard. Apart from unearthing the entangled histories of people from the metropolis and the colonies who fought together in World War II (in the "Before" chapters), Levy's novel recasts popular British constructions of the Empire Windrush generation as a unit of young male Caribbeans only. Instead, in the "1948" chapters of *Small Island,* men and women, members of different social classes, immigrants from the Caribbean as well as white Londoners and even English racists (Bernard), all appear as entangled actors of the Windrush generation.

This effect is heightened by the relatively equal distribution of first-person narrators: in alternating chapters, each of the four protagonists articulates his or her way of experiencing the Windrush years. The novel thus "gives voice" to four different perspectives on Windrush. In this way, it extends our notion of the racial and gendered boundaries of the "first immigrant generation" and makes us realize that Windrush as a sociopolitical event shaped the memories and generational identities of very different constituencies and that in fact we are dealing with highly diverse but entangled generationalities.

What *White Teeth* and *Small Island* show in their own ways is the entanglement of generations, in their synchronic as well as their diachronic genealogical aspects, through enmeshments that cut across what is constructed as the boundaries of family, gender, race, nation, colonizer, and colonized. These new fictions of generational memory make a strong case for recognizing the power of affiliative relationships as they were first theorized by Edward Said, not only among the writers themselves (Stein 6) but also among the fictional characters, who all deal with intersecting histories, shared spaces of experience, and sometimes, as when Archie coremembers Samad's would-be ancestor Mangal Pande in *White Teeth,* even with affiliative memories in Marianne Hirsch's sense (Hirsch 36).[6]

SECOND GENERATION ONCE REMOVED: CARYL PHILLIPS'S *IN THE FALLING SNOW*

Caryl Phillips's *In the Falling Snow* occupies a somewhat different place in the field of the recent black British literature of generation and memory. In *Small Island,* the Windrush generation takes center stage, and in *White Teeth* it is shown as a powerful presence, shaping the fortunes of the second generation (a graphic instance is Samad's autocratic rule over his children). Phillips's novel, however, gives expression to the fact that roughly since the turn of the millennium the configuration of immigrant generations in Great Britain has significantly changed.

As the first generation of Windrushers is getting old, firsthand witnesses of postwar immigration will soon pass away, and with them the embodied experience, the episodic memories, and the oral stories they may tell in situations of face-to-face interaction. What will remain are mediated representations of the first generation: photographs, documentary footage, videotaped oral history interviews, movies, and novels. Such a transition from (mainly) embodied to (exclusively) mediated memory has been theorized by Jan Assmann and Aleida Assmann as the change from the register of "communicative memory" to "cultural memory" (J. Assmann). In such times of mnemonic transition, which are fundamentally generational—even biological—transitions, literature tends to become more sensitive to issues of remembering and questions of generation.

With both Phillips and his fictional protagonist Keith born in the 1950s, raised in Britain, and sons of Windrushers, *In the Falling Snow* lends itself to being read as a second-generation novel.[7] Mark Stein defines the second generation as the children of Caribbean and South Asian immigrants and as "the authors who started writing in the 1970s and 1980s, a period also marked by racial hostility" (5). In this sense, the second generation is distinct from the Windrushers, who immigrated into Great Britain after World War II, as well as from "the third generation who started writing in the 1990s" (5). Stein shows convincingly that novels by and about the children of Caribbean and South Asian immigrants tend to draw on patterns of the bildungsroman. According to Stein, these are therefore "novels of transformation" in a double sense, as they show the "formation of its protagonists as well as the transformation of British society" (22).

However, Phillips's novel marks the "biological" or "natural" development of this second-generation genre, which is a result of the simple fact that this generation has become older.[8] The issues that are negotiated in *In the Falling Snow* are different from those that we find in the mainstays of the black British bildungsroman genre, as in Hani Kureishi's *The Buddha of Suburbia* (1990), in Andrea Levy's *Fruit of the Lemon* (1999), and even in the depiction of intergenerational interaction in Zadie Smith's *White Teeth.* This is not only because sociopolitical circumstances have changed over time, but also because the concerns that inform these coming-of-age novels revolve around "subject formation" (Stein 22)—that is, around a process that is closely tied up with what in theories of generation is called the "impressionable time" ("Zeitalter der Empfänglichkeit"; Dilthey 37). In "The Problem of Generations," Karl Mannheim locates this "formative phase"—or the "critical years"—of a young adult, which will bring forth his generational affiliations and shape his or her memories, between ages seventeen and twenty-four.

The second-generation novel has moved on, and in Caryl Phillips's case this move is connected with a strong and critical reflectiveness about the very idea of generation. In *In the Falling Snow,* the fictional protagonist and main focalizer Keith, a middle-aged man in his late forties, has to grapple with many different aspects of generation: generational transitions, generationality, and familial and cultural genealogy. First of all, *In the Falling Snow* features a rather conventional midlife crisis plot: Keith finds himself enmeshed in problems with his wife, his son, and his workplace.

Three years ago, his white wife Annabelle turned him out of the house after he had confessed he was cheating on her; he has become estranged from his seventeen-year-old son Laurie, who appears to associate with the wrong crowd; and his boss suspends him from his office, after Yvette, a much younger colleague, makes public the emails he wrote to her during their short-lived affair. All this, however, gives Keith time to embark on a long-planned project of writing a book on soul music. Keith experiences these changes as manifestations of a transitional phase in his life, apparent, for example, in his self-admonishment that he "must now begin to *act his age* and stop associating with young girls" (106; my emphasis).[9]

More crucial are the ways in which the idea of generation is connected to issues of collective memory and identity. In Keith, we can observe an emphatic identification with "*his generation* of kids, who were born in Britain and who had no memory of any kind of tropical life before England" (41; my emphasis). Keith shows a strong sense of generationality, which shapes his most fundamental decisions in life. As a conscious member of *his* generation, Keith was aware of race riots in the 1970s and 1980s, when he was a young man, and decided to respond to these generation-defining events by choosing not to do postgraduate work but to leave university with only a bachelor's degree and go into social work, as he realized that Britain needed "people who could help explain black anger to white people, and white liberal do-gooding to disgruntled black people" (45). One of the novel's ironies is that Keith welcomes the "merging [of] his Race Equality unit with Disability and Women's Affairs," because it means for him "more money, a bigger office, and double the number of staff to manage" (33).[10]

In his family, Keith is the only one to show such a strong, identificatory sense of generationality. Still, the other black male family members are also given their own generational location—their *Zeitheimat,* to use WG Sebald's term (261). The reader finds three generations, three different versions of black youth experience, and three reservoirs of memory mediated in three different ways. The dying Earl's rambling monologue, addressed to his son Keith, evokes the image of the young Windrush generation in the early

1960s trying to gain a foothold in English cities, faced with bad housing and rampant racism. Keith's internally focalized memories paint the picture of the second generation's problematic position in a predominantly white society, exemplified by the open racism encountered from his father-in-law and, it seems, significant parts of the English village his wife, Annabelle, was born in.

The exploits of his seventeen-year-old son, Laurie, belong to the primary story set in the present. The worried exchanges between his estranged parents and his teachers suggest the son's preference for American-style gang life. Laurie makes it very clear that despite his own encounters with racism (being called a "halfie" as a child; 17), he and Keith do not share the same space of experience: "The thing is, Dad, I don't know if things are the same now as they were when you were my age ... It isn't just about discrimination and stuff" (167).[11] Laurie's generational self-description amounts to the belief that "it's got a lot to do with respect" (167)—a concept that Keith, from the viewpoint of his generational location, does not understand: "What have they done to earn respect?" (167).

Earl, Keith, and Laurie represent three generations of black people in Britain, with their respective experiences and memories. At the same time, they form the tripartite genealogy of a British family of Caribbean descent. This diachronic perspective (which is copresent with the synchronic one, as genealogy always intersects with generational locations) raises a different set of questions: that of biological and social inheritance in the diaspora. Sonali Thakkar speaks of the "logic of diaspora, which pairs geographical displacement with cultural continuity and transmission. Continuity, frequently framed as familial transmission, is what supposedly allows for the transmission of identity *despite* dislocation. It is this emphasis on cultural reproduction as familial reproduction that makes diasporic discourse so dependent on family forms" (207–8). In Keith's case, however, familial transmission turns out to be a key problem.

Phillips's novel places its focus on patrilineal genealogy and transmission. It is the men whose stories are told in detail and who are granted extended passages of focalization and intradiegetic narration. However, transgenerational processes appear to be severely disrupted, as both fathers are—to a larger and lesser extent—absent, Earl having spent years in a mental asylum and only been able to take his son Keith into his house when the boy was already thirteen, and Keith having split up with his wife when his son was fourteen. There are small hints at transmissions between the three men, though, such as a certain inheritance of reticence and stubbornness palpable among all of them and Keith's predilection for spending evenings brooding in his local pub, just as his father does.

Yet apart from these masculine (dis)connections, the memory of Keith's loving stepmother Brenda comes into view as a generative force. Brenda died when Keith was at university. It is her photograph that he still keeps on the living room wall. When Keith exhorts his son to "put in more effort and try twice as hard as anybody else" (167), he clearly echoes Brenda's "Keep your chin up, love, your clothes nice and tidy, and your language decent … mind you come back with A's on that report card" (16)–the only difference being that these exhortations are lost on his son, who, as Keith suspects, may be wondering "what a square tosser his dad is" (168). Given the fact that Brenda is female, white, and not even Keith's biological mother, the novel thus makes a strong point about the generative force of affiliative relationships and the power of transgenerational transmission beyond the biological and the racial.

The main genealogical theme of the novel, however, is Keith's "search for the father." Earl's stubborn silence about his experience as a migrant in Britain and his family history prevent Keith from developing a sense of identity: "His father's silence has meant that his son has never been able to properly explain himself to anybody" (285). It is only in the novel's powerful finale, on Earl's deathbed, that the old man finally discloses in a long monologue addressed to Keith what he had held secret all his life: his memories of his experience as an immigrant in Britain in the 1960s and of extreme racial violence, which turns out to have been a trigger of his mental illness,[12] and his memories of Keith's mother Shirley, also an immigrant from the Caribbean, who got pregnant after one sexual encounter and whose offer to marry he did not accept.

For Keith, and for the reader, Earl's monologue delivers the long-awaited solutions to many riddles in Keith's life. This is, of course, a strategy of suspense, but in terms of character psychology, it also means the possibility for Keith to reconnect with, imagine, and remember a diasporic genealogy. Intergenerational conflicts, which, according to Mark Stein, are "part and parcel" of the black British bildungsroman, thus appear modified in *In the Falling Snow:* conflicts between first- and second-generation immigrants are either remembered conflicts (Keith's memories of the 1980s) or conflicts about memory (Earl's denial and eventual overflow of intergenerational remembrance), while conflicts between the second and third generations are shown to play out along different lines.

Keith's search for familial genealogy broadens into an interest in cultural genealogies—"a search for forefathers"—when he embarks on a book project about the history of soul music. Keith is interested in "how black cultural heritage is passed on from one generation to the next" (95). But the history of the black presence in Britain—all the way from the African soldiers "the Romans brought … to build Hadrian's wall" (95)—offers little to inspire him. Instead, he "is trying to write about a deeper and more sub-stantial tradition of cultural inheritance, and this means that he has to look across the Atlantic for his models" (95).[13]

While Keith tends to work on small familial genealogies, for example when he charts the relationship between "Cissy Houston and Whitney Houston, and of course, Whitney's aunt, Dionne Warwick" (142), the overall book project, which connects American soul music with his British iden-tity, suggests the kind of interactions that Paul Gilroy has described in *The Black Atlantic;* in fact, Caryl Phillips has long been known as a Black Atlantic writer. Uncovering the historical interconnections of the African diaspora in the Caribbean, the United States, and Britain has characterized much of Phillips's earlier work, most notably perhaps the novel *Crossing the River* (1993) and the travelogue *The Atlantic Sound* (2000). Both of these works giv-ing evidence to the idea that the construction of a cultural genealogy of black people in Britain requires the practice of transcultural memory across and beyond the Black Atlantic (Ward, "An Outstretched Hand" 32).

Despite Keith's focus on black genealogies, what his family history dis-plays is an instance of the entangled genealogies typical of modern post-colonial and multicultural societies. Ironically, perhaps, but no longer uncommonly as a genealogical constellation in British society, Annabelle's racist father, who had served the empire as a soldier, becomes grandfather to mixed-race Laurie. Such entanglements, too, are a major preoccupation of Phillips's fiction and structure novels such as *Cambridge* (1991) and *A Dis-tant Shore* (2003). Even if these connections may be conflictual or remain unacknowledged, their representation in the literary text is a practice of transcultural remembrance.[14]

On the level of the novel's structure, there is yet another striking in-stance of cultural genealogy: Earl's extended monologue in his hospital bed, which amounts to a story within the story (269–82, 287–319), is clearly an expression of *literary* genealogy. It is a self-conscious reference, a homage to one of the literary founding fathers of black fiction in Britain: Sam Selvon, the author of *The Lonely Londoners* (1956). In this now classic novel, Selvon gave fullest expression to the experience of the Windrush generationality. The novel revolves around the adventures of a group of "boys," young im-migrants from the Caribbean in postwar London, bound together by the generation-defining "communal voice" of character-narrator Moses Aloetta. Earl's monologue is reminiscent of Selvon's style. Just as Selvon's novel first and famously did, it features "modified forms of the oral vernacular" to create a distinctly Caribbean voice (Nasta 70), and it echoes Moses Aloetta's similarly breathless extended stream-of-consciousness passage that can be found at the center of *The Lonely Londoners*.

Earl's monologue is a Windrush mininarration. It is marked as such as it starts with a generation-defining voice: "I want to go home, Keith ... I'm not from here. I land in England on a cold Friday morning. It is April 15, 1960" (269). This precision of historical reference echoes the oral testimonies of his generation as they were given in the context of the Windrush anniversary (Phillips and Phillips). The representation of Earl's memories draws on well-established topoi of Windrush remembrance, such as the Caribbean immigrants' realization upon arrival at the London docks that England was not full of the well-to-do white colonial administrators and landowners they knew back home: "The people don't look like the type of white men I used to see back home wearing club blazer and tie and walking about the place ramrod straight. Jesus Christ, I don't know England have such poor white men" (269).

All in all, Earl's monologue is much darker in tone and content than its genealogical pretext. The "sons of Empire" (196), as Earl's friend Baron calls their group with an ironic nod to genealogical empire metaphors (Nünning, "Metaphors"), have not been able to make England their home. Earl's last words are a testament to his lifelong failure to cope with the realities of his life in England: "The idea of England is fine. I can deal with the idea. You understand me, son? I can deal with the idea" (319).

In his 1999 essay "Following On: The Legacy of Lamming and Selvon," Caryl Phillips describes Selvon and George Lamming in a typical generational-genealogical figure as "our literary antecedents ... In the seventies and eighties I know that these writers had a profound effect on my generation, the second generation in this country who found themselves trying to deal with loneliness, ambivalence, and confusion about their relationship to British society" (36). In this essay, Phillips is rather cautious about the significance of black American culture for black writers in Britain. He describes his realization in the 1980s that for him, African American authors were "from a different world," just like "their British contemporaries of the Golding-Lessing school" (35); the "simple fact was, I was not an American" (35). Phillips muses that as a reader from Britain, he could only "respond to the universal elements of African-American fiction" (35). It is perhaps for this reason that in *In the Falling Snow* it is soul music, with its allegedly "universal appeal," which is used as a marker of a shared cultural heritage.[15]

"IN THE FALLING SNOW": FROM RACIAL TO GENEALOGICAL METAPHOR

The genealogical finale, as it were, is prepared by the gradual narrative development of the novel's main literary image, which we find already in its

title. With "in the falling snow," Phillips establishes yet another literary genealogy reaching across the Black Atlantic. As Abigail Ward has pointed
out, "in the falling snow" is an intertextual reference to a haiku written by
the African American author Richard Wright, one of Phillips's main literary
influences ("Looking across the Atlantic"):

> In the falling snow
> A laughing boy holds out his palms
> Until they are white. (Wright 92)

Phillips retains Wright's thrust of the snow metaphor as an image of black
people in a dominantly white environment, an image that reminds the
reader of the continuity of racialized thinking in British society, while it
implies—with the "laughing boy"—a certain levity.[16] In fact, Phillips's novel
can be read as a diachronic phenomenology of "being *in the falling snow*," of
being black in Britain across three generations. At the same time, and in a
double move, Phillips develops Wright's metaphor of race into a metaphor
of generation. In the ensuing narrative elaboration, "being in the falling
snow" is turned into an impressive image of familial genealogy, a condensed
figure that captures the essential relatedness of father and son, of Earl and
Keith.

As a way of structuring the many different temporal planes of the story
world, which is mainly focalized through Keith, memories of key incidents
keep coming back to Keith's mind in the form of textual blocks inserted into
the flow of his thoughts—just as haunting memories come back to us, triggered either by internal or external cues. The memories connected with the
image of being in the falling snow are first introduced in the second part of
the novel, when Keith, once again sitting alone in his apartment with white
wine and cheese, contemplates Brenda's photograph on the wall. Memories
of his childhood are triggered. Keith remembers his thirteenth birthday,
when his father suddenly turned up again after having spent a long time in
a mental hospital.

Earl presents Keith, who has lived with Brenda for years now, with a
birthday card. It is the time of the year when "the clouds were high and
heavy with snow" (88). One week later, Earl comes back to take his son to
the movies (just as Keith later will take Laurie). The snow already in the air
a week earlier is now coming down: "huge white flakes were tumbling down
from the sky and coating the pavement white" (320). This second encounter
between Earl and Keith is accompanied by a rhetoric of memory, which
indicates that Keith is repeatedly revisiting this part of his past: "He *couldn't
remember* if his father bought him any sweets or anything to drink, but he

clearly recalls that ..." (320; my emphasis). These acts of reconstructive remembering are characteristic of autobiographical memories, and they build
up to the key moment of Keith's childhood memories:

> They began to walk back in the direction of the bus stop, past the parked cars
> that were already clad in snow, and as the flakes continued to fall on their bare
> heads he could feel his hand tight and safe in his father's hand. He looked be-
> hind him and saw two sets of footprints where they had walked, a large pair and
> his own smaller ones ... As they turned a corner, he tugged his father's hand.
> His father looked down at him and smiled. He pointed to the sky. "Look at all
> the snow!" His father continued to smile. (320–21)

Here, suddenly, in the description of a rare moment of peace and hap-
piness between father and son, all qualifiers that would point to the act of
remembering have disappeared. With young Keith as internal focalizer, and
with the immediacy and vividness of the narrated events, the passage clearly
represents what psychologists would call a "field memory" or "event-specific
knowledge." It is a representation of the detailed recall characteristic of episodic remembering, providing it with a sense of veridicality and a "truthful-
ness" we associate with memories that we feel are "etched" into our minds,
usually because the remembered events were perceived as momentous.[17]
With the retrieval of the memory of walking in the falling snow alongside
Earl, Keith appears to have worked his way to the very core of the meaning
he attributes to their father-son relationship.

The two pairs of footsteps in the snow work as a genealogical metaphor,
indicating the movement of generations through time (older and larger footsteps next to younger and smaller ones). In fact, this metaphor is extended
when Keith remembers standing at the door of Brenda's house and watching his father walk away: "As he walked, his father left behind a single set
of footprints, and he remembered lingering by the doorstep and watching
closely as the falling snow steadily erased all evidence of his father's presence" (321). This is a powerful, condensed image of the transitory nature
of all generations: the older generation inevitably disappears, is "erased"
by nature. Afterward, "all evidence" of their "presence" is that which will
remain in the autobiographical memories of a younger generation—just as
the ones reemerging in Keith's mind—and, importantly, in media, such as
Earl's box of old photographs.

After Keith's retrieval of his key childhood memory, the narrative
switches back again to the primary storyline. Keith learns that his father
Earl has just died. Back at home, he realizes: "His father has gone and there
is nobody ahead of him" (326). A generational turnover has taken place.
This means that Keith is now also confronted with the dynamics typical

of the transition from communicative to cultural memory. After having lis-
tened to his father's oral memories at his hospital bed for several days and
nights, what remains after his death as the sole source to an understanding of Earl's life are media of memory. The old photographs kept by Earl,
which are mentioned repeatedly in the novel and which in the end "remain
scattered on [Earl's] kitchen table" (323), await, the reader is led to assume,
Keith's perusal—as "*evidence* of his father's life" (324; my emphasis).

Ironically, perhaps, it is not those photographs but an altogether different one that is mentioned on the novel's last page: the picture of Annabelle's
parents in the bedroom of the house Keith used to share with his wife. Her
"father is looking confidently into the lens of the camera, while her mother's
gaze is altogether more mournful" (330). With this, the novel retains as a final
image the certainties and the anxieties of empire, its continued presence in
Britain, and its complex genealogies, which are, for better or for worse, an
integral part of Keith's own family. And although Keith muses, "There is
no reason for him to spend a night here in this small terraced house with all
these people" (330), the reader knows by then that these are indeed *his* people
and that it is quite likely that Keith will stay and reunite with his wife.

With *In the Falling Snow*, Phillips, who was then mainly known as a
writer of historical fiction, participates for the first time in the genre of the
second-generation novel.[18] Being a latecomer to this genre means also that
he inevitably transforms it. In this novel, we see a "second generation once
removed"—to middle age, to a state in which the first generation is disappearing and can therefore no longer be held accountable (a theme also developed through the dementia Annabella's mother is suffering from), and
to the new questions that arise in this situation. These questions are about
the memories and identities of people of Caribbean descent in Britain and
about their abilities to place themselves in generational locations and in
familial and cultural genealogies.

CONCLUSION: FICTIONS OF GENERATIONAL MEMORY TODAY

What we find in *In the Falling Snow* and increasingly in black writing in Britain today, as the examples of *White Teeth* and *Small Island* have shown, is not
only reflections on different immigrant generations but also the problema-
tization of generational identities and of transgenerational family dynamics
within migrant settings, the unearthing of far-reaching cultural genealogies
and postcolonial entanglements, and, last but not least, critical perspectives
on the biologist notions that pervade contemporary discussions of genealogy and transmission in multicultural societies. In short, a recent kind of

black writing produces fictions of generational memory in almost all aspects that the multifarious idea of generation implies. Novels such as *In the Falling Snow* can be read as seismographs of the shifting meanings of *generatio* in contemporary British society.

Fictions of generational memory are not produced only in Great Britain (this essay's focus) but have also emerged in Germany (A. Assmann), South Asia (Butt), and elsewhere. They seem to be a truly global phenomenon, a specific literary mode to cope with generational, and hence also mnemonic, transitions: from a generation of witnesses (of war, genocide, and migration) to their children and grandchildren, from "memory" to "postmemory" (in Marianne Hirsch's words), from "communicative" to "cultural memory" (in Jan and Aleida Assmann's terms). In our age of self-reflective remembrance, the ever-ongoing shifts between generations become visible—and problematic—as shifts in memory culture. They affect how the key events of the twentieth century (the Holocaust and World War II, decolonization and mass migration, the Partition of the Indian subcontinent, and so on) can be remembered today, and they evidently give rise to a type of literature that imaginatively addresses the set of problems connected with generation and memory.

Astrid Erll is a professor of Anglophone literatures and cultures at Goethe-University Frankfurt am Main. She has worked on memories of the First World War, the Spanish Civil War, British colonialism in India, and the Vietnam War. She is general editor of the book series Media and Cultural Memory (De Gruyter, since 2004), a coeditor of *A Companion to Cultural Memory Studies* (De Gruyter, 2010; with Ansgar Nünning) and *Mediation, Remediation, and the Dynamics of Cultural Memory* (De Gruyter, 2009; with Ann Rigney), and author of *Memory in Culture* (Palgrave Macmillan, 2011), an introduction to memory studies. She is part of the editorial board of the journal *Memory Studies* (SAGE) and the Memory Studies book series (Palgrave Macmillan).

NOTES

1. On Phillips's complex play with racial markers in *In the Falling Snow,* see Collier.
2. For a very good overview of black British literature, see Ledent.
3. On "fictions of memory," see Nünning, *Fictions.* On cultural memory in black British writing, see Eckstein; Pirker; Rupp. For a study on the representation of generation in British Asian literature, see Weingarten.
4. Karl Mannheim developed his theory of synchronic generations in the 1920s. Substantial overviews of genealogical thinking can be found in Weigel, *Genealogik* and in Parnes, Vedder, and Willer.

5. For an in-depth discussion of such programs see Korte and Pirker. On "tangled roots," diaspora memories, and genetics, see also the contributions to Hirsch and Miller.

6. In his essay "Secular Criticism," Edward Said describes the "filial relationship" as "held together by natural bonds and natural forms of authority—involving obedience, fear, love, respect, and instinctual conflict" (20). In contrast, "the new affiliative relationship changes these bonds into what seem to be transpersonal forms—such as guild consciousness, consensus, collegiality, professional respect, class, and the hegemony of a dominant culture. The filiative scheme belongs to the realms of nature and of 'life,' whereas affiliation belongs exclusively to culture and society." What Said neatly distinguishes here are the fundamental ambiguities at the core of all thinking about "generation": the "natural" aspect in the idea of genealogy (as procreation, as familial relationships) becomes entangled with ways of establishing "cultural" generativity (which, as Said emphasizes, tends to return to the filial patterns).

7. Phillips was born in St. Kitts in 1958 and came with his parents to Leeds when he was four months old. Keith, too, was raised in the north of England. Although the novel may thus invite its readership to think about the possibilities and limits of an autobiographical reading, I would argue that its extratextual reference concerns the generational and not so much the individual dimension.

8. I am indeed making a "biological argument" here, arguing with Karl Mannheim that the new second-generation novel is *based* on biological rhythm but can of course not simply be *deduced* from it: "The sociological phenomenon of generations is ultimately based on the biological rhythm of birth and death. But to be based on a factor does not necessarily mean to be deducible from it, or to be implied in it ... The *sociological* problem of generations therefore begins at that point where the sociological relevance of these biological factors is discovered" (Mannheim 290–91).

9. There are many poignant reflections in the novel on the transition between different stages of life: Annabelle's mother's complaint that the old are "all being kept alive so that like old fruit they can just rot" (232); Keith's observation that there is a time when "a single woman becomes a spinster" (260); his observation that his wife "was slowly, despite her youthful looks, becoming her mother" (51); Laurie's "'big man' behaviour" (168). Later in the novel, "Act your age and not your colour" (168) will be Keith's unuttered advice to his son Laurie.

10. This, too, is a generational point with a clear extrafictional reference. In an interview in 2007, Paul Gilroy commented on "some of the things that New Labour has done. A whole generation of activists—my generation—seem to be management consultants! Even the black nationalists are busy managing the health service and the police" (Gilroy qtd. in Richardson 3). Keith not only is middle aged but has also risen to the middle class. The novel is riddled with middle-class markers, such as the ubiquitous white wine, Gruyère cheese, and careful choice of language. The novel shows how race, class, and generationality intersect in the making of identities—and of identity-related problems.

11. The following passage has a similar effect: "'Did the police abuse you in any way?' Laurie looks up at his father. 'What?' 'I'm talking about racial abuse. Did the interviewing officer verbally abuse you in any way?' 'What are you on? The copper who interviewed me was black'" (227).

12. English racists killed Earl's friend Ralph. Earl's psychic illness is reminiscent of Frantz Fanon's work on the psychopathology of the experience of racism in *Black Skin, White Masks*. Brenda explains to Keith that "England had hurt his head" (221). See also the discussion of Fanon's work in relation to postcolonial trauma in Craps.

13. This reflectiveness and interest does not mean that Keith is free from stereotypical thinking about generations elsewhere. In the subplot about Britain's most recent "first generation of immigrants," those from Eastern Europe in the wake of the 2004 enlargement of the European Union, Keith notes one Danuta's Polish descent and contemplates in all seriousness: "Home of Treblinka and Auschwitz. You don't change people's minds in a couple of generations" (79).

14. Another focus of Phillips's transcultural memory fictions is on black-Jewish relatedness. Both Rothberg and Craps discuss the travel report *The European Tribe* (1987) and the novels *Higher Ground* (1989) and *The Nature of Blood* (1997) in this light.

15. For a discussion of soul music as a carrier of transcultural memory, see Kennedy.

16. Ward emphasizes that "the imagery is clearly loaded and evokes a contrast between black and white spheres … [in] other works by Wright, snow frequently symbolizes an unfeeling, white-dominated world." She suggests that the image of the laughing boy "perhaps chimes with Phillips's desire for a kind of racial 'transcendence,' or an understanding which goes beyond the confines of racial binaries" ("Looking across the Atlantic" 300).

17. For these concepts, See Pillemer; for an overview of the psychology of memory and its relevance for literary studies, see Erll, *Memory in Culture* 77–94.

18. Phillips's first two novels, *The Final Passage* (1985) and *A State of Independence* (1986), featured immigration from the Caribbean to Britain (and back) as a theme, albeit not in the form of a second-generation novel. However, as Rini Vyncke points out, "It might become even more interesting to compare *In the Falling Snow* (2009) further with two of Phillips' earlier plays. Both *Strange Fruit* (1981) and *Where There Is Darkness* (1982) deal with … intergenerational friction" (117).

WORKS CITED

Assmann, Aleida. *Cultural Memory and Western Civilization: Functions, Media, Archives.* Cambridge: Cambridge University Press, 2011.

Assmann, Jan. *Cultural Memory and Early Civilization: Writing, Remembrance, and Political Imagination.* Cambridge: Cambridge University Press, 2011.

Brunow, Dagmar. "Rethinking Remediation and Reworking the Archive: Transcultural Reappropriations of Documentary Images of Migration." *In Search for Transcultural Memory in Europe* 2013. Web. 30 Mar. 2015.

Butt, Nadia. *Transcultural Memory and Globalised Modernity in Contemporary Indo-English Novels.* Berlin: De Gruyter, 2015.

Collier, Gordon. "The Dynamic of Revelation and Concealment: *In the Falling Snow* and the Narrational Architecture of Blighted Existences." *Caryl Phillips: Writing in the Key of Life.* Ed. Bénédicte Ledent and Daria Tunca. Amsterdam: Rodopi, 2012. 375–406.

Craps, Stef. *Postcolonial Witnessing: Trauma Out of Bounds.* Basingstoke: Palgrave Macmillan, 2013.

Dilthey, Wilhelm. "Über das Studium der Geschichte der Wissenschaften vom Mensch, der Gesellschaft und dem Staat (1875)." *Die Geistige Welt: Einleitung in die Philosophie des Lebens. Erste Hälfte: Abhandlungen zur Grundlegung der Geisteswissenschaften. Gesammelte Schriften Vol. 5.* Leipzig and Berlin: Teubner, 1924. 31–73.

Eckstein, Lars. *Re-membering the Black Atlantic: On the Poetics and Politics of Literary Memory.* Amsterdam: Rodopi, 2006.

Erll, Astrid. "Generation in Literary History: Three Constellations of Genealogy, Generationality, and Memory." *New Literary History* 45.3 (2014): 385–409.

——. *Memory in Culture.* Trans. Sara B. Young. Basingstoke: Palgrave Macmillan, 2011.

Eyerman, Ron, and Bernard S. Turner. "Outline of a Theory of Generations." *European Journal of Social Theory* 1.1 (1998): 91–106.

Fanon, Frantz. *Black Skin, White Masks.* New York: Grove Press, 1967.

Gilroy, Paul. *The Black Atlantic: Modernity and Double Consciousness.* London: Verso, 1993.

Hirsch, Marianne. *The Generation of Postmemory: Writing and Visual Culture after the Holocaust.* New York: Columbia University Press, 2012.

Hirsch, Marianne, and Nancy K. Miller, eds. *Rites of Return: Diaspora Poetics and the Politics of Memory.* New York: Columbia University Press, 2011.

Kennedy, Rosanne. "Soul Music Dreaming: *The Sapphires,* the 1960s, and Transnational Memory." *Memory Studies* 6.3 (2013): 331–44.

Korte, Barbara, and Eva U. Pirker. *Black History, White History: Britain's Historical Programme between Windrush and Wilberforce.* Bielefeld: Transcript, 2011.

Ledent, Bénédicte. "Black British Literature." *The Oxford Companion to English Literature.* Ed. Dinah Birch and Margaret Drabble. 7th ed. Oxford: Oxford University Press, 2009. 6–22.

Levy, Andrea. *Small Island.* London: Headline Review, 2004.

Mannheim, Karl. "The Problem of Generations." *Essays on the Sociology of Knowledge. Collected Works Vol. 5.* Ed. Paul Kecskemeti. London: Routledge, 1997. 276–322.

McLeod, John. "Extra Dimensions, New Routines." *Wasafiri* 25.4 (2010): 45–52.

Nasta, Susheila. *Home Truths: Fictions of the South Asian Diaspora in Britain.* Basingstoke: Palgrave, 2002.

Nünning, Ansgar. "Metaphors the British Thought, Felt, and Ruled by, or: Modest Proposals for Historicizing Cognitive Metaphor Theory and for Exploring

Metaphors of Empire as a Cultural Phenomenon." *Literature and Linguistics: Approaches, Models, and Applications. Studies in Honour of Jon Erickson.* Ed. Marion Gymnich, Ansgar Nünning, and Vera Nünning. Trier: WVT, 2002. 101–27.

——, ed. *Fictions of Memory.* Spec. issue of *Journal for the Study of British Cultures* 10.1 (2003).

Parnes, Ohad, Ulrike Vedder, and Stefan Willer. *Das Konzept der Generation: Eine Wissenschafts- und Kulturgeschichte.* Frankfurt a. M.: Suhrkamp, 2008.

Phillips, Caryl. *Strange Fruit.* London: Amber Lane Press, 1981.

——. *Where There Is Darkness.* London: Amber Lane Press, 1982.

——. *The Final Passage.* London: Faber and Faber, 1985.

——. *A State of Independence.* London: Faber and Faber, 1986.

——. *The European Tribe.* London: Faber and Faber, 1987.

——. *Higher Ground.* London: Viking, 1989.

——. *Cambridge.* London: Bloomsbury, 1991.

——. *Crossing the River.* London: Bloomsbury, 1994.

——. *The Nature of Blood.* London: Faber and Faber, 1997.

——. "Following On: The Legacy of Lamming and Selvon." *Wasafiri* 14.29 (1999): 34–36.

——. *The Atlantic Sound.* London: Faber and Faber, 2000.

——. *A Distant Shore.* London: Secker and Warburg, 2003.

——. *In the Falling Snow.* London: Vintage, 2010.

Phillips, Mike, and Trevor Phillips, eds. *Windrush: The Irresistible Rise of Multi-racial Britain.* London: Harper Collins, 1998.

Pillemer, David B. "Momentous Events and the Life Story." *Review of General Psychology* 5.2 (2001): 123–34.

Pirker, Eva Ulrike. *Narrative Projections of a Black British History.* New York: Routledge, 2011.

Reulecke, Jürgen. "Generation/Generationality, Generativity, and Memory." *A Companion to Cultural Memory Studies.* Ed. Astrid Erll and Ansgar Nünning. Berlin: De Gruyter, 2010. 119–26.

Richardson, Brian. "Stories of Black Britain in Pictures." *Socialist Review* Oct. 2007. Web. 30 Mar. 2015.

Rothberg, Michael. *Multidirectional Memory: Remembering the Holocaust in the Age of Decolonization.* Stanford: Stanford University Press, 2009.

Rupp, Jan. *Genre and Cultural Memory in Black British Literature.* Trier: WVT, 2010.

Said, Edward. "Introduction: Secular Criticism." *The World, the Text, and the Critic.* Cambridge: Harvard University Press, 1983. 1–30.

Sebald, WG. "Hitlers pyromanische Phantasien: Interview mit Volker Hage." *Zeugen der Zerstörung: Die Literaten und der Luftkrieg.* Ed. Volker Hage. Frankfurt a. M.: Fischer, 2003. 259–79.

Selvon, Samuel. *The Lonely Londoners.* London: Allan Wingate, 1956.

Schuman, Howard, and Jacqueline Scott. "Generations and Collective Memories." *American Sociological Review* 54.3 (1989): 359–81.

Smith, Zadie. *White Teeth.* London: Penguin, 2001.

Stein, Mark. *Black British Literature: Novels of Transformation.* Columbus: Ohio State University Press, 2004.

Thakkar, Sonali. "Foreign Correspondence." *Rites of Return: Diaspora Poetics and the Politics of Memory.* Ed. Marianne Hirsch and Nancy K. Miller. New York: Columbia University Press, 2011. 200–15.

Vyncke, Rini. "From *The Final Passage* (1985) to *In the Falling Snow* (2009): Caryl Phillips as a Second Generation Postcolonial Author." MA Thesis. Ghent University, 2010.

Ward, Abigail. "An Outstretched Hand: Connection and Affiliation in *Crossing the River.*" *Moving Worlds* 7.1 (2007): 20–32.

——. "'Looking across the Atlantic' in Caryl Phillips's *In the Falling Snow.*" *Journal of Postcolonial Writing* 47.3 (2011): 296–308.

Weigel, Sigrid. *Genea-logik: Generation, Tradition und Evolution zwischen Kultur und Naturwissenschaften.* Paderborn: Fink, 2006.

——. "'Generation' as a Symbolic Form: On the Genealogical Discourse of Memory since 1945." *The Germanic Review: Literature, Culture, Theory* 77.4 (2002): 264–77.

Weingarten, Jutta. "Narrating Generations: Representations of Generationality and Genealogy in Contemporary British Asian Narratives." Diss. University of Giessen, 2012.

Wright, Richard. "*In the Falling Snow.*" *Ebony* 16 (1961): 92.

Chapter 6

The Uses of Facebook for Examining Collective Memory

The Emergence of Nasser Facebook Pages in Egypt

Joyce van de Bildt

⊷⬦⬦⊶

INTRODUCTION

Over the past few years, social media have proven to be an effective tool for opposition groups in authoritarian states to voice their demands and interests. Facilitated by the Internet, local experiences have evoked national or international responses and have been a cause for mass mobilization. This raises questions about the power of social media for collective memory as well. Over the past few years, Egypt has witnessed the emergence of Facebook pages with historical themes, on which video and photo material and other historical documents are posted. Especially in the period after the January 2011 revolution, the past has been invoked more than ever in order to benefit the present, on Facebook and elsewhere.

This essay demonstrates that contemporary Facebook pages function as another platform on which people express their different views of a shared past, evoking rivalries but also dialogue. As a case study, this essay explores the emergence of Facebook pages dedicated to the late Egyptian president Gamal 'Abd al-Nasser. It investigates how they relate to Nasser's regime, his failures, and his achievements and how these are made relevant to contemporary Egyptian political concerns. It examines how the pages' historical themes stand for a larger, more complex trend of nostalgia for the past, which is closely related to current social and political agendas.

It is safe to assume that the Nasser Facebook pages were founded by a younger generation of Egyptians whose members did not experience his period of rule. Therefore, the *transgenerational* dimension of cultural memory is particularly relevant in the examination of historical Facebook pages. By way of language and images, the memory of Gamal 'Abd al-Nasser has been transferred to those who did not live "within the spatial and temporal reach" of his rule, and his memory has become "negotiable and useable" for generations that grew up after he died (A. Assman 39). This transgenerational transmission enabled the development of a memory discourse of nostalgia for Nasser among Egyptians who were not yet born when he was president but still relate to his image on an individual and collective level as if they themselves remember him.

The transnational characteristics of these forums, such as their potential to reach out to the Egyptian diaspora and other sympathizers abroad, are also relevant. This essay seeks to draw broader conclusions as to whether Facebook can be considered an appropriate object for examining collective memory and aims to discuss the opportunities and limitations of such a methodology. It suggests that an adequate methodology should follow the basic rules that have been put forward in more traditional memory studies, for example regarding mediated memory, measuring reception, representativeness, and the connection between the past and the present. While the use of Facebook does not call for an entirely new conceptual approach, this essay concludes that using Facebook as a source can be problematic and that its use as a source should never stand in isolation from other archives.

FACEBOOK AS A COMMEMORATIVE PLATFORM

Over the past two decades, digital technologies have become more important in the dissemination of memory on the nonstate level. The computer and the Internet have facilitated the collection, storage, and distribution of commemorative materials by individuals and groups within civil society. In Egypt, there has been a rise in commemorative websites, both on state and nonstate levels.[1] In addition, Facebook is increasingly starting to serve as a digital tool for commemoration. For example, in the aftermath of the Egyptian Revolution of 25 January 2011, a new type of Facebook page was created, honoring "Egypt's Revolution Martyrs." On these pages, users could post names, pictures, and stories of people who had died as a result of mistreatment under the Mubarak regime or during the uprisings of January 2011.[2]

The creation of these online memory environments calls for new methodologies to conceptualize the dynamics of collective memory. Collective memory can be described as the way in which groups construct versions of an imagined shared past and employ them to buttress self-understanding and legitimization in an ever-changing present. Keeping in mind Maurice Halbwachs's observation that collective memory is a social construct that is shaped in interaction with others, it seems almost inevitable that memory scholars will come to incorporate Facebook and other social media into their research—as indeed they have, as José van Dijck and Amanda Lagerkvist show in the next section of this volume.

However, the study of social networking platforms forces us to think carefully about the terms we use when discussing online memories. Jan Assman introduced a distinction between "communicative" memory and "cultural" memory as two different forms of collective memory. Communicative memory, on the one hand, is mainly passed on orally in day-to-day life and dies along with its living carriers. Cultural memory, on the other hand, refers to memories that may be transferred from one generation to the next through mnemonic institutions, objects, symbols, and commemorative traditions (J. Assman 111).

Facebook serves as a medium for the expression of both forms of collective memory. As a means of everyday communication between individuals, it is an excellent platform for communicative memory; at the same time, Facebook has become a storage place for cultural memory—a place where people save and transmit memories with the aim of sharing them with a wider audience so that they may crystallize into a collective experience, be readopted across different generations, and contribute to the construction of personal as well as shared identities (J. Assmann 110–11).

Since Facebook can function as a platform for both communicative and cultural memory, in this essay I use the overarching term "collective memory" when discussing the general use of Facebook as a commemorative tool. However, I have characterized the particular memory discourse about Nasser as a form of cultural memory, since it is expressed on public pages and objectified and stored in symbolic forms with the aim to transmit it to future generations. This does not mean that none of the interactions I examine could belong to the category of communicative memory. One qualifying feature for distinguishing cultural memory from communicative memory is time, but since digital platforms are a fairly recent form of storing memories, their role in shaping future collective memory obviously remains to be determined.

One thing that is certain is that the emergence of online memory platforms has resulted in the increased visibility of "vernacular memory." The distinction between official and vernacular forms of collective memory was originally introduced by John Bodnar. While the official narrative originates in the concerns of leaders or authorities at all levels of society who share a common interest in social unity, the continuity of existing institutions, and loyalty to the status quo, vernacular culture, in contrast, represents an array of specialized interests originating from different units within society (75). The latter has also been termed "countermemory" and seeks to complement or pose a challenge to the "commemorative master narrative" (Zerubavel 12).

Vernacular memory is not always as easily discernible as official or state-sponsored memory—especially not in authoritarian states, where freedom of the press and of publication has been restricted. However, in the last two decades, the Internet has emerged as a powerful tool for the expression of vernacular memory. Even more recently, social media have made commemoration yet more interactive and dynamic.

While José van Dijck elsewhere in this volume points to the significant ethical and political problems besetting the success of Facebook, it has several undeniable advantages over other memory tools in terms of speed, scope, accessibility, and costs, among other things. First of all, the potential for generating a large audience in a very short time span is an advantage that social media and the Internet have over other instruments used by memory agents. Monuments, textbooks, archives, and other tangible memory aids take much longer to establish and are slower in their transmission. In contrast, the Internet, including Facebook, can have an almost direct effect, enabling practices of "mobile witnessing" (Reading 246).

Second, Facebook can easily reach a relatively large audience compared to fixed memory aids such as monuments. It is not tied to a geographic location and is accessible globally, even from people's living rooms. Third, in authoritarian states, the Internet is one of the few tools available to the public for the creation and distribution of memory. In addition, Facebook is an inexpensive way of generating, preserving, and distributing memory. Finally, Facebook makes commemoration more participatory. It encourages the public's contribution to the formation of collective memory, inviting every individual to take an active part in the process of creating, structuring, and negotiating collective memory through posting, commenting, or liking. Facebook is therefore preeminently a platform that allows expressions of vernacular discourse.

Aside from serving as a commemorative platform, Facebook is a handy tool of communication that serves memory agents in their efforts to mobilize the public to engage in nondigital acts of remembrance. For example, Facebook pages may be used to spread information about memorial services, protest marches, and other popular events. At the same time, Facebook may be used to make nondigital memory work accessible and known to a larger audience. In Egypt, for example, graffiti has recently become a prominent vehicle for popular commemoration in the postrevolutionary period (van de Bildt). Pictures of commemorative graffiti are distributed via Facebook and can in that way be viewed by a larger audience. Facebook has also fulfilled the function of preservation in cases in which the Egyptian government has ordered the removal of dissident graffiti, while the pictures of the graffiti remained available online. This transmediality reinforces vernacular expressions of memory by supporting, promoting, and preserving them, thus increasing their outreach.

In Egypt, where the print media and broadcasting services as well as public space have been largely state controlled for decades, platforms for the expression of vernacular memory have historically been restricted. In these circumstances, the Internet has proven a useful medium for the Egyptian public to disseminate various nonofficial narratives regarding the history of the country. Among other things, Facebook has served as an outlet and catalyst for feelings of nostalgia for selected episodes of the Egyptian past that spread among the public in the period leading up to the 2011 revolution and afterward.

NOSTALGIA AND THE NASSERIST LEGACY IN EGYPT

The term "nostalgia" comes from the Greek words *algos* (pain) and *nostos* (to return home; Boym xiii). Nostalgia is a sentimental yearning for the past, typically downplaying its negative aspects. A revival of the past is most common in times of searches for identity or stability and is particularly likely to emerge during periods of political upheaval. Pierre Nora famously noted, "Temporal and topographical memory sites emerge at those times and in those places where there is a perceived and constituted break with the past" (7).

Present grievances and mistrust toward the future have led people to turn to history for answers, glorify past periods, and sink into nostalgia. Nick Hodgin argues that nostalgia has the important mnemonic function of connecting people to the past "as a way of barricading themselves against the present" by clinging to talismans of continuity (154). But scholars have questioned whether nostalgia really does constitute a genuine desire to return to the past, as nostalgia can be a longing for something that may have never existed. Susan Stewart describes nostalgia as a form of sadness without an object that wears a distinctly utopian face; she argues that, like any form of narrative, nostalgia is thoroughly ideological: the past it seeks has never existed, except as a narrative, and it is this narrative, and the longing it expresses, that is of crucial importance.

During the recent years of political upheaval in Egypt, the younger generation of secular Egyptians has tended to glorify the period of the rule of Gamal 'Abd al-Nasser in what can be recognized as an expression of nostalgia. Typical for this nostalgia is that they express a longing not so much for what they have lost but rather for an ideal situation that was not actually attained during Nasser's rule, yet is retroactively associated with a period of "real" freedom, prosperity, equality, and dignity. It is common for people to revive or reshape the past in order to make sense of the present, and, indeed, the trend of nostalgia for Nasser says more about this generation's attitude to the present than it says about its actual connection to Nasser.

Gamal 'Abd al-Nasser, who was president of Egypt from 1956 until his death in 1970, is credited with achieving sovereignty for Egypt and "Egyptianizing" the national economy through the introduction of socialist measures. The successes of large Nasserist projects such as the building of the Aswan Dam, the nationalization of the Suez Canal, and the expulsion of the British are little debated. With his charismatic style of leadership, Nasser successfully courted both Egyptians and a large part of the Arab world with his vision of Arab nationalism. Nevertheless, the darker, authoritarian side of his system of rule was already clear in the 1950s. Moreover, in the 1960s, Nasser's policies failed to fulfill the dream of Arab unity and social justice. Increased state control over the economy, land reforms, and nationalization did not rid Egypt of rural poverty, unemployment, and social injustice.

Although a champion of nonalignment during the Cold War, Nasser became militarily and economically dependent on the Soviet Union. Egypt's humiliating defeat in the 1967 war with Israel dealt the—as the recent nostalgia makes clear, provisional—final blow to Nasser's public image and his pan-Arabist ideology. Politically, Nasser died a broken man in 1970; still, he had won the hearts of a large part of the Egyptian people. Nasser's successors, Anwar al-Sadat and Hosni Mubarak, gradually diverted from Nasser's domestic and foreign policies and at times went as far as reversing Nasser's policies. But they too failed to solve Egypt's problems of poverty, unemployment, and inequality and only succeeded in creating new reasons for public resentment as they opened up the economy and drew closer to the West.

Since Nasser's death, his legacy has remained contested in Egypt. During the Mubarak years, however, Nasser's reputation seems to have undergone a substantial popular revival. In a critical assessment of the Nasserist legacy on the thirtieth anniversary of his death, Egyptian journalists Hosni Guindi and Hani Shukrallah acknowledged:

Gamal 'Abd al-Nasser continues to inhabit Egypt because ... he is the representative of an age of certain national glory, despite any mistakes or setbacks ... Above all, he symbolises for Egyptians the expression of their independent national will. It is this that remains. It is in this that we must seek our project for the future. (Guindi and Shukrallah)

In a 1997 article, Joel Gordon argued that Nasserist nostalgia provides Egyptians with a sense of unity and stability. This sentiment emerged at a time when neither Islamism nor the state was seen to offer viable political alternatives to a lost civic culture. Nostalgia for Nasser should be interpreted as a search for "hope, purpose, Arab unity, and, not least, national unity and stability ... Nasserism produced a sense of nation and citizenship that transformed the way Egyptians looked at themselves and their world" (105).

The historian Carl Becker has argued that no matter what is written in history books, the memory of the past will always remain the dominant factor in how people perceive the past and that "this picture, however little it corresponds to the real past, helps to determine their ideas about politics and society" (61). As David Lowenthal argues, in the minds of the people, the accurate version of historical events is of only minor importance; most important is what people *believe* happened, or what they *want* to have happened. The majority "does not seek historical veracity nor mind its absence" ("Fabricating Heritage" 13). They may believe in anything that unites them or strengthens their identity, which is something that is based on "faith, not rational proof" (13).

Indeed, Nasser nostalgia is based on an imagined Egyptian utopia that was not achieved during his rule but that nevertheless provides people with a fascination for the past that helps them look toward the future. This confirms David Lowenthal's assertion that "nostalgia is often for past thoughts, rather than past things" (*Past* 8). The memory of Nasser was increasingly revived in the 2000s and was used as a vehicle to express contemporary political grievances and a yearning for better times. Gabriel Ben-Dor has argued that Nasser's commitment to "the restoration of pride in being Egyptians, the immense increase in the status of Arabism and Arabs throughout the region and the world [and] the confrontation with imperialism and the West" are values that still resonate with the Egyptian people, especially in periods of political upheaval (x).

Facebook provides an indication of the ways nostalgia for Nasser has been expressed and given shape in the twenty-first century and can be a useful archive for memory scholars in examining the characteristics of a certain nostalgic discourse by looking at the content of the Facebook pages. Examining photos and videos considered memorable enough to upload gives an indication of what it is exactly that Nasser embodies for the communities the pages foster. In addition, the Facebook pages show the links that people make between history and the present when current events and current political leaders are identified with Nasser. In the rest of this essay, I map out the major Nasser Facebook pages and demonstrate how their content supports and shapes the nostalgia for Nasser in contemporary Egypt. I will also draw attention to the caveats of using Facebook as an aid for examining the cultural memory of Nasser.

THE EMERGENCE OF NASSER FAN PAGES ON FACEBOOK

A search for the words "Gamal 'Abd al-Nasser"[3] in Arabic on Facebook results in a list of more than one hundred pages dedicated to his memory. A closer look at the content of the most important pages (that is, the pages with the largest number of likes) reveals a few recurrent themes that demonstrate how the memory of Nasser is constructed on Facebook. As is often the case with nostalgia, these Facebook pages romanticize the type of leader Nasser represents in cultural memory: a strong leader, a proud Egyptian, a man of the people, and a family man. For example, Nasser is known to have mixed standard literary Arabic with colloquial Egyptian (the dialect of everyday communication) when addressing the nation in order to strengthen his connection to the masses and to present himself as one of them.

A post on "Gamal 'Abd al-Nasir Za'im al-Umma al-'Arabiya (Gamal 'Abd al-Nasser, Leader of the Arab Nation)" confirms this image of Nasser as a man of the people, as it features a picture of the late president in the middle of a crowd, with the caption: "He feels safe only among the people and the masses." This emphasis on Nasser as a leader close to the masses reflects a contemporary desire for a strong national leader who acts in the interest of the people he is close to.

The Facebook pages generally feature iconic pictures of Nasser: greeting the people, giving a speech, meeting world leaders, or posing with his family. Moreover, they include pictures and written accounts of memorable Nasserist projects such as the Aswan Dam and the nationalization of the Suez Canal. It is telling that there are multiple pages titled "Nasir 56" in reference to Nasser's decision of 26 July 1956 to nationalize the Suez Canal. The move was followed by a military confrontation with Israel, the United Kingdom, and France and ended in a political victory for Egypt that forced the Anglo-French withdrawal from its territory. It is seen as one of several heroic deeds of Nasser and a significant step in recovering Egyptian sovereignty and national pride. "Nasser 56" is also the title of a popular movie that came out in Egypt in 1996 and that narrates the July 1956 events, highlighting Nasser's leadership. This example illustrates how the Nasser Facebook pages commemorate the bright sides of the Nasser era, citing only the more glorious episodes of his period of rule, as is typical for nostalgia.

The numbers of likes of the Nasser fan pages range from a few dozen to 100,000 followers. The largest page is called "Shabaka Nasser Akhbariya–Nasser News Network 3.N" and has 142,000 likes. It was founded on 28 September 2011, the forty-first anniversary of Nasser's death. The second largest page, founded on 24 July 2008, is "Gamal 'Abd al-Nasir" (written in Arabic), and it has managed to gather more than 78,000 likes. Another page with the exact same name was established on 4 January 2013 and has more than 44,000 likes. There are other popular pages, such as "Min Aqwal al-Za'im Gamal 'Abd al-Nasir (From the Words of the Leader Gamal 'Abd al-Nasser)" (15,119 likes), "Jamal Abdel Nasser II By Mahmoud ElSheikh" (1,931 likes), "Gamal Abdel Nasser" (8,759 likes), "Nasir 56" (11,733 likes), and "Gamal 'Abd al-Nasir Za'im al-Umma al-'Arabiya" (1,442 likes). Notably, one of the pages examined is called "Gamal 'Abd al-Nasir al-Gha'ib al-Hadir," which may be translated as "Gamal 'Abd al-Nasser, who is both absent and present."[4]

Reference to statistics such as the number of likes, which are made available on every public Facebook page, immediately draws the question of how to interpret these numbers. I highlight four problems here. First, although the number of likes a Facebook page displays makes it tempting to draw conclusions about the popularity of a topic or personality, there is no way to exactly know what audience the likes represent. One of the reasons for this is that liking an interest page or a cause on Facebook is also subject to what has been called "slacktivism." This term is a portmanteau of the words "slacker" and "activism" and refers to "actions performed via the Internet in support of a political or social cause but regarded as requiring little time or involvement," yet leaving a person with a feeling of satisfaction of having contributed something ("Slacktivism").

Thus, the number of likes can be misleading when measuring the popularity of a page, and the Facebook statistics feature in this regard gives no clue as to users' motivation behind liking a particular page or, indeed, as to what such an action is intended to signify. Neither, and this is a second problem, does Facebook provide the tools to examine the transcultural (Islamist, secular, Coptic) participation in these pages. Moreover, the virality of topics and fan pages on Facebook may depend on marketing strategies. The role of different agents in the dynamics of Facebook memory is difficult to pin down, since many of the medium's operations are automated, as José van Dijck explains in the next section of this book. This makes Facebook as much a platform for memory agents as a force by itself.

Third, there are additional variables to be taken into account when attempting to analyze collective memory on Facebook, such as the overall number of Internet users who might connect to a certain topic as well as the degree of Internet participation among different segments of the population. In developing and newly industrialized countries in particular, it is an open question to what extent long-time Internet users represent the lower to middle classes and their political demands.

Fourth and finally, it should also be noted that the date of the establishment of a Facebook page does not pinpoint the start of a certain trend, since the establishment of the page on that particular date may be the result of other factors, such as the degree of access to the Internet as described above or the popularity of Facebook as a medium in general. The fact that the most popular Nasser pages were all established between 2008 and the present does not mean that the trend of nostalgia for Nasser started in 2008. The creation of a fan page is best understood as one element within an existing trend, in which Facebook is used as an additional platform of expression.

These are among the multiple caveats that should be taken into account when using Facebook as a tool for examining collective memory. The statistics that Facebook provides are only a rough indicator of the popularity of the subject of the page, of the page's "most popular week," and of the age and location of the users. Certainly, it would be an ambitious, and perhaps futile, project to carry out comparative studies of the popularity of topics or personalities using only Facebook. Nevertheless, as I want to argue in the rest of this essay, if approached reflexively, Facebook can illuminate certain trends within public discourse, even if we also need to track these trends in other platforms and contexts.

THE CHANGING MEMORY OF NASSER ON FACEBOOK

The Nasser Facebook pages clearly illustrate how Nasser's memory has assumed different meanings over time, depending on the current state of political and socioeconomic affairs. During the Mubarak years, the image of Nasser was invoked, among other things, in opposition to the rise in food prices and education costs, unemployment, the privatization of companies, and cooperation with the United States and Israel. The overthrow of the Mubarak government coincided with an intensified interest in Nasser, even though Mubarak was often perceived as the continuation of a line of presidents that ruled Egypt since Nasser established the republic. The slogans and goals of the 2011 revolution were often linked to those of the 1952 revolution because of their common call for change, freedom, social justice, and dignity (El-Tonsi).

After the overthrow of Mubarak and the subsequent dissatisfaction with the leadership of the democratically elected Muslim Brotherhood in 2012, Nasserist nostalgia assumed a new dimension, centering on the belief that Nasser was right when it came to the Muslim Brotherhood and his policy of suppressing it. Facebook pages cite Nasser quotes in order to show that Egyptian politics was better off when it marginalized the Muslim Brotherhood. Other posts invoked the memory of Nasser to express a longing for his secular policies and to call for a separation between religion and state, among other things. For instance, the page "Jamal Abdel Nasser II By Mahmoud ElSheikh" includes a long post about "what Nasser offered Islam," promoting interpretations of Islam that contrast with those of the Muslim Brotherhood, which was in power at the time.

Also "Gamal 'Abd al-Nasir" posted a picture of Nasser praying, with the accompanying text "Leader Gamal 'Abd al-Nasser and the correct understanding of Islam." The page "Suwar Qadimahu li-Misr / Gamal 'Abd al-Nasir (Old Pictures of Egypt / Jamal 'Abd al-Nasser)" features a series of photos of Nasser making the hajj pilgrimage to Mecca together with Anwar al-Sadat. Both former presidents are dressed in the ihram, a white, seamless garment that all pilgrims are supposed to wear during the performance of the hajj rituals. Thus, the memory of Nasser is used to express people's views regarding the "correct" understanding of Islam and what its place should be in Egyptian society at a time when the country was governed by an Islamist movement seeking to promote its religious agenda and especially the introduction of sharia law.

In 2013, as General al-Sisi came to power, Nasser's image assumed yet another dimension and started to become used to legitimize the role of the military in Egyptian society. For example, the Facebook page "Gamal 'Abd al-Nasir" includes a picture of Nasser and 'Abd al-Fatah al-Sisi, both in uniform, with the text "'Abd al-Nasir and 'Abd al-Fatah: Thank you. Signed by the Egyptian and Arab people." Significantly, this picture was posted on 18 July 2013, two weeks after the Egyptian army ousted President Morsi and while the situation in the country remained very unstable.

The political criticism or endorsement expressed on Facebook as illustrated above highlights a major consequence of the rise of the Internet as a commemorative tool: I mean the way it has affected the traditional balance of power between official and vernacular memory. Traditionally, the most powerful memory agents were those who had both the power and the money to institutionalize memory, for example through the establishment of museums, monuments, and archeological excavations and the organization of commemorative services. In the age of social media and graffiti, no large sums of money are needed to enter the public and virtual spaces with narratives that oppose those projected by government officials and state media.

Increased nostalgia for Nasser is also a reaction to what is perceived as continued Western domination in the region and the unquestioned decline of Egypt's standing and influence in the Arab world. The Facebook page "Shabaka Nasser Akhbariya–Nasser News Network 3.N" includes photoshopped pictures that mock Morsi's relationship with US leaders. The page "Gamal 'Abd al-Nasir Za'im al-Umma al-'Arabiya" also includes a picture of Nasser meeting Che Guevara, placed next to a picture of Morsi meeting John Kerry. The page "Nasir 56" contrasts popular attitudes toward the government in 1967 to those of 2011. On one side is a picture of the 2011 demonstrations demanding Mubarak's downfall, and next to it is a picture of the 1967 June demonstrations demanding Nasser stay on as Egypt's president after the *Naksa,* the Egyptian defeat in the war of June 1967.

The picture is accompanied by the text *Ayna taran min at-turayya,* a proverb used to compare things of disproportionate value. These examples show how on historical Facebook pages, contemporary images are articulated with past events (and vice versa) in order to send a critical message about present politics. It also shows clearly how the image of Nasser functions as a "screen" on which we "project present or timeless needs and desires" (Hirsch 120). The memory of Nasser is not a recollection of past events, but rather it constitutes a set of "preestablished forms" that serve the promotion of a contemporary political goal.

MEDIATION AND TRANSFORMATION: THE IMAGE OF NASSER IN TRANSNATIONAL CONTEXTS

The Nasser fan pages are almost entirely in Arabic and rarely include posts in other languages. This indicates that the pages' followers may include domestic as well as overseas Arabic-speaking groups with various connections to the personality the page deals with. The icon of Nasser means different things to these different audiences, and the themes of the Facebook pages may vary, even though they were all established in Nasser's name. For example, while some pages use the image of Nasser to call for strong leadership within Egypt, other pages promote Nasser's vision of Arab unity, emphasizing Nasser's promise to restore Arab dignity. "Shabaka Nasser al-Akhbariya," for example, presents itself as "the voice of Arabism," declaring, "There is no place for neutrality here, we are biased in favor of the Arab homeland and the poor, who both have a leader: Gamal 'Abd al-Nasser."

The page "Jamal Abdel Nasser II By Mahmoud ElSheikh" echoes Nasser's discourse of Egypt as the leader of the Arab world and the importance of the restoration of Arab unity: "If Egypt is weak, the entire Arab struggle is weak. When Egypt is paralyzed, the Arab struggle is paralyzed. This is not a new fact but the effect of history and nature." Furthermore, it states:

> Arab nationalism is not embodied in one man or group nor is it represented just by 'Abd al-Nasser and those who worked with him, but millions of Arabs carry the flame of nationalism in their hearts and it is irresistible and cannot be destroyed by any force in the world as long as one continues to believe in it with confidence."

Such a formulation has the potential of being adopted by a larger Arab collective outside of Egypt. Thus, Nasser has become an icon that has the potential of expressing and condensing different ideals associated with him. Comparing the Nasser pages to other Facebook pages of legendary historical or contemporary personalities, it is notable that for these icons, there are always multiple Facebook pages, almost never just one. This reinforces the observation that it is not exactly the popularity of people but rather the ideals they embody that make them into a trending topic.

For example, Aung San Suu Kyi has more than ten very popular Facebook pages, and so does Che Guevara. They seem to embody widely shared ideals that many different people identify with in their own ways. While for the founders of one page, Aung San Suu Kyi "symbolises the struggle of Burma's people to be free," other pages invoke her as an icon for peace and freedom for suppressed peoples in the world at large. This example illustrates how the Internet facilitates the transition from local memory to global memory, creating transnational and sometimes transcultural memories. These icons are almost always overdetermined, as they provide an outlet for more than one single wish or need.

The memory of Nasser, like any other cultural memory, should not be seen as a stable or homogenous entity but as something that evolves as it is (re)interpreted by diverse individuals and collectives across time and space, depending on time, place, and context, as demonstrated in the previous sections. Facebook accelerates this evolution in and the transformation of the significance of certain memories. In *The Texture of Memory,* James Young explains how, once available in the public space, memory objects are reinvigorated and acquire new meanings, often stubbornly resistant to the maker's original intentions (3).

In his work on Holocaust monuments, Young argues that by themselves, monuments are mere stones in the landscape and that they depend on visitors for whatever memory they end up producing. Public memory and its meanings depend not just on the forms and figures in the monument itself but on the viewer's response to the monument, on how it is used politically and religiously in the community, on who sees it under what circumstances, and on how its figures enter other media and are recast in new surroundings (Young xii). Thus, every memorial space possesses a fundamentally interactive, dialogical quality. One could argue that this effect is exacerbated when memory is diffused via social media, since the interactive nature of this medium is fundamentally larger than that of monuments or other analogue memory objects.

As do all media, Facebook shapes the memories it mediates. One could argue that online commemoration causes an even higher degree of mediation of memory than do traditional channels. As Wulf Kansteiner observes, memories are always mediated phenomena, since "all memories, even those of eyewitnesses, only assume collective relevance when they are structured, represented, and used in a social setting" (190). The Nasser Facebook pages illustrate that the activity of structuring, representation, and usage reaches a whole new level on the World Wide Web.

For example, "Shabaka Nasser Akhbariya—Nasser News Network 3.N" published a picture that portrays a map of Israel and Palestine covered in the flag of the United Arab Republic (as Egypt used to be called since it formed a union with Syria in 1958 and continued to be called even after the union was dissolved, until the name and the flag were changed again by Anwar al-Sadat in 1972) and a picture of Nasser accompanied by the text: "All of Palestine is Arab. No to reconciliation, recognition and negotiation." Anna Reading has examined the high degree of intermediation that results from digitization visible in such pictures, noting that online memorial items easily intersect with other images, resulting in "an assemblage of discursive formations" (248).

The highly mediated picture described above gives Nasser's memory the potential to send different political messages to various collectives: For Palestinians, it may signify support for their cause. To the Arab world at large, it may symbolize a call for Arab unity. The Egyptian government, for its part, may interpret it as criticism toward its relations with Israel—a policy starkly opposed to the one pursued by Nasser, who is generally viewed as a champion for the Palestinian cause (Sharnoff). As such, the memory of Nasser can be adopted in different social settings, depending on the time, place, and context in which it is viewed. Reading also notes that memories can be "deterritorialized" and subsequently "reterritorialized." This means, for example, that an uploaded cell phone video can easily be exported to other places in the world, where it is adopted and popularized by a local audience and shaped and adjusted according to local interpretations and interests. Eventually it may "return" to the place of origin in its new form, where it assumes different connotations once again.

CONCLUSION

An examination of Facebook as an object for studying collective memory should address questions of the reception, transmission, and mediation of memory across different generations and transnational contexts. Only limited conclusions can be drawn about reception based on Facebook statistics and trending topics, as there is no way to establish who the founders and followers of a page are representing or, even, think they are representing. In many ways, this caveat is analogous to what historians encounter while carrying out discourse analysis based on "traditional" sources such as newspapers and books: there is no hard evidence on the representativeness of the author or the impact of the writing.

Although it is difficult to establish the makeup of the followers of the Nasser pages, we can safely assume that it concerns a younger generation of both Egyptians and Arabs from other countries, with diverging motivations for taking an interest in Nasser. Yet, in order to use Facebook as a source, one has to be aware of the limitations of the medium. For instance, Facebook cannot be taken as a tool for pinpointing trends in society, if only because the pages represent at best a limited part of society. Moreover, online commemoration reveals a high degree of mediation in the construction of the meaning of memory. What is most interesting and productive, I believe, is to track trends of nostalgia and other types of memory on Facebook—a process for which Jessica K. Young, in her contribution to this volume, provides valuable tools—and see how they are given shape with audiovisual material, texts, and comments.

The transgenerational aspect of historical Facebook pages is especially worth noting. It is important to remember that over a longer time span, the persistence of cultural memories of a particular individual, event, or experience requires explanation, since the passage of memory from the generation that experienced the event to the following generations cannot be taken for granted. This makes the existence of Nasser fan pages on Facebook highly interesting. The fact that there *are* Nasser Facebook pages, and that there is recorded activity among the public on such pages, testifies to the ongoing currency of his memory and, importantly, suggests that his image serves the purpose of promoting present political goals. This makes Facebook a useful tool for memory scholars, since it gives an indication of which memories are "alive" or are being revived. In addition, Facebook can give insight into vernacular memory, which is often expressed only at informal levels or may be restricted by the state, as is the case in Egypt.

Facebook is increasingly part of the mediascapes that keep memory traces alive in the process that Jay Winter and Emmanuel Sivan have defined as "renewing the shelf-life of a memory" through "constant rehearsal, group action and ingenuity in mobilizing resources" (31). Facebook and other Internet platforms create an opportunity for opposition parties and minority groups in particular to represent themselves and their identities and to recruit "followers." Even if Facebook pages are not exclusively grassroots initiatives, since the state is also represented on Facebook,[5] Facebook provides nonstate actors with a more powerful voice in the formation of collective memory.

In this atmosphere, the Internet has served as one of the most productive tools available to the public for the creation and distribution of memory. Indeed, the advantages of using Facebook as a tool for memory agents apply mostly to nonstate actors, especially when it comes to low costs and easy accessibility. Also the speed and scope, that is, the potential for generating a large audience in a very short time span, constitute an advantage over traditional memory aids. Thus, the rise of the Internet as a commemorative tool affects the traditional balance of power between official and vernacular memory.

Joyce van de Bildt is a Ph.D. candidate in history at Tel Aviv University, writing her dissertation about the contested memory of the 1952 revolution in Egypt during the periods of rule of Anwar al-Sadat and Hosni Mubarak. She is also a junior research fellow at the Moshe Dayan Center for Middle Eastern and African Studies. Her research interests include contemporary Egyptian history and politics, collective memory, commemoration, and identity politics.

NOTES

1. See, for example, the Memory of Modern Egypt project on the website of Bibliotheca Alexandria and the websites egyptmemory.com, lan-nansahom.org, tahrirdocuments.org, and anwarsadat.org.

2. See, for example, the following Facebook pages: "Al-shuhada' al-thawra al-misriya (Egyptian Revolution Martyrs)," "Shuhada' 25 yana'ir al-ward ila fatah fi al-jana'in (Egypt Martyrs)," and "Shuhada' thawra 25 yana'ir al-misriya (Martyrs of Egyptian Revolution's 25th January)."

3. All Arabic to English translations are mine.

4. The number of likes was retrieved on 1 September 2014.
5. See, for example, the Facebook pages "Mathaf al-Sadat–Sadat Museum" and "Majalla dhakira Misr al-mu'asira–Memory of Modern Egypt."

WORKS CITED

Assmann, Aleida. "Re-framing Memory: Between Individual and Collective Forms of Constructing the Past." *Performing the Past: Memory, History, and Identity in Modern Europe.* Ed. Karin Tilmans, Frank van Vree, and Jay M. Winter. Amsterdam: Amsterdam University Press, 2010. 35–50.

Assmann, Jan. "Communicative and Cultural Memory." *Cultural Memory Studies: An International and Interdisciplinary Handbook.* Ed. Astrid Erll and Ansgar Nünning. Berlin: De Gruyter, 2008. 109–18.

Becker, Carl L. "What Are Historical Facts?" *Detachment and the Writing of History: Essays and Letters of Carl. L. Becker.* Ed. Phil L. Snyder. Ithaca: Cornell University Press, 1958. 3–28.

Ben-Dor, Gabriel. "Foreword." *Rethinking Nasserism: Revolution and Historical Memory in Modern Egypt.* Ed. Elie Podeh and Onn Winckler. Gainesville: University Press of Florida, 2004. ix–xii.

Bodnar, John. "Public Memory in an American City." *Commemorations: The Politics of National Identity.* Ed. John R. Gillis. Princeton: Princeton University Press, 1994.

Boym, Svetlana. *The Future of Nostalgia.* New York: Basic Books, 2001.

El-Tonsi, Ahmed. "Nasser and Egypt's Two Revolutions." *Al-Ahram Weekly* 29 Sept. 2011. Web. 3 Sept. 2014.

Gordon, Joel. "Secular and Religious Memory in Egypt: Recalling Nasserist Civics." *The Muslim World* 87.2 (1997): 94–110.

Guindi, Hosni, and Hani Shukrallah. "Liberating Nasser's Legacy." *Al-Ahram Weekly* 28 Sept. 2000. Web. 3 Sept. 2014.

Halbwachs, Maurice. *On Collective Memory.* Chicago: University of Chicago Press, 1992.

Hirsch, Marianne. "The Generation of Postmemory." *Poetics Today* 29.1 (2008): 103–28.

Hodgin, Nick. *Screening the East: Heimat, Memory, and Nostalgia in German Film since 1989.* New York: Berghahn Books, 2011.

Kansteiner, Wulf. "Finding Meaning in Memory: A Methodological Critique of Collective Memory Studies." *History and Theory* 41.2 (2002): 179–97.

Lowenthal, David. "Fabricating Heritage." *History and Memory* 10.1 (1998): 5–24.

———. *The Past Is a Foreign Country.* Cambridge: Cambridge University Press, 1985.

Nora, Pierre. "Between Memory and History: *Les Lieux de Mémoire.*" *Representations* 26 (1989): 7–24.

Reading, Anna. "On Media Memory: Collective Memory in a New Media Age." *On Media Memory: Collective Memory in a New Media Age.* Ed. Motti Neiger, Oren Meyers, and Eyal Zandberg. Basingstoke: Palgrave Macmillan, 2011. 241–52.

Sharnoff, Michael. "Academic Perspective: Revisiting Nasser and Palestine after the 1967 War." *Al-Arabiya News* 11 June 2011. Web. 3 Sept. 2014.

"Slacktivism." *Oxford Dictionaries.* Oxford: Oxford University Press. Web. 3 Sept. 2014.

Stewart, Susan. *On Longing: Narratives of the Miniature, the Gigantic, the Souvenir, the Collection.* Baltimore: Johns Hopkins University Press, 1984.

Van de Bildt, Joyce. "Revolutionary Graffiti in Egypt: Resistance and Commemoration." *Tel Aviv Notes* 7.24 (2013): 1–5.

Winter, Jay, and Emmanuel Sivan. *War and Remembrance in the Twentieth Century.* Cambridge: Cambridge University Press, 1999.

Young, James E. *The Texture of Memory: Holocaust Memorials and Meaning.* New Haven: Yale University Press, 1993.

Zerubavel, Yael. *Recovered Roots: Collective Memory and the Making of Israeli National Tradition.* Chicago: University of Chicago Press, 1995.

Part III

Transmedial Memory

Chapter 7

Connective Memory

How Facebook Takes Charge of Your Past

José van Dijck

⬦

INTRODUCTION

In September 2011, Mark Zuckerberg introduced Facebook's novel interface at a public event, saying, "Timeline is the story of your life. It has three pieces: all your stories, all your apps, and a new way to express who you are" ("Mark Zuckerberg Unveils"). He then continued to explain how Timeline lets you "tell the whole story of your life on a single page." The advent of Timeline signaled Facebook's transformation from a social networking site into a connective memory tool: rather than a mere instrument for interpersonal or mass self-communication, the platform has also become a prime means for shaping personal and social memory. People's stories, apps, and expressiveness, if we believe Zuckerberg's promises, are all combined into a single new interface. For many people, their Facebook site has become indispensable in their efforts to build an online persona that is both private and public—an intricate knot of *self-expression,* recollection, and *self-promotion.*

Does Facebook transform the way individual memory is shaped in the public mind? This chapter will analyze how users struggle with platforms to control their personal online manifestation—a process that is played out at the level of the *interface.* Users deploy social network services for several purposes, and over the years, they have adapted their strategies in online presentation as platforms changed their functionalities. Initially, platforms like Facebook were commonly regarded as a space for (personal) self-expression and for making connections between people. Gradually, users have come to understand the art of online self-presentation and the importance of social network services as tools for (professional) self-promotion.

Since each form of self-communication brings along a specific concept of audience, users had to learn how to handle privacy settings accordingly. Parallel to the shift in users' needs, there has been a shift in platform owners' ambitions in operating social network services. Whereas in the first stage of their development these sites were primed to facilitate *connectedness* between people, after 2009 most corporate networks shifted their focus to monetizing *connectivity* by maximizing lucrative data traffic between people, things, and ideas (van Dijck, *Culture of Connectivity* 31). Along with this shift came a change in platforms' architectures: rather than being *databases* of personal information, they became tools for (personal) *storytelling* and *narrative* self-presentation.

The next section will explain how these shifts are intricately intertwined and how they force us to raise questions also discussed elsewhere in this volume: about human agency in digital environments (a topic also broached by Amanda Lagerkvist), about the performativity of memory (as discussed by Max Silverman), and about the relation between memory and personal identity (addressed in many of the chapters). In light of the "transmedial memory" theme of this section, this chapter will focus on the dynamics of memory between technology and users; media interfaces are never neutral carriers of content but actively coconstitute the meanings and dynamics of commemorative culture.

Social media's changing digital architectures form the necessary backdrop for asking critical questions about online self-presentation: how are personal memories and public identities shaped through platform interfaces? How do these features enable and constrain the sculpting of personal and public personas? And what are the consequences of imposed connectivity and narrativity on people's online identities? To answer these questions, I will use the method of platform analysis. While Facebook emphasized self-presentation and personal memory as its most important platform qualities from the very outset, the site gradually began to foster public self-promotion. This dual strategy can be distinctly revealed in recent interface changes. In 2011 and 2012, Facebook rolled out its new Timeline layout, a feature that enforced a uniform presentation of self on all its members' homepages and implicitly encouraged a formatted style of self-promotion.

At the same time, individual users' data are increasingly used as input for data crunching and the detection of "social" trends. Facebook's Page Insights stimulate users to find aggregated anonymous insights about people's activity on their page and thus keep track of their online behavior, and already a few years before the introduction of Timeline, Facebook had introduced Facebook Memology, the total sum of all Facebook status up-dates and expressions on individual pages. As we read on the Facebook site, "When taken as a whole, these words offer a unique barometer into the issues, world events and thoughts that are connecting people" ("Facebook Memology Blog"). Facebook, in other words, has not only become a prime tool for shaping individual memories but also created a novel form of social memory.

Facebook's strategies epitomize the emergence of a more general in-dustrial logic called *life mining*—identifying, analyzing, coding, and project-ing social events on the basis of user-generated data. Data assembled by networks like Facebook are in particular regarded as indicators of social memory and shared collective experiences of the recent past. Considering the immense speed at which social network services continue to grow, the larger concerns underpinning their technological and economic impera-tives are systematically understated. How are individual personas shaped through platform interfaces, and how are these data regarded in the face of increasingly commercialized environments? In other words, what does "social memory" mean in an ecosystem dominated by principles of online connectivity? And what are the consequences of imposed connectivity and narrative on online spaces of personal and what I prefer to call "connective memory" (van Dijck, "Flickr" 402)?

These kinds of questions are increasingly relevant when we enter legal and political discussions about information control. They also complicate claims for the political efficacy of social media, such as those investigated in the case of contemporary Egypt in Joyce van de Bildt's chapter in this vol-ume. In the rest of this essay, I attempt to deconstruct the strategies of plat-forms promoting the online self as a tradable product and theorize about its cultural implications.

MAKING MEMORY CONNECTIVE:
DATABASES TURNING INTO NARRATIVES

The emergence of what Manuel Castells has called "mass self-communica-tion" refers to a global system of networked interaction, a system that har-bors platforms like Facebook, LinkedIn, Google Plus, and Twitter, all of-fering crucial means to galvanize identity performance online. From the earliest days of social media, platforms were presented as "magical" tools for self-expression while at the same time enabling participants to connect endlessly with others. As facilitators of networks, they promoted human connectedness as a profound value. Being well connected, both offline and online, generally defines a human being's success as a social creature. As danah boyd and Nicole Ellison observed in 2007, social network sites were about enhancing human relationships already existing in real life as well as about supporting expansive networks of "friends of friends" (2). Social networks enhanced connections rooted in offline sociality while also enabling weak ties through algorithmic computations.

Facebook thus became a primer for promoting the self as the center of an extensive network of friends and friends of friends; over the years, one's personal Facebook page has come to signal an individual's capacity to build and maintain a substantial network of contacts. In online environments, people want to *show* who they are; they have a vested interest in identity construction by sharing pieces of information because disclosing information about oneself is closely linked with popularity.

Psychology researchers Emily Christofides, Amy Muise, and Serge Desmarais have argued, "Identity is a social product created not only by what you share, but also by what others share and say about you," concluding that "the people who are most popular are those whose identity construction is most actively participated in by others" (343). Since Facebook is the largest social network, it offers the best potential for mass self-communication. In contrast to other mass media, social network services in general—and Facebook in particular—offer individual users a stage for crafting a self-image and for popularizing this image beyond intimate circles.[1] Popularity and disclosure are two sides of the same coin, and they mirror the double meaning of "sharing," which is often regarded as a synonym of "friending."

The function of social network services as instruments of self-expression and the building of personal memory is closely related to their function as network tools for everyday communication. It is important to recall how most social network sites, notably Facebook, started out in protected environments such as college campuses. It took two years for Facebook to expand its service to a general global audience, changing the nature of the game: Facebook's interface was gradually adapted to meet the demands of many more groups of users and a rapidly expanding user base. As audiences became less homogeneous and more general after 2007, online manifestation on Facebook increasingly implied presenting a public persona that could be seen and contacted by users worldwide. Online connections no longer automatically paralleled offline contacts but favored instead weak and latent ties. Networked connectedness quickly came to dominate the organization of everyday sociality (Christakis and Fowler; van Dijck, "Facebook as a Tool").

Toward the end of the first decade of the millennium, a noticeable change occurred in the organization and architecture of social media platforms, shifting their gravitas from connectedness to connectivity. Key terms denoting routine humanoid activities of bonding and socializing—such as "friending," "liking," "sharing," and, of course, the very adjective "social"—rapidly penetrated the discourse of platforms. However, these terms increasingly referred not just to human contacts but also to automatic connections between nonhuman objects: platforms translated relationships between people, ideas, and things into algorithms in order to engineer and steer humans' social performance.

Most algorithms are coded quantifications of sociality, implemented to trigger and enable as many connections as possible, even though users are often unaware of the effects these algorithms have upon them (Beer, "Power through the Algorithm," "Social Network(ing) Sites"). Personal and behavioral (meta)data, once a mere byproduct of connectedness and online sociality, have now become a valuable resource in the exploitation of platforms. Friending increasingly refers to people you *may know* or *ought to know* according to an algorithm's computation (think of the People You May Know button). "Liking" has turned into a provoked automated gesture of appreciation that yields precious information about people's unconscious desires and predispositions.

As Nicole Ellison, Charles Steinfeld, and Cliff Lampe have argued, the more connections users make to both human and nonhuman entities, the more social capital they accumulate. And the more social capital people assign to things and ideas, the more economic capital can be gained from connectivity. The automatic mining of personal and behavioral data has developed into platform owners' most important driver for promoting online traffic.

This so-called connective turn—from connectedness to connectivity—in social media platforms has also had a noticeable effect on how people present their online personas. Since roughly 2009, social acts of self-expression on social network services have begun to give way to more conscious acts of self-staging as people's public presence and popularity are increasingly measured by their online manifestation. The online self has turned into an object of marketing and promotion, fueled by the understanding that connectivity can transform social value into monetary rewards. Stars and politicians can now eminently exploit the possibilities of marketing individual personalities as products. Celebrities' exuberant self-presentation via Twitter or Facebook uncovers the lucrative side of the connective turn: their online personas equal their brands, and the ultimate successful presentation of self is to have millions of followers.

For celebrities such as Justin Bieber and Barack Obama, sculpting one's online persona has become an indispensable part of self-branding. PR teams use—in contrast to previous public staging by mass media, such as television—social media channels to control their personal messages and maximize their "brand's" profitability, whether in terms of votes or money. It has become fairly common for people with large followings to take on brand promotion for products or causes; if Madonna recommends a particular kind of shoes or takes a stance against child labor, she cashes in on the connective value of her personal popularity among millions of followers.

Promoting and branding the self has also become a normalized, accepted phenomenon in people's everyday lives (de Certeau). Following the example of celebrities' self-promotion, many users (especially young adults and teenagers) shape their online identities in order to gain popularity and reach a comfortable level of recognition and connectedness.[2] Indeed, teenagers have always modeled their self-image after celebrities' exposure through mass media such as television and movies—a phenomenon theorized by British sociologist John Thompson well before the advent of social media. But in addition to enhanced personal visibility, common users have gained instruments for self-promotion that may actually pay off. Those users who attain high levels of acknowledgment from their peers are regarded as "influencers" on Facebook and Twitter; as such, they may receive offers from companies to distribute promoted messages (e.g., in the form of messages distributed to people's Walls) and be rewarded materially or symbolically.

Online self-promotion is not just for teenagers: adults of all ages manifest themselves online to emphasize their professional skills and proficiency, attracting contacts, contracts, customers, or employers, and put up personal profiles to emphasize their hobbies and affinities. There are many ways to shape online identities for a variety of purposes and, in theory, there are a number of platforms to choose from—platforms that, over the years, have specialized in catering for specific functions and to specific audiences, such as LinkedIn and JobLink for professional labor markets, eDating for dating markets, Flickr for posting photographs, Pinterest for publishing creative ideas, and so on. In principle, users utilize various platforms concurrently to satisfy different aspects of their need for personal expression, professional presentation, and interpersonal and public communication. However, despite a seemingly diverse ecosystem of platforms, major platforms like Facebook are central to all this connectivity.

Facebook is not only the largest but also the most generic social networking site, servicing the general social needs of users, in contrast to more specific niches, such as LinkedIn and Academia.edu, which serve primarily professional markets (Bukvova; Papacharissi). Over the years, Facebook's interface has become less generic and more purposeful, thus restraining users' modes of self-presentation. Whereas in the early years of social media there was still a relative freedom in online presentation, Facebook and other platforms have gradually tweaked their interfaces and protocols not just to help users but also to serve businesses and maximize connectivity.

The introduction of standardized presentation formats on users' home-pages helps to instantly recognize a pattern in the layout of information; for instance, on the basis of their Timelines, advertisers can target women with small children to advertise diapers or send direct mail to Stanford alumni with offers for credit or mortgages. Moreover, algorithms work better if input is uniform, making it easier to automatically detect patterns of behavior and manipulate them. Platform owners are interested in standardization as well as in customization: data need to be inserted and presented uniformly, while users can still give a personal touch to their sites. In other words, standardized input via interfaces serve platform and advertisers' needs more than they serve users.

Not only did the connective turn in social media change platforms into harbingers of coded and branded sociality, it also brought along a shift in the organization of platforms from database structures into *narrative* structures. In the early years of Web 2.0, new media scholar Lev Manovich theorized about the distinct architectural nature of interactive platforms as databases—organized collections of textual, audiovisual, and numerical data supported by a database management system. Unlike previous media, interactive platforms forced users to present information in a nonlinear, nonnarrative fashion. Databases in themselves do not tell stories with a beginning or end; in fact, "they do not have any development, thematically, formally, or otherwise that would organize their elements into a sequence" (Manovich 218). Instead, Manovich argued, the user interface of digital media relies upon a concept of spatial montage in which the retrieval of data is highly dependent on search systems (322).

For the first decade of the twenty-first century, the dominance of databases over narratives presented users with a new logic of the information order, and it was exactly this new logic that distinguished social media platforms from other types of communication media. The applicability of Manovich's concept could be discerned in the contingent ordering of information on social network sites, which centered on users' needs rather than on platform owners' interests. Facebook's interface, as Joanne Garde-Hansen observes, used to be presented as a database *of* users and *for* users in which "each user's page is a database of their life, making this social network site a collection of collections and collectives" (141).

As a result of the database logic in the visible interface, each user could very well define the distinctive functionality of his or her profile. For some users, their page presented a personal archive, a way to share life histories and memories with selected others or open it up to the public at large. For others, social network services appeared to be a "stage for digital flâneurs," a place to "see and be seen" (boyd 155). In sum, Facebook's visual interface initially served users' desires for variable modes of self-presentation, allowing for openness and randomness; drawing on Manovich's distinction between database and narrative, social network services used to favor a spatial-visual ordering of information over a linear-narrative one.

But what happened to database logic in light of the recent connective turn, and how did these changes show in social media platforms' interfaces? In many respects, social network services still function as databases, and yet their interfaces show an inclination toward a directive narrative ordering of information. When you enter a personal page on Facebook—or any other social media site, for that matter—it is hard to escape the trend toward "storytelling" and personalization. The presentation of self is increasingly molded in a prescribed format that espouses many coercive features: fields to be filled with data, pictures in specific spaces, prompts to highlight specific events, a chronological order of personal information, and much more.

Facebook has crept deeper into the texture of life, its narrative principles imitating proven conventions of storytelling and thus binding users even more tightly to the fabric that keeps them connected. At the same time, the site's database logic has not vanished, even though it is now veiled by the narrative layout of the visible user interface. Database and narrative appear to be complementary yet hierarchical structures. In the next sections, I will analyze recent interface changes to Facebook, first with regard to personal users and subsequently with regard to companies, to understand how acts of self-expression and personal memory are implicitly aligned with self-promotion and brand publicity.

FACEBOOK AND THE MIXING OF PERSONAL MEMORY AND SELF-PROMOTION

The introduction of Timeline profoundly reshaped the functional use of the social networking site. If we compare Facebook's interface in 2004 with the latest one introduced in 2011 (see Illustration 7.1), we can hardly miss the huge transformation from connectedness to connectivity. If the original interface centered almost entirely on personal communication and making contacts, the interface structured by Timeline instead focuses on promoting and presenting the self as a persona with a smooth past, a cheerful present, and a clear ambition for the future.

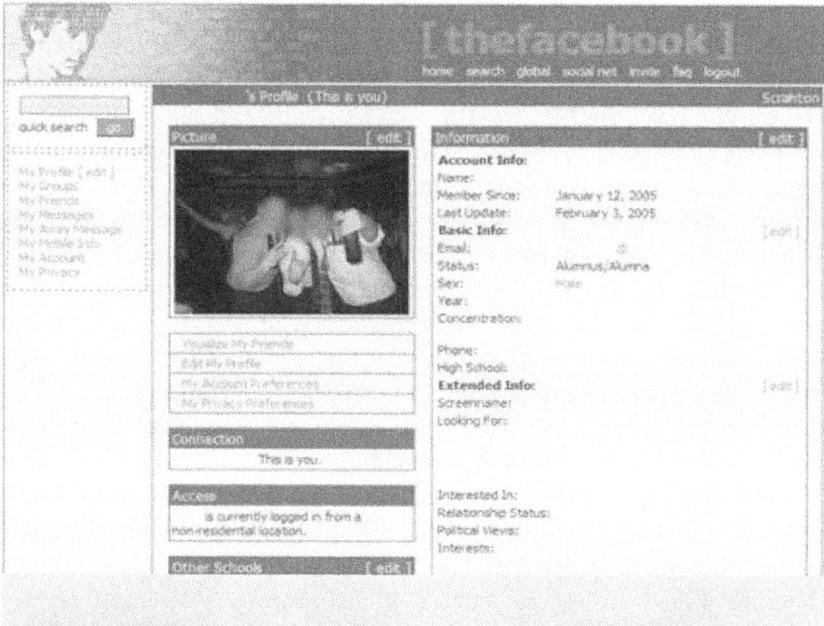

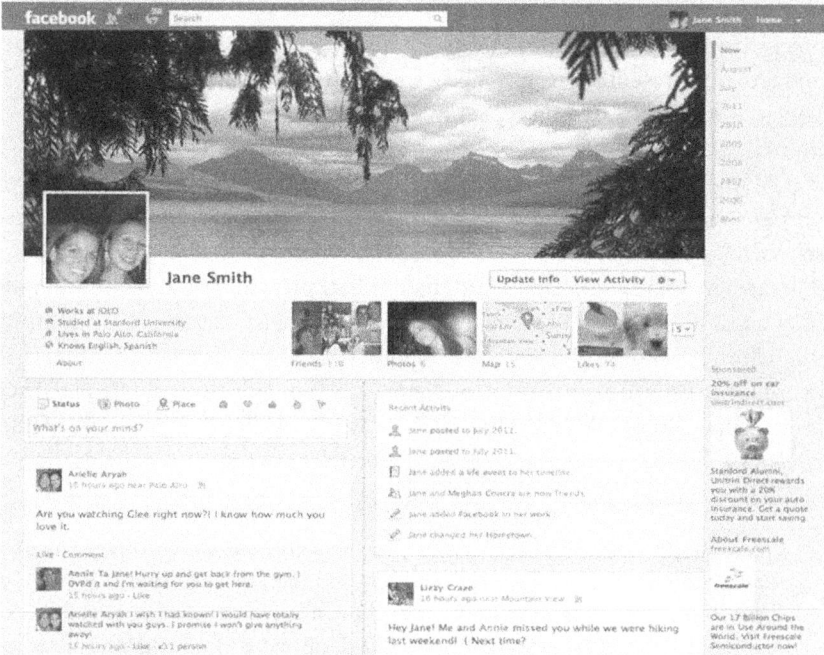

Illustration 7.1. Top: Facebook's original interface in 2004. Bottom: Facebook's Timeline interface in 2012.

The most significant ordering principle of the new interface layout is a vertical bar on the right indicating a chronological line from the present to the past, starting with the most recent months, which slip into years when you scroll toward the bottom. The entire left side and center of the page are filled with events, "stories of your life" in the form of pictures, posts to friends, music that you like(d), recipes you exchange(d), all your likes and pokes, updates, maps of the places you have been, and a lot more. Every single piece of data (text, picture, video, sound) you ever uploaded on Facebook is automatically transferred onto the Timeline upon opening it in the new format—a format that became compulsory for every user after it was rolled out and implemented in 2012. But the new Timeline is much more than a glitzy new interface feature: it is a complete architectural overhaul that smartly disciplines its users into combining self-expression—in this case memory and emotion—with self-promotion into one standardized format.

Timeline's format is organized as a narrative biography, a story chronicling life up to the present day by rearranging bits and pieces uploaded previously. The resulting narrative is a construction in hindsight, a retroactive ordering of life events at one moment in time. Facebook's encoded activity resembles the analogue real-life shoebox experience: people reassembling pieces from their old photo albums, diaries, scrapbooks, and weblogs into one smooth presentation of the present past (van Dijck, *Mediated Memories*). Due to the Timeline format, all online Facebook pages contain the same key ingredients.

At the bottom of the Timeline, you are cued to post a baby picture, and as time moves on, standard milestones pass in review: family pictures, school classes, old friends, college years, wedding pictures, honeymoon, (partner) pregnant with first child, baby's first picture, first step videos, holiday trips, and so on. Since few user profiles contain pictures or posts from one's "pre-Facebook" life—which is before 2004 at the earliest—the interface overhaul urged all users to fill in "gaps" in their life stories and illustrate them with pictures. Memory and emotion are explicitly made part of the Facebook Timeline experience as a tool for self-expression. As blogger Jodie O'Dell explains:

> Years-old memories flashed before me—old friends, old places, things I hadn't thought about in ages. I got sucked back into the past the same way I would have in front of my mother's old cedar chest, a trunk packed full of childhood tchotckes [*sic*] and pictures that holds our family's history. This innocuous social web tool had just made a powerful and convincing bid for more than my information or my time. Facebook was grasping at my emotions by way of my memories, and it was doing a damn good job. (O'Dell)

Triggering memory and self-expression by telling one's life story is exactly what Facebook intended to accomplish by rolling out its mandatory new interface. Facebook is not alone in applying this strategy: around the same time that Facebook introduced Timeline, LinkedIn updated its interface to introduce a more linear-chronological ordering; and Google, in 2011, completed a prominent offline and online advertising campaign for its browser Chrome featuring a remarkable commercial (called "Dear Sophie") in which the browser is presented as a unique instrument for obliging fathers to document their child's life story from the day the baby is born.

However, on Timeline, the acts of self-expression and the creation of personal memory are subtly superseded by the act of self-promotion in which the self is increasingly regarded as an online production—not unlike a performance or enactment. Transforming a database into a narrative not only requires the addition of new data to already existing content but also triggers a new awareness of *how* you want your life story be told, *to whom*, and *for what purpose*. The *how* question is all about layout and polishing. Timeline's new look is much more picture heavy than the old interface: the opening image requires a large eye-catcher, friends become big pictures, and many posts carry much larger versions of pictures than originally posted.

Users are asked to emphasize some events by inserting streamers and pictures, thus adding "highlights" in retrospect. The month-by-month and later year-by-year ordering gives personal pages the look and feel of a magazine. Your former profile suddenly becomes the center of a slick publication ("your life in review") with you as the protagonist. Upgrading to Timeline involves a number of layout decisions that are heavily steered by the interface's default settings.

At the same time, the questions *to whom* and *for what purpose* you craft your self-image raise more profound issues of personal and professional branding. When one switched to Timeline in 2012, all previous posts were automatically transferred into the chronological preformatted layout. By default, every formerly inserted piece of data was set to "public" even if you had previously set it to "friends only." As the site explains, users received a grace period of seven days to make decisions about their self-presentation.

We can read on the Facebook site: "When you upgrade to timeline, you'll have seven days to review everything that appears on your timeline before anyone else can see it. If you decide to wait, your timeline will go live automatically after seven days. Your new timeline will replace your profile, but all your stories and photos will still be there" (Tow). For those users who take their online profile seriously, the transfer to Timeline implied a precarious balancing act between self-expression and self-promotion. With every piece of data—both new and old—one had to decide to whom it would be accessible: to friends, a wider circle, or the general audience.

In other words, every post from the past had to be reassessed in terms of *current* audience and potential effects—a typical act of projecting the past that raised dilemmas such as if I add a picture of my wedding, will this upset my jealous ex-spouse displayed in the picture? Should the picture of a rowdy student party really be open to the general public if it also affects the image of former roommates? Each decision to customize your Timeline was hence not only a decision about the (private) reassembling and remembrance of one's past life (how was it?) but also a conscious effort at (public) self-promotion (how is this perceived?). Users were forced to combine reflections on self-expression and self-promotion in terms of reimagining their audience when turning on their revamped Facebook profile.

In addition, the introduction of Timeline exposed the interface as a site of struggle between owners and users. On the one hand, users deployed the new tool to redesign their strategy for self-presentation. As Alice Marwick and danah boyd have demonstrated, Facebook users have gradually become more skilled in the techniques of audience appraisal and personal branding. For those users who put in the time and effort to really work on their profile, this revamping exercise indeed increased their audience awareness. However, the overwhelming majority of Facebook users lack the necessary skills or interest to control their privacy settings the way they want (Leon et al.). Since Facebook's default settings force users to "opt out" when it comes to keeping information private, user profiles have likely become more public than before the feature was implemented.

Timeline's coercive effect on users to provide more personal details, according to a user poll in early 2012, caused more than 50 percent of all subscribers to worry about their data (a concern also contextualized and theorized in Amanda Lagerkvist's chapter), and yet, relatively few of them actually signed off ("Facebook Timeline"). Over time, Facebook users will likely become more experienced in promoting their online selves, but the seemingly innocuous transformation into personal-yet-public personas, as enforced by the new interface, caused an acceleration of this process.

MAKING COMPANIES AND ADVERTISING SOCIAL

Just as Facebook's Timeline turned an individual's personal page into a stage for public self-promotion, the new interface also prompted businesses to adopt Facebook's strategies for personalized branding: like users, companies were urged to switch their presentation strategies from sending messages to telling stories in order to render advertising more "social." Examples of storytelling include relating the history of a company, its goals, ambitions, and ways of bonding with customers. Narratives are supposedly the lubricant for connecting people to products and products to people. For companies, the idea of driving traffic to a page through ads was declared passé; rather, they were prompted to turn products or businesses into stories that could be shared with "friends."

Social advertising means trying to blend promotional messages with a user's sense of belonging or becoming part of a "grander story": for instance, a coffee company on Facebook might narrate the story of how it came to serve a network of local communities to explain how the chain of stores supports local gatherings and neighborhood initiatives. The insertion of so-called Sponsored Stories—posts from "friends" to your Facebook page that are paid for by businesses or organizations—into a user's Timeline was widely promoted as an effective sales strategy.

According to Facebook, a company relating its corporate life story in a personal narrative is likely to be perceived as an ally by customers, as, like people, businesses not only have a past and a present but need to show off their social face to present potential customers with their intrinsically noble intentions. Sponsored stories, as part of the company's sales strategy, are claimed to be almost 50 percent more effective than targeted ads (Constine). User recommendations derived from like buttons are in turn deployed to promote brands or products without a user's consent: users automatically approve of this tactic by signing Facebook's terms of service.

Virtually all multinationals, from Coca Cola to BMW, deploy Facebook for marketing and so-called mouth-to-mouth at scale promotion. Facebook urges companies to use Timeline for adjusting their ad strategies to include its insidious but rather effective architectural principles. Another tactic is to pay influential Facebook connectors (or influencers) to endorse their brand through the intersecting groups and networks they are involved in. Making everything social—from ads to apps and from people to companies—means making everything narrative as well as connective: Facebook's new interface smoothly integrates the two principles. The more people buy into a story, the better the brand is promoted and the better a company's public image will be liked.

And yet, the narrative architecture of Facebook's interface has not diminished the importance of databases and data management. On the contrary, another feature of Facebook that was released simultaneously with Timeline but that received much less attention was its real-time Page Insights data. The feature enables marketers to access real-time analytics that measure the effectiveness of their ads moment by moment. Leveraging these insights, companies can make decisions about what works and what does not, subsequently tweaking content in order to optimize their strategies. Whereas the linear, narrative structure has taken the driver's seat on the visible user interface, the data engine indiscernibly steers and manipulates users' abilities to enact sociality. Products or ideas that "do well" in terms of popularity are commonly products whose data flow ubiquitously through the arteries and veins of connective media—not just Facebook but also Twitter, YouTube, and a host of other platforms—and whose movements can be minutely tracked and rechanneled through real-time data systems.

Products and people are thus increasingly presented with similar narrative strategies, rendering the personal public and the public personal and so underpinning Facebook's strategy to "make everything social." In a video roadshow released several weeks before the IPO (initial public offering), Facebook pitched its bright future outlooks to prospective investors (Facebook IPO Promo Video). Facebook's top managers and CEOs, along with two of the platform's biggest advertisers (Ben & Jerry's and American Express), explained their business strategies in an almost evangelical way, professing the company's "social" mission as an economic boon. A spokesperson for the ice cream company echoes the rhetoric of Facebook when he states, "Messages on Facebook spread not just from business to consumer, but from friend to friend. At Ben & Jerry's, we're not just a company, we really are a friend to people. We want a holistic relationship with our community, our customers. We engage in a large scale conversation."

In virtually every line of text in the thirty-minute promotion video, values of connectedness and community are equaled to connective commercial values, smoothly aligning business models with user interests. Clients are communities and customers equal friends, warranting the identification of a new category of "frustomers." Facebook's mantra to make the world social is presented as a win-win business proposition. The double logic of connectivity and narrative, as we have seen, penetrates every fiber of the site's interface.

The similarities between the online presentation of people and products, individuals and brands are striking: the same interfaces and tactics apply to both, making them even more exchangeable than before. Facebook's interface is an attempt at smoothly integrating self-expression and self-promotion into one uniform interface strategy. Connectivity and narrative are two important principles by which platforms and companies galvanize their economic and symbolic currency, and users and companies alike are forced to strategically adapt their self-presentation to these principles.

MAKING MEMORY SOCIAL?

As argued above, Facebook uses the Timeline interface layout to increase the platform's control over personal data: individual users are prompted to give uniform input of data in a specific narrative order, which helps platform owners to distill overall behavioral patterns from members' likes and other information left on the site, consciously or unconsciously. The narrative presentation format in fact improves platform owners' ability to keep track of users by means of database analytics. The more companies know about their customers—the more stories they share about their lives—the more relevant data can be traced and translated into potentially successful marketing strategies. Recognizing the common denominators of desire, interests, needs, and wants is thus a very important strategy for social networks like Facebook; in fact, all personal data combined are said to form a giant automated polling machine of current and future user trends.

A typical manifestation of this strategy is Facebook Memology: a tracking tool implemented in 2009 that "takes the pulse of this global community by comparing this year's status updates to last year's, unearthing the most popular topics and cultural trends—or memes—emerging on Facebook" (Facebook Memology Blog). The term "memology" derives from the study of memes as units for the transmission of cultural ideas or practices, analogous to genes in that they mutate and respond to pressures in their evolutionary environment. Popular ideas spreading through Facebook are thus "naturally selected" winners in the race for users' attention; those ideas or events finishing on top of the memology are granted cultural longevity and have a chance to survive social media's temporality.

Facebook Memology claims to form a "social barometer" of online interaction. Through analyzing likes, popular keywords, acronyms used in discussions, and favorite subjects, actors, or singers, Facebook's Memology stats allegedly measure communal interest and emerging trends culled from personal data and formatted input. Memes of the recent past are first tracked and then analyzed and interpreted to predict the next global fashion or common interest.

The implicit assumption underlying Facebook Memology is that all individual members' expressions and triggered data combined form the "pulse" or underbelly of social communities, culminating in a top 10 of the most popular memes in that year. In 2011, memes as varied as the death of Osama bin Laden and the release of a new video game (*Call of Duty: Modern Warfare 3*) were among the most talked about on Facebook. Like Twitter, the social media platform presents itself as a life-mining tool that enables data collectors to draw conclusions about social trends and popular topics. However, the idea of Facebook as a giant Internet poll of current trends presents only one side of the coin: the social networking site is not an innocent or representative poll but is itself a strategic instrument used by individuals and companies to promote and manipulate interests and products.

In this respect, Facebook's new strategy of life mining—the extraction of user data in order to predict and influence popular trends—squarely puts the site at the heart of an ecosystem of platforms driven by the same principles of connectivity and standardized content input. Twitter, for instance, claims to be a network with the capability of resonating with the "roar of the crowd." Scientists and information analysts tend to take the incessant stream of Tweets circulating through the platform's veins as a real-time data flow of people's opinions, sentiments, likes, and dislikes—metaphorically feeling the pulse of a life stream of online data to take the masses' heartbeat.

And yet, by the same token, the platform encourages its users to influence trends, to *create* and manipulate social memes or "trend" certain topics. Twitter users engage in massive maneuvering not only of their own public persona (think of Justin Bieber's or Barack Obama's millions of followers) but also of topics and ideas by actively promoting specific hashtags. Twitter and Facebook are thus not simply echo chambers of popular ideas but rather control rooms of public opinion and social trends.

A claim rapidly gaining credibility is the assertion that social network sites like Facebook—and, for that matter, Twitter—are going to make collective experience and memory more "social," meaning that the history of ideas and public consciousness plays out through social media platforms. After all, collective memories organize themselves according to our perceived participation in a (temporary) collectivity, according to Maurice Halbwachs. People's participation in collective events indeed happens increasingly through sites like Facebook and Twitter, and this participation leaves many traces in their individual log trails—traces that are subsequently picked up by the tracking monitors of data miners and life miners. However, what social media advocates like to defend as social or collective memory is in fact connectivity: the very platforms by which ideas are transmitted are not intermediaries but active mediators in the constitution of popular memes or ideas. British media scholar Andrew Hoskins articulates this very precisely when he says:

> Contemporary memory is thoroughly interpenetrated by a technological unconscious in that there occurs a co-evolution of memory and technology. Memory is readily and dynamically configured through our digital practices and the connectivity of our networks … The increasingly digital networking of memory not only functions in a continuous present but is also a distinctive shaper of a new mediatised age of memory. (96)

As part of the "technological unconscious," interfaces are important instruments of identity formation and meme construction whose steering mechanisms (algorithms, protocols, and other interface features) are hidden behind simple buttons and implicit business models, as convincingly argued by David Beer ("Power through the Algorithm?"). Facebook Memology and Twitter Trends are instruments of life mining as well as tools for steering public opinion. Ever since the invention of writing utensils, media have been devices that "mediate" between individual and collective ideas while simultaneously manipulating this connection (van Dijck, *Mediated Memories*). We need to thoroughly understand the technological and commercial mechanisms of social media platforms to understand how social memes are constructed and deconstruct far-reaching claims about social media's ability to "take the pulse of society."

CONCLUSION

Facebook's Timeline, Page Insights, and Memology have pushed the art and science of self-presentation as well as the promotion of ideas to a new level. Users have become increasingly skilled at playing the game, while advertisers and other interested parties are getting leverage out of these tools for their own purposes. The power over interfaces naturally resides with platform owners, but they have to constantly balance users' demands with business interests—a struggle that reveals the deeper ideological and economic interests at stake in online identity formation. At the core of this tussle we find three stakeholders: users who want to secure their connectedness and deploy multiple modes of self-presentation; advertisers who seek out information about users' online behavior, needs, and desires; and, finally, platform owners who have a vested interest in truthful information and uniform narratives to maximize connectivity. All three stakes are rooted in strategic paradoxes: each act of self-performance requires tactical maneuvering and awareness of the power plays involved in the game.

Users, for their part, have various sociodiscursive needs—expressive, communicative, or promotional—in defining their identity, and each of these needs necessitates different levels of confidentiality or publicity. If users' strategic aim is self-promotion, they shape a consistent image of themselves across platforms and adopt Facebook's Timeline interface toward achieving that goal. Facebook's new layout surreptitiously integrates various needs for self-expression, memory, communication, and promotion through one and the same interface. With the imposed Timeline format, users may surrender more personal data than they would like, while the need for self-promotion motivates many to carefully craft their profiles. The fine line between what Gina Hernez-Broome, Cindy McLaughlin, and Stephanie Trovas have called "authentic" and "inauthentic" (or idealized) self-promotion requires a precarious balancing act, which users are not always aware of or are not always good at.

And yet, the site's interface blurs the differentiated needs of self-expression, self-promotion, and communication by conflating them into one narrative structure. Ever since Erving Goffman launched his theory of symbolic interactionism, it has been commonly accepted that people live their daily lives as staged performances in which they deliberately use the differentiation between private and public discursive acts to shape their identity. Each construction of self entails a strategy aimed at *performing* a social act or achieving a particular social goal—a strategy meticulously explained by Nancy Van House. In that respect, individuals and companies have in common that in an online environment they need to mix personal identity with brand promotion if they want to gain popularity. As demonstrated in the previous paragraphs, Facebook's Timeline smoothly aligns the narratives of people as brands and brands as personalized stories so that commercial objectives become less explicit.

Of course, disgruntled users have protested the Promoted Stories strategy and even taken Facebook to court, forcing the platform to offer a settlement, but the normative effect of this gradual change has become so pervasive that it is almost impossible to turn back the clock on these new frustomer tactics.[3] Facebook shapes user behavior as much as users (re)shape the platform's interface. The subtle adjustments of interface strategies show how platforms deploy users' need for connectedness to stimulate connectivity and how they push narrative forms to enhance the traceability of social data.

Just as personal pages on Facebook are not a *reflection* of one's identity, as Facebook's Mark Zuckerberg wants us to believe, the list of most popular memes on Facebook does not represent a *sensor* of collective experiences. Facebook profiles and memologies are part and parcel of a power struggle between users, advertisers, and platform owners to steer online information and behavior. Historically, social media platforms like Facebook grew big on the promise of global self-communication and personal expression, but gradually, the technical and commercial directives built into its interface have come to emphasize connectivity and (self-)promotion at the expense of connectedness and self-expression.

Timeline represents the conflation of online self-expression and self-promotion in one and the same tool, which is similarly utilized to promote products and establish brands in personalized narratives. Facebook Memology is both a tracking tool and a pushing tool: ideas circulate through pipelines that are subject to constant manipulation, by individuals, companies, and owners themselves. The technical and economic logic underpinning this apparatus signals the ideological tendency to create an online social space that renders expression interchangeable with promotion, friends with customers, commercial products with personal brands, and trends with memes. Evidently, social media are not neutral stages for the presentation of self and society, but they are the very tools for shaping identity and sociality.

Facebook's Timeline, Page Insights, and Memology are just a few examples of the ongoing struggle between the platform's owner and its users to define personal identity and social memory in the online ecosystem of interrelated platforms. Timeline lets you "tell the whole story of your life on a single page," while Facebook Memology offers "a unique barometer into the issues, world events and thoughts that are connecting people." We need to critically examine the ideological claims and arguments in the grand story, told over and over again by Mark Zuckerberg and other CEOs, that the goal of social media platforms like Facebook is to make everything social, from ads to apps and from personal to collective memories.

Making everything social, though, is the equivalent of engineering sociality, and it takes a critical eye to render visible the principles and mechanisms by which this new social reality is created. Narrative and connectivity, as I have argued in this chapter, are two of the core principles underpinning this ideology, and by deconstructing their role in the evolution of Facebook's interface I have tried to make users more aware of the platform's strategies. In fact, these are two of the core principles underlying the ecosystem of connective media as a whole. By analyzing the detail of these strategies, we may become more aware of how social media in general (and Facebook in particular) "code" personal and cultural memory.

As more and more memories move to online contexts—platforms through which they are generated, framed, archived, and retrieved—it is extremely important to complement the "sociophenomenological" approach that Amanda Lagerkvist outlines in the next chapter in order to understand how their technocommercial mechanisms work. The future of memory studies is partly dependent on our understanding of digitally born communication; user interfaces are much more than replacements of photo albums or home videos. Analyzing the technical and economic apparatus of social media is vital to understanding memory production today.

José van Dijck is a professor of comparative media studies at the University of Amsterdam. Her work covers a wide range of topics in media theory, media technologies, social media, television, and culture. She is the author of six books, three coedited volumes, and approximately one hundred journal articles and book chapters. Her latest book is *The Culture of Connectivity: A Critical History of Social Media* (Oxford University Press, 2013). Van Dijck served as dean of the Faculty of Humanities at the University of Amsterdam and is currently president of the Royal Netherlands Academy of Arts and Sciences.

NOTES

1. Mass self-communication platforms, such as Facebook, operate in the same economic, political, and legal space as personal media and mass media—a space dominated by powerful telecom and media industries. As Manuel Castells explains in *Communication Power:* "It is mass communication because it can potentially reach a global audience, as in the posting of a video on YouTube, a blog with RSS links to a number of web sources, or a message to a massive e-mail list. At the same time, it is self-communication because the production of the message is self-generated, the definition of the receiver(s) is self-directed, and the retrieval of specific messages or content from the WWW and electronic networks is self-selected" (55).
2. Some psychologists, such as Soraya Mehdizadeh, have argued that young adults with low self-esteem can be correlated with a greater amount of self-promotional content on their Facebook pages; my point in this essay is not to investigate the psychological effects of social media use.
3. Facebook settled a lawsuit outside a California court; the lawsuit was brought by a consumer group protesting the platform's invasion of privacy by using likes as unwitting recommendations. For more information, see Sengupta.

WORKS CITED

Beer, David. "Power through the Algorithm? Participatory Web Cultures and the Technological Unconsciousness." *New Media & Society* 11.6 (2009): 985–1002.

——. "Social Network(ing) Sites ... Revisiting the Story So Far: A Response to danah boyd & Nicole Ellison." *Journal of Computer-Mediated Communication* 13.2 (2008): 516–29.

boyd, danah. "None of This Is Real: Identity and Participation in Friendster." *Structures of Participation in Digital Culture*. Ed. Joe Karaganis. New York: Social Science Research Council, 2007. 132–57.

boyd, danah, and Nicole Ellison. "Social Network Sites: Definition, History, and Scholarship. *Journal of Computer-Mediated Communication* 13.1 (2007): 1–11.

Bukvova, Helena. "Scientists Online: A Framework for the Analysis of Internet Profiles." *First Monday* 16 Oct. 2011. Web. 28 Feb. 2015.

Castells, Manuel. *Communication Power.* Oxford: Oxford University Press, 2009.

Christakis, Nicolas, and James Fowler. *Connected: How Your Friends' Friends' Friends Affect Everything You Feel, Think, and Do.* New York: Back Bay Books, 2009.

Christofides, Emily, Amy Muise, and Serge Desmarais. "Information Disclosure and Control on Facebook: Are They Two Sides of the Same Coin or Two Different Processes?" *Cyberpyschology and Behavior* 12.3 (2009): 341–45.

Constine, John. "Facebook Sponsored Stories Ads Have 46% Higher CTR, 18% Lower Cost Per Fan Says TBG Digital Test." *SocialTimes.* Adweek Blog Network 3 May 2011. Web. 28 Feb. 2015.

De Certeau, Michel. *The Practice of Everyday Life.* Berkeley: University of California Press, 1984.

Ellison, Nicole, Charles Steinfeld, and Cliff Lampe. "The Benefits of Facebook 'Friends': Social Capital and College Students' Use of Online Social Network Sites." *Journal of Computer-Mediated Communication* 13.1 (2007): 210–30.

"Facebook IPO Promo Video." *YouTube* 19 May 2012. Web. 28 Feb. 2015.

"Facebook Memology Blog." *Facebook* 21 Dec. 2009. Web. 28 Feb. 2015.

"Facebook Timeline a Concern to Users—Survey." *Digital Strategy Consulting* 3 Feb. 2012. Web. 28 Feb. 2015.

Garde-Hansen, Joanne. "MyMemories? Personal Digital Archive Fever and Facebook." *Save As … Digital Memories.* Ed. Joanne Garde-Hansen, Andrew Hoskins, and Anna Reading. Basingstoke: Palgrave, 2009. 135–50.

Goffman, Erving. *The Presentation of Self in Everyday Life.* New York: Anchor Books, 1959.

Halbwachs, Maurice. *On Collective Memory.* Chicago: University of Chicago Press, 1992.

Hernez-Broome, Gina, Cindy McLaughlin, and Stephanie Trovas. *The Truth about Sucking Up: How Authentic Self-Promotion Benefits You and Your Organization.* Greensboro: CCL Press, 2009.

Hoskins, Andrew. "Digital Network Memory." *Mediation, Remediation, and the Dynamics of Cultural Memory.* Ed. Astrid Erll and Ann Rigney. Berlin: De Gruyter, 2009. 91–108.

Leon, Pedro G. et al. "Why Johnny Can't Opt Out: A Usability Evaluation of Tools to Limit Online Behavioral Advertising." *Cylab.* Carnegie Mellon University 31 Oct. 2011. Web. 28 Feb. 2015.

Manovich, Lev. *The Language of New Media.* Cambridge: MIT Press, 2001.

"Mark Zuckerberg Unveils Facebook Timeline." *YouTube* 22 Sept. 2011. Web. 28 Feb. 2015.

Marwick, Alice, and danah boyd. "I Tweet Honestly, I Tweet Passionately: Twitter Users, Context Collapse and the Imagined Audience." *New Media & Society* 13.1 (2011): 114–33.

Mehdizadeh, Soraya. "Self-Presentation 2.0: Narcissism and Self-Esteem on Facebook." *Cyberpsychology, Behavior, and Social Networking* 13.4 (2010): 357–64.

O'Dell, Jodi. "Once Facebook Launches Timeline, You'll Never Want to Leave." *VB Social* 6 Oct. 2011. Web. 28 Feb. 2015.

Papacharissi, Zizi. "The Virtual Geographies of Social Networks: A Comparative Analysis of Facebook, LinkedIn and ASmallWorld." *New Media & Society* 11.1 (2009): 199–220.

Sengupta, Somni. "To Settle Lawsuit, Facebook Alters Its Policy for Like Button." *New York Times* 21 June 2012. Web. 14 July 2012.

Thompson, John B. *The Media and Modernity: A Social Theory of the Media.* Cambridge: Polity Press, 1995.

Tow, Slater. "Timeline: Now Available Worldwide." *Facebook* 15 Dec. 2011. Web. 28 Feb. 2015.

van Dijck, José. *The Culture of Connectivity. A Critical History of Social Media.* Oxford: Oxford University Press, 2013.

——. "Facebook as a Tool for Producing Sociality and Connectivity." *Television & New Media* 13.2 (2012): 160–76.

——. "Flickr and the Culture of Connectivity: Sharing Views, Experiences, Memories." *Memory Studies* 4.4 (2011): 401–15.

——. *Mediated Memories in the Digital Age.* Stanford: Stanford University Press, 2007.

Van House, Nancy. "Collocated Photo Sharing, Story-Telling, and the Performance of Self." *International Journal of Human-Computer Studies* 67.12 (2009): 1073–86.

Chapter 8

Embodiments of Memory

Toward an Existential Approach
to the Culture of Connectivity

Amanda Lagerkvist

◈

INTRODUCTION: SEARCHING FOR
SENTIENT INHABITANTS OF THE DIGITAL ECOLOGY

What does it mean to say that "digital memories become us" (Garde-Hansen, Reading, and Hoskins 1) or *have* become us? In recent debates in media memory studies, this statement does not stand in isolation; it comes together with the trope of the digital ecology, which signifies, besides its naturalizing bent, a notion of an environment in which previously held boundaries between media, subjects, and the physical world dissolve. It conveys the idea that we have become posthuman, that we are now informational-material entities and subjects "dispersed throughout the cybernetic circuit" (Hayles 27). When digital memories have become us—as we carry around portable archives, as we leave our digital traces, or as we are affectively engaging in endlessly revisable memory work online—the body itself seems radically implicated (Gies). Media are not just environmental but also wearable and incorporated.

Memory technologies are enmeshed in our bodies, while our embodied selves and memory traces are embedded in the technologized everyday within our so-called culture of connectivity (van Dijck, *Culture of Connectivity*). By connectivity, I will in this chapter refer to the sense in which platforms, as the introduction to this volume delineates, "*construct* and *exploit* rather than merely *enable* connections between users" but also, and more profoundly, to the way their automated operations seem to force certain memories upon us.

Such a cybernetic ontology is thoroughly rooted in bodies; as N. Katherine Hayles notes, "information, like humanity, cannot exist apart from the embodiment that brings it into being as a material entity of the world: and embodiment is always instantiated, local and specific" (49).This is a situation, I propose, that does not only apply to the technologically savvy—those happy to connect, share, thrive, prevail, play, and self-promote (Rainie and Wellman). It is above all an *existential moment,* which also entails heightened anxieties, interruptions, vulnerabilities, and uncertainties.

In this metareflexive essay, I contend that it is precisely because digital memories have become us that the field of media memory studies needs to be embodied; at the same time, and paradoxically, it is precisely because of the posthuman condition that some kind of a "human" has to be retained. In other words, abandoning anthropocentrism does not necessitate abandoning subjectivity altogether. Instead, it requires a reconceptualization of the human in terms of a responsible sense of subjectivity (Braidotti) as well as in terms of more humble and diversified visions of selfhood. More specifically, I propose that, because the media is where we "live and move and have our being" (Mitchell and Hansen xiv), the digital memory ecology awaits being theoretically inhabited by embodied and precarious human selves—by "sentient bodies" (Gonzales-Arnal, Jagger, and Lennon; Sobchack). These should be conceived as navigating and struggling within the torrents of our digital age, whether they are making or losing meaning (or sense) or affectively and emotionally relating to, or retorting from, these torrents.

At first glance, such a call to focus on the inhabitants of this ecology—drawing them out from the long shadows of the memory site or the memory object, as it were—may not seem like an entirely original step. In *On Media Memory: Collective Memory in a New Media Age,* Motti Neiger, Oren Meyers, and Eyal Zandberg end up in a similar corner of the pitch. Having launched the field of media memory studies in the conviction that modern media of communication have assumed an increased significance in the formation of memories, they conclude by looking forward to more empirical research into audiences' memory repertoires, the lived and collected memories of people, as opposed to the well-traveled roads of the collective memory of monuments, texts, canons, and archives.

In another key intervention, Astrid Erll describes the plural contexts of reception of mediated memory as vital for understanding how certain media become powerful media of memory in culture. Along these lines, I suggest a theoretical engagement with the various debates about embodiment in feminist new materialism, posthumanism, and media phenomenology (Gonzales-Arnal, Jagger, and Lennon; Koivunen; Hayles; Hong; Mitchell and Hansen; Sobchack) and in the field of Internet and emotions

(Garde-Hansen and Gorton; Karatzogianni and Kuntsman) in order to find ways to bring the body to the fore on what I call "the existential terrains of connectivity" (Lagerkvist, "New Memory Cultures").[1]

In an earlier contribution to these debates, I have myself pushed toward what I call a sociophenomenological approach for analyzing the transmediality, globality, and performativity of mediated memory (Lagerkvist, *Media and Memory*). As an umbrella term for capturing the project of embodying media memory—or at least for taking us some way in that direction—I suggest that sociophenomenology is apposite since it subsumes at least four central aspects of what the different fields I engage with all share.

First, it conceives of memory as processual, emergent, and forged through practice and performance; second, and in line with the new materialism, it puts emphasis on embodiment, emotion, and lived experience. Here I supplement the affective turn and the new materialism in one crucial respect. While these moved beyond the linguistic models of textuality and subjectivity, and beyond the representational level toward the affective as "the real" (Koivunen), I instead follow the phenomenological tradition and film scholars such as Vivian Sobchack to argue that the point is not to discard the textual, the mediated, and the discursive but rather to juxtapose them with embodiment, affect, and emotion and situate all these forces in a dynamic relationship of mutuality. My approach relies on Sobchack's existential and phenomenological deliberations in her *Carnal Thoughts: Embodiment and Moving Image Culture,* in which she discusses the radically material nature of human existence. Her argument, drawing on Maurice Merleau-Ponty's comprehensive study of perception, is that the lived body makes meaning out of bodily "sense." Embodiment is defined through "the lived body as at once both an objective subject and a subjective object: a sentient, sensual, and sensible ensemble of materialized capacities and agency that literally and figuretivelly makes sense of, and to, both ourselves and others" (2). The key assertion is that there is always an entanglement of matter and meaning. Here my project also connects with how Gonzales-Arnal, Jagger, and Lennon provisionally define their version of the new materialism as a theoretical turn that reconceives of the interrelationships between the material and discursive realms, between lived embodiment and mediation.

As a third central aspect, which connects directly with the other contributions to this section of this volume, memory is seen as transmedial and forged across bodies, artefacts, and different forms of media and mediation (not least across the online and offline; Refslund Christensen and Sandvik). This reasoning echoes feminist theorizations of affect and emotions in culture. Emotions are, as Sara Ahmed argues, about things—they shape things and they also take shape in relation to these objects that are in turn pervaded by and "sticky" with affect. Here emotions are conceived as simultaneously and irreducibly individual, material, cultural, and social.

The fourth aspect thence concerns the "socio-" in sociophenomenology, which stresses the communal, collective, societal, and material aspects of the lived and affective experiences of our technologized existence. This means in addition that affect is placed outside neither individual perceptions nor intersubjective experiences. Anu Koivunen similarly refutes the rejection of the experiential landscapes of subjectivity for understanding the affectivity of media (and film in particular) and retains an interest in "identity, history and experience" (90). So rather than "calling forth a new materialist notion of experience as beyond the realm of the subject," she deploys the concept of affect as a sense of *cultural weight* and stresses the affectivity of the embodied subject through the necessary "relationality, intersubjectivity, and worldliness of all selves" (98).

This implies conceiving of the self as socially and contextually forged. This essay proposes, furthermore, that it is precisely due to the ways in which affective bodies and (social) selves are implicated in sociotechnological ensembles (van Dijck, *Culture of Connectivity*)—that is, to our subjectivity of connectivity—that we need an existential approach to digital memories. This means taking the sociophenomenology of memory one step further. Due to the vulnerabilities and uncertainties of the culture of connectivity, we are compelled to both revisit and embody basic and "eternal" existential questions: Who am I? How am I presented before others? What is my/our purpose? What is the nature of human life and of existence itself? In this pursuit we need to carefully conceptualize "the human" anew, beyond the fiction of a universal and unchangeable human being and a coherent, disembodied self.

I argue that without an embodied sense of self (or rather of selves in the plural) there is a risk that digital memory studies will end up ridding us both of agency and of the ability to pursue the profound conditions of our lifeworld; indeed, our *being-in-and-with-the-digital-world* comprises both freedom and necessity, both ethical decisions and compulsions of connectivity.

TOWARD MEDIA BODIES: MEDIA MEMORY STUDIES TODAY

The push toward embodiment in media memory studies is not merely a question of remedying theoretical negligence; it is also a propulsion felt across our contemporary media geographies and lifeworlds. How did we end up here? In the following I will offer my perspective on how both media and memory studies in a way lost their analytical objects, leaving them in the company of the body. Indeed, in light of the incessant processes of digitalization and globalization, both media and memory studies are challenged with the rapid reconstitution of their fields of study and their object(s). Both are forced to acknowledge that previously discrete and relatively fixed matters have been rendered *trans*itional, *trans*medial, and *trans*cultural—a transformative movement in contemporary memory cultures that this volume as a whole seeks to address.

It seems far from exaggerated to suggest that scholars in both fields are currently faced with a horror vacui, as they are confronted with newly appearing and emerging phenomena that remain semantically vacant. Both media and memory studies are simultaneously experiencing intense and rich debates, which amount not simply to a "cluttering up" of the void but to a veritable moment of reaching out and painting the conceptual canvas anew, resulting in increased creativity and sometimes audacious leaps of the imagination. Both fields seem reciprocally fated to renew themselves, and this provokes and produces, in effect, a mutual recognition, since they find that in the mirror reflection of one's new emergent self stands the other.[2]

The media is no more. Trying to grasp a situation in which the key analytic tools as well as the analytical object itself—the text, the audience, the media institution—have been liquefying and have become processual has challenged media and communication studies during the past decade (Kember and Zylinska). Scholars have repeatedly struggled to understand "the new," launching successive concepts to describe it: "new media," "participatory culture," "convergence," "netizens," "citizen journalism," "prosumers," "networked individualism," "tethered selves." Such efforts have been rapidly followed by a (re)problematization of "the new" and its grasp on our imagination, turning scholars' attention to remediation processes, media historical continuities, and the materialities of residual media.

Indeed, before any of the new concepts could mature or the new methodological approaches could be solidified, some of the developments launched by the term "Web 2.0 environment" and what has more recently been called the "culture of connectivity" burst upon the scene of media studies, leaving media scholars in an identity crisis—or, alternatively, with a tremendous momentum. What was formerly known as "the media" has, as Mike Featherstone argues, "become embedded in material objects and environments, bodies and clothing, zones of transmission and reception. *Media pervade our bodies, cultures and societies*—a shift made possible by miniaturized electronic circuitry" (3; my emphasis).

Memory studies has equally found itself in perpetual transition. Conventionally, memory is a selective process of reconstruction through which the past is represented or reinvented to serve the needs, goals, and politics of the present. Typically, memory is related to the identity work and interests of a particular nation, group, or community (Halbwachs) and has been conceived as forged through different technologies such as monuments, artefacts, texts, and photography (Sturken). However, and as the introduction to this volume lays out, these "memory sites" (Nora) seem to be vanishing as the locus of memory (and memory studies) in a world of global, connective, mediatized, digital, transnational, transcultural, cosmopolitan, and multi-directional memories.

The notion of a collective memory has thus been challenged on both theoretical and empirical grounds. Memory is forged transnationally across cultural contexts that in turn shape new communities of memory; memory, that is, is located neither in one physical place nor within the nation, nor is it ever determined by one institution alone. As the contributions to this section of the volume discuss, there is also a renewed emphasis on the fact that memories are forged *transmedially* across texts, photographs, film and television footage, the Internet, and—last but not least—*the body*. After the so-called connective turn, moreover, memory is now also subject to socio-technical flux (Hoskins, "7/7 and Connective Memory"), at once implicating and forging entwinements of sociality and identity, the technologies in use, the spaces we inhabit, and our biological bodies.

As José van Dijck's contribution to this volume explains, the notion of connective memory describes the molding force of algorithms and emphasizes that the infrastructures behind our connections compel us to remember certain things, trace our movements, record them, while the notion at once challenges the idea that any memory can be lasting, as memory processes are always subject to sociotechnological mutability and technological obsolescence (Lagerkvist, "Netlore of the Infinite"; Peters). These are profound existential predicaments of our time.

I argue that the current moment of mutual reflexivity and felt voids in media memory studies is first of all an existential moment in which the body and forms of embodiment await theorization. In moving toward embodying media memory, the objective is more pointedly to begin to bring the rich and diverse discourses on embodiment into dialogue with digital memory studies. Through a few examples, this essay picks up on and describes some of the challenges that await us in media memory studies if we take into account the debates about embodiment in the digital age. One premise for this ensuing tentative mapping of embodiment is that the present situation also further compels our attention to what Internet scholars have emphasized since the late 1990s, when they turned away from the dematerialized and disembodied discourses that prevailed in the late 1980s and early 1990s surrounding cyberspace.

This debate on posthumanism (re)introduced the body into the digital and hence enabled an important discussion on the materialities of the virtual. Initiating this discourse, N. Katherine Hayles distinguished, importantly, between *the body* as hegemonic cultural construct and *embodiment* as the experiential level that captures the particular individual articulation of discourse (193–94). There is no body; there are only bodies, and moreover, "embodiment is contextual, enmeshed within the specificities of place, time, physiology and culture, which together compose enactment. Embodiment never coincides exactly with the body ... Relative to the body, embodiment is elsewhere, at once excessive and deficient in its infinite variations, particularities and abnormalities" (196–97).

Inspired by this insight, I propose that we consider a plurality of embodied modes of being human in the digital memory ecology. This essay takes its cue from these debates through which four media bodies unfold for media memory studies: the performative body, the device body, the body as implicated, and the body as implied. Remaining attentive to these varying, while sometimes enmeshed, forms of embodiment and to the diversity of experiences of media memory cultures, I hope to illustrate some of the most important aspects of what an *existential take* on digital media and memory could mean.

THE BODY IN MEMORY STUDIES: MOVING BEYOND THE TEXT AND THE SITE

Before I turn to the most recent tides of theorization, I want to pause to reflect upon how the body has been figured (in relation to the mind and to culture) in earlier debates in cultural memory studies. In an important discussion on memory and embodiment, sociologist Rafael F. Narvaez argues that collective memory studies have traditionally dissuaded analyses of the embodied, unconscious dimensions of memory, thereby reproducing the Platonic body-mind dichotomy.

Against this tradition, and in order to further our understanding of the role of embodied mnemonic practices in both reproducing and contesting norms about behavior inherited from the past, Narvaez launches an approach that links mental, bodily, and social dimensions of memory. He argues that this approach "can help us understand how collective pasts become sedimented in individual and 'collective bodies,' so that the past thus becomes vivified in shared presents; and social groups thence 'naturally,' 'intuitively' march toward inherited futures" (52). Narvaez holds, moreover, that social actors may actually oppose values inscribed upon their bodies and choose to develop new practices and new standards and thereby produce new futures. The body is, as Marianne Hirsch has argued recently, a "site for change."

But what of the media? And how have the interrelations between mediated memories (externalized memory technologies, objects, and products) and embodied memory agents been conceived? Typically, key theorists in cultural memory studies have conceived of the body or embodied performances in opposition to media, which are considered as discrete phenomena. In Paul Connerton's groundbreaking work on the embodiment of memory, *How Societies Remember,* he distinguishes between *inscribed* and *incorporated* memory practices.

Inscribed—that is, mediated—memories are contained, stored, retrieved, distributed, and transmitted by modern media technologies of communication; incorporated practices, for their part, involve those memories that exist only when sustained by the body—that is, when being acted out as embodied performances. Connerton recognizes that bodily practices such as gestures, proverbial manners, habits, and choreographic movements in space that include affective gesture, prayer, and commemoration practices are essential for how societies remember, yet he stresses that they have been underplayed in our culture's emphasis upon texts as the prime carriers of meaning.

Similarly, Diana Taylor distinguishes between the mediated *archive* of "supposedly enduring materials (that is texts, documents, buildings, bones) and the so-called ephemeral *repertoire* of embodied practice/knowledge (that is spoken language, dance, sports, ritual)" (19). Archival memory exists in documents, on maps, in literary texts and letters, but beyond texts and next to videos, films, and CDs she also includes archaeological remains and bones—"all those items supposedly resistant to change" (19).

The repertoire, by contrast, enacts embodied memories, and these include performances, dancing, singing, gestural movements, and orality. These are phenomena that we typically read as ephemeral, she argues, and as knowledge that cannot be reproduced. It is through physical acts that the repertoire is activated: "The repertoire requires presence, people participate in the production and reproduction of knowledge by 'being there,' being part of the transmission. As opposed to the supposedly stable objects of the archive, the actions that are the repertoire do not remain the same. The repertoire both keeps and transforms choreographies of meaning" (Taylor 20). In line with Connerton, Taylor holds that live performance can never be fully captured and transmitted through the archive; still, the repertoire is not for all that completely bereft of all patterning or coding capacities. Taylor thus moves somewhat toward a position in which both the archive and the repertoire are seen as "mediated."

Recent developments in the field of memory studies continue this movement away from texts and sites toward the body. Astrid Erll stresses that the field of memory studies should not be restricted by a focus on intentional commemoration practices or by "narrative and a quest for identity." Instead, it should remain "open for the exploration of unintentional and implicit ways of cultural remembering, or of inherently non-narrative, for example, visual or *bodily forms of memory*" (2; my emphasis). In this formulation, bodily forms of memory are seen as a category distinct from intentional memory or from narrative. With the aim to mediatize memory discourse and dynamize the memory site, Ann Rigney launches a new definition of the notion of cultural memory by firmly underscoring "the extent to which shared memories of the past are the product of mediation, textualization and acts of communication" (14).

A model for collective memory, as she calls it, should then build on secondhand and mediated recollection, rather than on the ideal of a direct face-to-face situation. One critical, yet perhaps inadvertent, aspect of this definition of cultural memory, however, is that the mediated becomes separated from the individual lived experience: "People may have undergone comparable experiences, but the cultural memory of those experiences is the ongoing result of public communication and the circulation of memories in mediated form" (Rigney 15–16). Unintentionally, then, recent discussions in memory studies reinforce, to some degree, the opposition between media (the cultural and social level) and the face-to-face (the subjective and embodied level). This separation in memory studies, which reproduces the bifurcation we earlier encountered in Connerton and (to some extent) in Taylor, may run the risk of turning embodied and lived experience into something altogether separate from mediated experience, and hence separate mediated memory from lived memory. It is this bifurcation that I want to argue against.

In my book *Media and Memory in New Shanghai: Western Performances of Futures Past,* I tried to answer the call by Astrid Erll and Ann Rigney to shift our focus away from intentional or textual memory and the memory site. In situating embodiment and media texts in a dynamic and complementary relationship I develop a sociophenomenological approach to mediated memories, which implies embracing insights from performance studies in media memory studies. This entails further problematizing the split between *either* mediated memory products and fixed sites *or* the processes in which memories are made through embodied performances.

The book interrogates the relationship between media and urban memory and the role of memory in a particular space of futurity: New Shanghai. I focus on the visiting foreigners and their engagement with the city's spatial stories and place-identity formation through what I term "mediatized performativity." I conceive of this concept as a sensitizing conceptual merger that makes it possible to perceive, describe, and interrogate the relationship between media and memory as thoroughly performative—that is, as coming to light, transpiring, and in movement as people remember in, with, and through media in particular settings.

Memories of Shanghai's Golden Age of the 1920s and 1930s, defined by capitalism, decadence, debauchery, cosmopolitanism, and adventure, were expressed locally and internationally in various media forms, in museums, bars, cafés, and consumer culture. But it was not until a particular kind of visitor—the "cosmopolitan" Westerner (tourists, expatriates, and reporters)—arrived, whose presence was sought after during the reinvention of the city in the 1990s, that these memories were fully reenacted and became "alive." Hence, I argue that it was not until the visitors engaged in an embodied sense with a range of futures past that were present in the city and with the city's regenerative sense of nostalgia that these mediated memories were fully activated. I suggest therefore that what is needed in order to achieve a movement away from viewing memory as a fixity is an additional focus on embodied performances of memory as inherently entangled with mediation.

In questioning the sharp line between the two forms of memory posited by Connerton, I develop a theorization of the mediated memories of the archive (scripted and inscribed memories), lived memories of the repertoire (embodied performances, incorporated memories), and spatial materialities (settings) as thoroughly enmeshed and coproductive. Hence, I seek out the reciprocal exigencies of the city imaginary and various mediatized, mnemonic, scripted, and embodied performances among mobile elites in particular settings in this urban space: the colonial mansion garden, the restaurant, the rooftop bar, the expatriate compound, and others.

I thereby privilege the role of performances for the (re)production, navigation, negotiation, activation, and, importantly, potential transgression of the memories of legendary Shanghai. This possibility of transgression is essential since the concept of mediatized performativity attempts to capture tensions or even contradictions, as the performance will always resist the script (since the performance can never happen the same way twice, as it always necessarily reinvents itself) while the script resists the performance as well. There is an ineluctable otherness to the performance, and the performative is "that which is played out unhappily against representation in that it has no analogue in text" (Thrift and Dewsbury 420).[3] Embodiment in this perspective thus holds the potential to explain the complex dynamic through which media memories take hold, gain significance, become meaningful, or are resisted.

FOUR MEDIA BODIES

I have argued so far that the loss of the media as our unambiguously defined analytical object and of memory as a monolithically delimited concept coincides with a turn to questions of embodiment, feelings, and affect within new materialist approaches, and that these need to be theorized in conjunction with mediation. I now turn to four specific instantiations of media embodiment to further this approach.

The Performative Body

The first media body that emerges from the deliberations above is the *performative body* that animates our media scripts. It is also both a sensual and a sentient being, whose experiences of self and others are always already mediated. Vivian Sobchack further sketches out the role of experience and embodiment in our media culture:

> However direct it may seem, our experience is not only always mediated by the lived bodies that we are, but our lived bodies (and our experience of them) is [*sic*] always also mediated and qualified by our engagements with other bodies and things. Thus, our experiences are mediated and qualified not only through the various transformative technologies of perception and expression but also by historical and cultural systems that constrain both the inner limits of our perception and *the outer limits of our world.* (4; my emphasis)

Sobchack's analysis builds largely on the particularities of the film medium. But if we move beyond moving image culture in general and focus on the digital, we may ask where "the outer limits of our world" are in digital existence. How do we feel and move about in the digital memory ecology? Here, we arguably encounter the confines of the sociophenomenological approach that I have drawn on so far. This approach lacked the intention to describe those particular modes of embodiment, performance, remembering (and forgetting) that are forged through digital culture. In other words, it was not specifically addressing the digital, and it was not attuned to the emergent culture of connectivity, in which new predicaments as well as possibilities appear.

The most palpable of digital media bodies is the avatar; it is a performative and affective *second* body immersed in virtual environments. It is a playful being that has been relentlessly discussed in academic debates on cyberfeminism, gaming, or second life environments, encompassing a sense of embodied selfhood that is both ultraextended and highly localized, gen-

dered, and heteronormative. The difference between this type of embodiment and those of other story worlds, according to Jenny Sundén, is that
in the case of the avatar "the body is activated, involved in and propelled
into the unfolding of events, both physically and symbolically" ("A Sense of
Play" 47).[4] Today digital gaming environments are providing quasicomplete
sensory immersion, or what has often been termed an "augmented sense of
reality."

Cybernetic embodiment is more than a potent technofantasy of science
fiction, and it does not apply only to game worlds. In the rest of this essay,
I will retain from the above deliberations the gist of this notion of embodied performativity of mediated memories—as essentially becoming, gestural,
and animating—as I turn to three other entwined aspects of digital embodiment that belong to our everyday digital memory ecology (Garde-Hansen
and Gorton). Here the body is a carrier of media *devices* and hence of our
personal archives of images, text, music, and sound—it is a body that enables
connectivity; it is also *implicated,* that is, caught up in affective viral (and visual) representations, both in life and after death; finally, the body is *implied,*
in the sense that there exists an indirect and ambivalent, ephemeral, ghostly
and insubstantial sense of (un)certain presence and embodiment online.

The Device Body

At our current juncture, some of the early debates in Internet studies seem
reactivated, since the cybernetic has become a mundane mode of being, and
this brings to the fore the irreducible tensions and relations between materiality and immateriality, presence and absence, localization and global
dispersion. As Joanne Garde-Hansen and Kristyn Gorton argue, "Global
flows, technological flows and media flows converge with the body" (77). In
other words, these complex cybernetic modes of being are today far from
futuristic and they are no longer marked by the technological sublime.

Indeed, they are quite commonplace and ubiquitous, as media are
"always on, and always on you," as Sherry Turkle puts it (see also Garde-
Hansen and Gorton 11). Besides comprising the omnipresent keyboard
self—thoroughly discussed in earlier writings on online textual embodiment
(Sundén, *Material Virtualities*)—the *device body* is an intertwined aspect of our
entire mobile and connected physicality. While this relates to many different
aspects of today's communication culture, here I will focus primarily on the
mnemonic aspects of this form of media embodiment.

The device body is the carrier of media, whether we are talking about
ubiquitous mobile devices such as iPads and smartphones (including our

archives of images or our social networking service accounts and their time-lines and feeds) or lifelogging devices, means of self-quantification, body-worn cameras, or other wearables such as smartwatches. The device body thus carries around a number of different registering applications and tracking devices (for instance, health apps and fitness and activity trackers). Here, devices that enable or fire our personal digital archive fever are both mobile and thoroughly environmental. In addition, this body is an enabler of connectivity, which in turn produces selfhood, expressive sociability in extended networks, and a sense of value.

In her book *Mediated Memories in the Digital Age* (2007), José van Dijck shows that we now inhabit a digital memory ecology in which we are embed-ded in a social context, while embodying as well as being emplaced within digital memory cultures. Van Dijck puts personal memories in what she calls "digital shoeboxes," which are often on display before a public in social networking, and moves them to the center of attention for digital memory studies. Others have argued that memory in the connected age is a question of individually choosing one's affinities and, by consequence, of choosing what to remember (Pinchevski).

Memory is now paradoxically, as Ingrid Volkmer puts it, a question of subjective public horizons of consciousness. These accounts gravitate to the individual and suggest that memory in our digital age is principally subjec-tive. In this context Andrew Hoskins has suggested that memory is not so much about remembering the past, as it is about the very act of recording ("Mediatization of Memory"). In such subjective memory practices through our device bodies of recording and simultaneously connecting, savvy indi-vidual users increase their social value and popularity—through numbers of "likes," friends, and followers and through constant connectivity.

One key example of such practices of recording is the selfie. The selfie, Paul Frosh argues, calls upon its viewer to "see me when I show you me" (or perhaps more precisely, "when I show you my body"). He defines the selfie as a "gestural image" that "inscribes one's own body into new forms of me-diated, expressive sociability with distant others. These are incarnated in a *gestural economy of affection* as the reflex bodily response by which we interact with our devices and their interfaces: the routinely dexterous movements of our hands and eyes" (1622; emphasis in original). Thus, while selfies are an expression of hyperindividualism, they also reveal, perhaps more than any-thing, our sociality, since they are performative and constitute what Frosh terms "a technocultural circuit of corporeal social energy" or a "kinesthetic sociability" (1608).

The device body, while at once highly performative, is thus in Frosh's reading inclined to reflex response and to affective relational positioning vis-à-vis others. What does this imply? Here I wish to introduce the implicated body and the implied body into the affective ecology of digital culture in order to emphasize that memory is also and crucially still communal and that, while it is seemingly utterly subjective, it is also sometimes beyond subjective control.

The Implicated and the Implied Body

According to recent scholarship on the Internet and emotions, affect is now emerging as the prime mover in analyses of digital culture (Garde-Hansen and Gorton 76; Karatzogianni and Kuntsman). Online worlds are able to create rich immersive experiences and to afford a felt sense of intimate co-presence (Benski and Fisher). The individualized yet social memory practices that I discussed above may also, however, invoke a different and less jovial subdivision of experience. Here a precarious body emerges: *the body as implicated.* This body is often visualized in acts of self-presentation that are seemingly consensual, but these practices may also involve experiences of suspicion, detachment, and alienation online. The implicated body bespeaks the vulnerabilities of the digital memory ecology, as our bodies, and parts of ourselves, are visually and graphically recorded and sometimes become viral through sharing and representation in circuits of affective social energy and reflex response (Frosh).

This is not seldom an area of pain. Our technologized existence sometimes seems ethically hollowed out as it is replete with trolling (often with gendered and racialized dimensions), cyberbullying, and revenge porn, causing a crisis for accountable presence and enhancing human guardedness, dissatisfaction, vulnerability, and harm (Garde-Hansen and Gorton 153–76; Miller). Suffering is even more pointedly the case at self-mutilation sites where bodies become marked and thence turned into mnemonic media of pain (Johansson) or in the case of real-time suicide online where "the final hour" becomes a hyperpublic memory, often reiterated online. This register also emerges when recordings of atrocity and trauma are similarly featured in the globital memory field (Reading; Westerlund, Hadlaczky, and Wasserman).

Another example of an implicated body within this spectrum of online vulnerability has to do with the loss of a person and concerns the ways in which the dead are kept socially alive online in, for instance, digital memorials or memorialized Facebook profiles (Brubaker, Hayes, and Dourish; Lagerkvist, "New Memory Cultures"). These practices mark a "re-presencing" of the lost person and his or her body through mourning and memory work with pictures and texts. The Internet is sometimes conceived as a place for immortal souls through which one fantasy of the posthuman (or rather transhuman) seems to be replayed: that of disembodied immortality (Lagerkvist, "Netlore of the Infinite"). It seems here, however, that while the physical body is inevitably disintegrating after death, the implicated embodied self may be under simultaneous and ongoing "resurrection": it is given new social life in persistent acts of posthumous commemoration that entail reediting and revising.

This verges on another type of embodiment: *the implied body*. Adding to the challenges of the digital age that I have described elsewhere—subjectively orchestrated and endlessly revisable memory work, the accelerated evaporation between the public and private, and the temporality of instantaneity (Lagerkvist, "New Memory Cultures")—we also observe a tendency to make memory automated and connective. Through connectivity the biological, technological (algorithmic), and social have been interlaced and enmeshed, turning memory into a process beyond individual purview and intention and beyond any sense of either subjective or collective control, as José van Dijck illustrates in her contribution to this volume (Hoskins, "Mediatization of Memory"). Hence, digitalization and our present moment of hyperconnectivity have consequences for both individual and collective memory.

Andrew Hoskins stresses these predicaments in our age that follow from the fragmentation and multiplication of memories and the connectivities through which they are fashioned. He argues that contemporary memory has less to do with bringing the past to the present through representation than with embedding memories in and spreading them through our sociotechnological practices. The dynamics of mediated memory makes it "created when needed, driven by the connectivities of digital technologies and media and inextricably forged through and constitutive of digital social networks: in other words, a new 'network memory'" ("Digital Network Memory," 92). Most importantly, in the digital age, memory is subject to "sociotechnical flux," which Hoskins describes as follows:

> [Sociotechnical flux is] the principal shaper of 21st century remembering through the medial gathering and splintering of individual, social and cultural imaginaries, increasingly networked through portable and pervasive digital media and communication devices so that a new "living archive" is becoming the organizing and habitual condition of memory. *Indeed memory's biological, social and cultural divisions and distinctions seem increasingly blurred if not collapsed under the key active dynamic and emergent media-memorial relationship: hyper-connectivity.* ("Mediatization of Memory" 661; my emphasis)

This new network memory, I argue, enhances the fears and anxieties of what it means to be human. Simultaneously it invokes a sense of implied digital embodiment. Today opaque digital assemblages are imbricated in our embodied existence; they are ripe with insecurities as to the status of our digital data traces and our uncertain capacity to gain a hold on them. There is also a related anxiety about the possibility to secure or keep track of our memories and "trace bodies" when we simultaneously know that they exist, that they are present, yet cannot feel their exact clout and whereabouts; they are confusingly unbeknown to us, as are (for a majority of people) the surveillance systems we have surrendered ourselves to (Hong).

This body is uncannily invoked also by our knowledge that we are distributed across digital systems. The implied body is invisible and more indirectly engaged, but it is nonetheless somewhere: there are traces of "me" out there. In an unclear sense I am somewhere (else): my body is intimated. I suggest that the longevity of data and the knowledge that search engines such as Google remember all our virtual steps leave us ambivalent, anxious, and quite vulnerable about where our traces may be situated and how they may bear on our lives and afterlives (Mayer-Schönberger; Peters). Our implied embodied selves concern those parts of us (what I have termed our digital "surrogates") that are circulating without our knowing precisely where and how, or even whether they are there (Lagerkvist, "Netlore of the Infinite").

Our embodied digital existence, one might conclude, has to a large degree to do with memory, with the ways we relate to the immediate and individual past as well as with the potential eternal life of data. We see this in recent debates about the right to forget or to be forgotten. May these media memories and this knowledge about us uncannily and disturbingly both outlast our needs and haunt our intentions? These deliberations point to profound existential challenges of our time. This constitutes an emerging situation, a way of being present in the world without clear demarcations and coordinates. And it will propel us toward a theorization of our embodied and diversified digital existence in terms of how we are implicated (precariously caught up or graphically represented) as well as how our bodies are implied (indirectly sensed or uncannily presenced) in this novel constellation.

CONCLUSION: THE EMBODIED EXISTENTIAL APPROACH IN MEDIA MEMORY STUDIES

This essay has shown that the field of media memory studies emerges at a precarious and rocky moment—a moment characterized by rapid and continuous reconfiguration: the mobile, global, and digital moment. This is also the moment of phenomenally experienced complexities of hyperconnectivity within the digital memory ecology. I have suggested that what anchors this fluid discourse, albeit in a plurality of modes, is a sense of embodiment.

In order to fruitfully embody media memories, I have suggested a sociophenomenological approach that involves recognizing the fundamental entanglement of embodied performances of memory, space, and mediation. On this holistic trajectory, we may begin to describe memory as both mediated (inscribed) and embodied (incorporated) at once—what I choose to term "memory as mediatized performativity"—while ultimately bound to places, infrastructures, and settings that need to be described.

The approach also stresses the performative, emergent, and processual character of memory practices. As I have shown, these insights will need to be supplemented in approaching the digital memory ecology. Performances of memory are produced across the realms of the body, media, physical artefacts, and space, but in the digital age, it seems that these entanglements of the mediated and the physical are even more accentuated than before and that the evaporating boundaries between biological, individual, social, public, and cultural regimes of memory have become intensified.[5] Memory is today increasingly forged across and through new hybrid but also automated forms.

The objective of an existential and embodied approach is to theorize human forms of being for media (memory) studies and digital culture more broadly, while moving beyond its current predilection for either one-sidedly describing the molding forces of automation, protocol, and algorithm (at the expense of human agency) or celebrating the developments as intrinsically liberatory or as natural parts of our "digital ecology" or "media life" (Deuze). This requires a careful reconceptualization of "the human," which describes the self as (to speak with Heidegger) thrown out into a universe of uncertainty (Lagerkvist, "Existential Media"). An embodied approach to media memory is, I contend, also an existential approach. In turn, it is a version of the existential that refutes conceptions of a disembodied and stable form of consciousness that is—as in classical logocentric approaches—conceived in opposition with the body.

Reenvisioning humans for the digital age implies conceiving of a plurality of ways of being. It is an approach sensitized to the diversifications of our embodied, uncertain, sentient, and vulnerable selves, which will also involve differentiating along the lines of gender, class, age, race, ethnicity, (dis)ability, sexuality, and cultural, religious, and historical contexts. In sum, the so-called media ecology presupposes and forges different yet often overlapping modes of embodiment that all entail different possibilities and challenges. These I have begun to summarize in terms of the performative body, the device body, the implicated body, and the implied body. In discussing these four media bodies, this essay has explored embodied senses of being-in-and-with-the-digital-world.

I will round up by further emphasizing that a shift toward embodiment and affect in digital memory studies should not be understood as a refutation of human agency, experience, ethics, or the quest for meaning. Indeed, endorsing an embodied sense of the human self means holding on to the possibility, or will, to achieve meaning and make ethical choices: the body is both sentient and sense making. And yet, our digital media bodies are examples of both implicated and implied forms of embodiment, and I have suggested that they are currently besieged by ambivalence and anxiety.

The approach I propose therefore makes it possible to focus less on the early adopters of new media, as is often implicitly done in media studies, and more emphatically on the less tech savvy, on those who worry about the culture of connectivity: stumbling agents who fall, embodied selves who underaccomplish, who fail to make sense, and whose concerns are with alienation, with not belonging, not managing, or not mastering. As is hopefully clear by now, the existential approach in this view is not about the cogito reasoning about his world, or about a subjective, disembodied consciousness, or even about radical "freedom"; it is instead an approach that allows us to describe online media and digital culture in terms of affectively being-in-and-with-the-digital-world, which includes the will to make sense as well as the failures of doing so. It further conceives of interruption as well as breakdown, asubjective and nonconscious affect, confusion, halt, and suffering as inevitable aspects of human existence and as part of the basic conditions of life—and of media life.

I want to end with an imaginative challenge: imagine if those of us who are never retweeted, who are unable to navigate and comprehend the fullness of the web, who can't make their devices work, who never post or seldom upload anything, who feel awkward and anxious about the traces we leave are recognized as the inhabitants of the digital memory ecology; and imagine if our vantage point for exploring our existential terrains of connectivity is not the early adopter but the disabled child. To further develop an approach that estimates, beyond the gloss of technological affordances and the clout of all-powerful corporate algorithms, the range of phenomenal, embodied, affective, and lived experiences of our digital existence is the formidable task of an existential approach in media memory studies.

Amanda Lagerkvist is an associate professor of media and communication studies and a Wallenberg Academy Fellow in the Department of Media Studies at Stockholm University. She is head of the research program Existential

Terrains: Memory and Meaning in Cultures of Connectivity (et.ims.su.se), which is funded by the Knut and Alice Wallenberg Foundation, the Marcus and Amalia Wallenberg Foundation, and Stockholm University (2014–2018). Probing our digital existence philosophically and ethnographically, she focuses on vulnerabilities in digital memory cultures relating to death and the digital afterlife. Her latest monograph is *Media and Memory in New Shanghai: Western Performances of Futures Past* (Palgrave Macmillan, 2013).

NOTES

The author wishes to acknowledge the valuable comments from Marta Zarzycka, Paul Frosh, Kristina Fjelkestam, and Mark Westmoreland on a previous draft of the essay. This article is part of the project "Existential Terrains: Memory and Meaning in Cultures of Connectivity" (et.ims.su.se), and was made possible through funding from The Knut and Alice Wallenberg Foundation, The Marcus and Amalia Wallenberg Foundation, and Stockholm University.

1. This is not the place for an in-depth engagement with the ontological foundations of these debates about bodies, science, and technology in feminist theory of the so-called ontological turn. For a good introduction to these debates, which accounts for their origins in quantum physics, cybernetics, and thermodynamics, see Clough. Clough argues that a retheorization of the human and the nonhuman, as well as of the human body in relation to technologies, will "alert feminist theorists to the changing definition of the body that is arising to fit what the body can now do but also what economic and governing interests, including science and technology, have and might yet invest, seek to control or modulate in relationship to life and *existence generally*" (104; my emphasis). For a useful discussion of the potential of posthumanism to retool the humanities to address the contemporary and utterly complex "human condition," see Åsberg et al.

2. Exemplifying this process, the birth of "media memory studies" (Neiger, Meyers, and Zandberg) introduces a field that focuses on the interface of media and memory in order to "explore each of these fields by using the insights gained from the other; utilizing the study of media in order to probe the field of collective memory research and vice versa—to investigate old and new questions concerning the operation of the media, by means of insights gained from the study of collective memory" (2).

3. As Connerton argues, the body always comprises its own materialized capacities, agency, and potentiality, and hence "no code of bodily performances, however elaborated that code is imagined to be, can comprehend the object described when the object described is a practice of bodily behaviour" (90). This means that the media script can never fully capture the performance, and hence the performance is never completely deployed by the script and can never materialize it exhaustively.

4. See Sundén and Sveningsson for a comprehensive overview of this field.
5. Another important strand of the field of memory studies has brought the body into connection with both cognition and culture in an attempt to create a dialogue across the cognitive sciences and the social sciences. The theory of "the extended mind" describes mental states as "spread across the physical, social, and cultural environments as well as bodies and brains" (Sutton 223). This approach of a *distributed memory* thus puts brain, body, and world together in order to assess the possible links and mutual benefits of integration between, for instance, neurobiologists' and narrative theorists' work on memory.

WORKS CITED

Ahmed, Sara. *The Cultural Politics of Emotion.* New York: Routledge, 2004.
Åsberg, Cecilia, Redi Kooback, and Ericka Johnson. "Beyond the Humanist Imagination." *Nora: Nordic Journal of Feminist and Gender Research* 19.4 (2011): 218–30.
Benski, Tova, and Eran Fisher, eds. *Internet and Emotions.* London: Routledge, 2013.
Braidotti, Rosi. *The Posthuman.* New York: Polity Press, 2013.
Brubaker, Jed, Gillian R. Hayes, and Paul Dourish. "Beyond the Grave: Facebook as a Site for the Expansion of Death and Mourning." *The Information Society: An International Journal* 29.3 (2013): 152–63.
Clough, Patricia Ticineto. "Feminist Theory: Bodies, Science and Technology." *Handbook of the Body.* Ed. Bryan Turner. London: Routledge, 2012. 94–105.
Connerton, Paul. *How Societies Remember.* Cambridge: Cambridge University Press, 1989.
Deuze, Mark. *Media Life.* Cambridge: Polity, 2012.
Erll, Astrid. "Cultural Memory Studies: An Introduction." *A Companion to Cultural Memory Studies.* Ed. Astrid Erll and Ansgar Nünning. Berlin: De Gruyter, 2010. 1–18.
Featherstone, Mike. "Ubiquitous Media: An Introduction." *Theory, Culture and Society* 26.2–3 (2009): 1–22.
Frosh, Paul. "The Gestural Image: The Selfie, Photography Theory and Kinesthetic Sociability." *International Journal of Communication* 9 (2015): 1607–28.
Garde-Hansen, Joanne, and Kristyn Gorton. *Emotion Online: Theorizing Affect on the Internet.* Basingstoke: Palgrave Macmillan, 2013.
Garde-Hansen, Joanne, Anna Reading, and Andrew Hoskins. "Introduction." *Save As ... Digital Memories.* Ed. Joanne Garde-Hansen, Anna Reading, and Andrew Hoskins. Basingstoke: Palgrave Macmillan, 2009. 1–21.
Gies, Lieve. "How Material Are Cyberbodies? Broadband Internet and Embodied Subjectivity." *Crime, Media, Culture* 4.3 (2008): 311–30.
Gonzales-Arnal, Stella, Gill Jagger, and Kathleen Lennon, eds. *Embodied Selves.* Basingstoke: Palgrave Macmillan, 2012.
Halbwachs, Maurice. *On Collective Memory.* Chicago: University of Chicago Press, 1992.

Hayles, N. Katherine. *When We Became Post-human: Virtual Bodies in Cybernetics, Literature, and Informatics.* Chicago: University of Chicago Press, 1999.

Hirsch, Marianne. "Mobile Memories." Budapest, 30 Sept. 2014. Keynote Address.

Hong, Sun-ha. "Presence, or the Sense of Being-there and Being-with in the New Media Society." *First Monday* 20 Oct. 2015. Web. 8 Dec. 2015.

Hoskins, Andrew. "7/7 and Connective Memory: Interactional Trajectories of Remembering in Post-scarcity Culture." *Memory Studies* 4.3 (2011): 269–80.

——. "Digital Network Memory." *Mediation, Remediation, and the Dynamics of Cultural Memory.* Ed. Astrid Erll and Ann Rigney. Berlin: De Gruyter, 2008. 91–106.

——. "The Mediatization of Memory." *Mediatization of Communication.* Ed. Knut Lundby. Berlin: De Gruyter, 2014. 661–80.

Johansson, Anna. "Hybrid Embodiment: Doing Respectable Bodies on YouTube." *Hybrid Media Culture: Sensing Place in a World of Flows.* Ed. Simon Lindgren. London: Routledge, 2014. 16–33.

Karatzogianni, Athina, and Adi Kuntsman, eds. *Digital Cultures and the Politics of Emotion: Feelings, Affect and Technological Change.* Basingstoke: Palgrave Macmillan, 2012.

Kember, Sarah, and Joanna Zylinska. *Life after New Media: Mediation as a Vital Process.* Cambridge: MIT Press, 2012.

Koivunen, Anu. "Force of Affects, Weight of Histories in *Love Is a Treasure.*" *Carnal Aesthetics: Transgressive Imaginary and Feminist Politics.* Ed. Bettina Papenburg and Marta Zarzycka. New York: IB Tauris, 2013. 89–101.

Lagerkvist, Amanda. "Existential Media: Toward a Theorization of Digital Thrownness." *New Media & Society.* Online first. Web. June 2016.

——. *Media and Memory in New Shanghai: Western Performances of Futures Past.* Basingstoke: Palgrave Macmillan, 2013.

——. "The Netlore of the Infinite: Death (and beyond) in the Digital Memory Ecology." *New Review of Hypermedia and Multimedia.* 21.1–2 (2015): 185–95.

——. "New Memory Cultures and Death: Existential Security in the Digital Memory Ecology." *Thanatos* 2.2 (2013): 1–17.

Mayer-Schönberger, Victor. *Delete: The Virtue of Forgetting in the Digital Age.* Princeton: Princeton University Press, 2008.

Miller, Vincent. "A Crisis of Presence: On-line Culture and Being in the World." *Space & Polity* 16.3 (2012): 265–85.

Mitchell, WJT, and Mark B. Hansen. *Critical Terms for Media Studies.* Chicago: University of Chicago Press, 2010.

Narvaez, Rafael. F. "Embodiment, Collective Memory and Time." *Body & Society* 12.3 (2006): 51–73.

Neiger, Motti, Oren Meyers, and Eyal Zandberg, eds. *On Media Memory: Collective Memory in a New Media Age.* Basingstoke: Palgrave Macmillan, 2011.

Nora, Pierre. "Between Memory and History: *Les Lieux de Mémoire.*" *Representations* 26 (1989): 7–24.

Peters, John Durham. "Proliferation and Obsolescence of the Historical Record in the Digital Era." *Cultures of Obsolescence: History, Materiality, and the Digital Age.* Ed.

Babette B. Tischleder and Sarah Wasserman. Basingstoke: Palgrave Macmillan, 2015, 79–96.

Pinchevski, Amit. "Archive, Media, Trauma." *On Media Memory: Collective Memory in a New Media Age.* Ed. Motti Neiger, Oren Meyers, and Eyal Zandberg. Basingstoke: Palgrave Macmillan, 2011. 253–64.

Rainie, Lee, and Barry Wellmann. *Networked: The New Social Operating System.* Cambridge: MIT Press, 2012.

Reading, Anna. "Memory and Digital Media: Six Dynamics of the Globital Memory Field." *On Media Memory: Collective Memory in a New Media Age.* Ed. Motti Neiger, Oren Meyers, and Eyal Zandberg. Basingstoke: Palgrave Macmillan, 2011. 241–52.

Refslund Christensen, Dorthe, and Kjetil Sandvik, eds. *Mediating and Remediating Death.* Farnham: Ashgate, 2014.

Rigney, Ann. "Plentitude, Scarcity, and the Circulation of Cultural Memory." *Journal of European Studies* 35 (2005): 11–28.

Sobchack, Vivianne. *Carnal Thoughts: Embodiment and Moving Image Culture.* Berkeley: University of California Press, 2004.

Sturken, Marita. *Tangled Memories: The Vietnam War, the Aids Epidemic and the Politics of Remembering.* Berkeley: University of California Press, 1997.

Sundén, Jenny. *Material Virtualities: Approaching Online Textual Embodiment.* New York: Peter Lang, 2003.

——. "A Sense of Play: Affect, Emotion, and Embodiment in *World of Warcraft.*" *Working with Affect in Feminist Readings: Disturbing Differences.* Ed. Marianne Liljeström and Susanna Paasonen. London: Routledge, 2010. 45–57.

Sundén, Jenny, and Malin Sveningsson. *Gender and Sexuality in Online Game Cultures: Passionate Play.* London: Routledge, 2012.

Sutton, John. "Memory and the Extended Mind: Embodiment, Cognition and Culture." *Cognitive Processing* 6 (2005): 223–26.

Taylor, Diana. *The Archive and the Repertoire: Performing Cultural Memory in the Americas.* Durham: Duke University Press, 2003.

Thrift, Nigel, and John-David Dewsbury. "Dead Geographies—and How to Make Them Alive." *Environment and Planning D: Society and Space* 18 (2000): 411–32.

Turkle, Sherry. "Always-on/Always-on-You: The Tethered Self." *Handbook of Mobile Communication Studies.* Ed. James Katz. Cambridge: MIT Press, 2008. 121–38.

Van Dijck, José. *The Culture of Connectivity: A Critical History of Social Media.* Oxford: Oxford University Press, 2013.

—— *Mediated Memories in the Digital Age.* Stanford: Stanford University Press, 2007.

Volkmer, I. (2014, May 22–27). Memory discourse as a 'reflective' dimension of network journalism. Paper presented at the ICA Conference "Communication and the Good Life," Seattle.

Westerlund, Michael, Gergö Hadlaczky, and Danuta Wasserman. "Case Study of Posts before and after a Suicide on a Swedish Internet Forum." *British Journal of Psychiatry* 207.6 (2015): 476–82.

Chapter 9

Metaphorical Memories of the Medieval Crusades after 9/11

Brian Johnsrud

I don't think books can change the world, but when the world begins to change, it searches for different books.

—Shlomo Sand

INTRODUCTION

Three days after the September 11, 2001 terrorist attacks, US president George W. Bush proclaimed, "Americans do not yet have the distance of history. But our *responsibility to history* is already clear: to answer these attacks and rid the world of evil" ("Remarks"; my emphasis). The "distance of history" in Bush's first sentence reflects norms drawn from a dominant thread of modern academic historiography: the attempt to gather all the facts and data to construct an objective, "distant" narrative account, often in book form, of "what actually happened."

However, in the subsequent sentence, President Bush reverses this initial call for a critical distance with an urgency of responsive decision making, a "responsibility to history" that includes remembering and contextualizing the attacks in order to devise an equitable reaction. With a similar impulse, a number of individuals and groups responded to the terrorist attacks by attempting to plot and sequence events leading up to 9/11 in order to assemble a narrative capable of connecting events from the past to the present catastrophe and, hopefully, of revealing a suitable course of action for the near future.

In times of crisis, comparative historical thinking provides a way for individuals and groups to construct narratives capable of placing the past in a relational dialogue with the present and future. This manner of temporal accounting assists the demands of the day, which often include an urgency at odds with slower, more distant modes of historical inquiry. Specific events from the past—even the distant past—often serve as anchors to quell a sense of temporal and mnemonic disorientation, for both individuals and the broader public. After 9/11, the history of the Crusades became one of the key historical and mnemonic benchmarks that individuals, groups, and institutions found useful and mobilized to frame their understanding of the attacks.[1]

When numerous actors introduced metaphors comparing the medieval Crusades to the US-led wars in Iraq and Afghanistan in global popular discourse, prominent American and British academic historians fervently condemned the professional, intellectual, and ethical appropriateness of these connections. Oxford historian of the Crusades Christopher Tyerman went so far as to levy a countermetaphor comparing any "Westerner" who discussed the Crusades alongside contemporary politics with the 9/11 terrorists themselves. Outside his academic circle, "the crusades and their history were *hijacked* by western supremacists," he argued (Tyerman, *Fighting for Christendom* 199).

The "Western supremacists" Tyerman rebukes are not political officials or elected leaders; rather, his disdain is reserved primarily for creative producers of the numerous Crusade-related films, novels, televisions shows, and mass-market popular products about the Crusades that proliferated after 9/11. For Tyerman, like many of the contemporary historians of the Crusades discussed here, these creative actors (or "supremacists," as Tyerman would have it) have "hijacked" the authority to represent the Crusades from the rightful keepers of knowledge of the past: academic historians.

Tyerman's condemnation of historical metaphors is extreme in its connotations, rhetorically comparing terrorist plane hijackers with nonacademics who use figurative language to "hijack" Crusader history. His disbelief that a millennia-old conflict could be practically relevant to the twenty-first-century public is worth considering. Perhaps, as Fredric Jameson claims, in the wake of the postmodern era's "end of history," "the recent past is always the most distant in the mind's eye of the historical observer" (704). To be sure, it is seemingly counterintuitive that the Crusades gained such popular historical significance when other, more recent historical events—the *First Gulf War*, for example—were surprisingly infrequent referents in American popular culture after 9/11, the War on Terror, and the invasions of Afghanistan and Iraq. Regardless, after September 11, 2001, dozens of alternative histories and popular metaphors sprang forth using the Crusades, religious violence, and a millennial "clash of civilizations" to try to understand present conflicts.

Professional historians are familiar with traditional, academic norms within their discipline, which generally eschew historical analogy in favor of mapping out the few empirically traceable continuities between past and present. A more common project of contemporary Western historiography is to emphasize the abundant breaks, ruptures, and divergence in historical patterns. In the aftermath of 9/11, leading Crusade historians did not issue condemnations against each other within a community with shared standards; rather, they imposed academic standards on nonhistorians making analogical comparisons between the Crusades and the War on Terror.

The academic historians discussed in this essay questioned the popular notion that 9/11 and the subsequent War on Terror could, or should, be perceived as a "new Crusade"—a cultural memory being remembered as if the Crusades and their medieval animosity lingered, ready to be relived between the "East" and the "West." In the face of such contentions, historians drew a line that echoes Pierre Nora's canonical distinction between history and memory, arguing that the Crusades should be considered inanimate history, not a living memory, and as such should be relevant to the present only through antiquarian or professional interest, not for presentist social or political purposes (7–8).

As this essay will show, the social and communicative functions of contemporary metaphors and metaphorical language have the capacity to breathe new life into seemingly "dead" histories. Just as memory scholars have conceptualized cultural memories as "dead" or "living" memories, theorists of metaphor also examine living versus dead, flattened, or inanimate metaphors. By combining these perspectives, "metaphorical memories" contrast "literal histories" by demanding their relevance to contemporary sociopolitical realities. In terms of transmediality, contemporary metaphorical memories often take advantage of the capacity for narratives to travel media landscapes, seeking out particular media affordances like audience agency, interaction, participant interpretation, and remediation.

Despite being condemned by academic historians, living, metaphorical memories of the Crusades, by which I mean those perceived as relevant to the lived present, persisted after 2001. Like the Hydra in Greek mythology, for each condemnation leveled by academic historians, dozens of popular comparisons between the old and "new" Crusades sprang forth. Contrary to what professional Crusade historians think, there is no way to police memory discourses by proscribing them; in the contemporary media ecology, alternative accounts come to take the place that authoritative historical discourse leaves unoccupied.

This essay reorients an understudied aspect of cultural memory studies, namely the linguistic and cognitive tendency to align distant historical events with the present through the act of metaphorical thinking. The first section details traditional definitions of history and memory to explain why memory is a useful term for describing the particular observable orientations to the past. I introduce the notion of metaphorical memory in order to help us understand the impulses behind creating popular narratives of the Crusades after 9/11 and to better understand on what "literal history" grounds traditionalist historians have challenged them.

The imaginative impulse surrounding popular histories, novels, films, television, journalism, and online blogs employing such metaphorical memories is often, and in my view unfairly, critiqued as an example of uneducated thinking, a stubborn refusal to submit to authorities, or callously politicized rhetoric. Rather, as this essay will show, it is important to carefully consider the motivations behind practices like historical analogies, temporal metaphors, or counterfactual thinking, all of which are cognitive acts that comprise what I call metaphorical memory.

The figurative constructions of metaphorical memories, as ways of engaging with traumatic events and complex pasts and presents, are much more than the antihistorical public doing bad history. Rather, acts of metaphorical memory come to terms with the present by creating new cognitive and historical frameworks through the imaginative transformations afforded by figurative language and by the media that provide room for them. More importantly, metaphorical memory offers a way for individuals operating outside strict historiographic norms to engage in the creative work of introducing the past to the present and ushering them into an imagined—and hopefully less violent—future.

LITERAL HISTORIES AND METAPHORICAL MEMORIES

Before introducing the ways that the Crusades have been constructed as metaphorical memories after 9/11, it is important to briefly clarify why the terms "history," "memory," and "metaphor" are necessary for understanding the cultural products discussed here and their reception. What, after all, does it mean to describe a perception of the past as memory? Despite the best efforts of notable scholars (Erll and Nünning; Olick, Vinitzky-Seroussi, and Levy; Radstone and Schwarz), there is no agreed upon solid ontological or theoretical distinction between history and cultural memory.

Rather than diagnosing cultural products as history or memory, it is more constructive in this case to consider these rhetorical *uses* of texts and objects presenting the past in the present. In doing so, out attention is drawn to how their production, reception, and uses generate different *orientations toward the past.* In a historical orientation to the past, individuals and groups typically perceive previous events as antiquarian objects of study that do not have daily or frequent relevance to their lived experience of the present. Here, Michael Oakeshott's definition of the historical past is useful, as he describes it as something tied to a "critical inquiry of a certain sort ... assembled in answer to a historical question" (36, 68).

The emphasis here is on a historical orientation to the past, as it relates to a question about the *past,* not the present (recognizing, of course, that no contemporary historiographical practices can be completely divorced from the demands of the present). A historical question asking, "What initiated the Crusades in 1095?" for example, does not explicitly tie the inquiry to the practical demands of the present but instead orients the respondent toward a kind of historical inquiry about the past *as past.*

The same question when reformulated as "How is the call to the Crusades in 1095 similar to or different from President George W. Bush's early speeches on the War on Terror?" on the other hand, asks something qualitatively different. This latter formulation explicitly orients the past *in relation to the present,* asking the respondents to draw on their individual memories of recent events, along with their memory of presentations of past events like the Crusades. These different memories—formally learned and informally acquired—connect disparate events in complex and creative ways.

As a practical orientation to the past, memory's creative versatility allows it to adapt to the diverse lived experiences it needs to accommodate, an adaptive trait that earns it the dubious attribute "subjective" in historiographical terms. This flexibility of cultural memory (as a pragmatic orientation toward the past) often draws on the affordances offered by figurative language, particularly metaphor. Metaphors, and metaphorical memories, serve numerous purposes above and beyond literality. As Ted Cohen explains, a key component of metaphorical language is the social creation of intimacy between the maker of the metaphor and the appreciator of the metaphor (if they are capable of appreciating it for what it is). This occurs when the creator of a metaphor issues a form of "concealed invitation" to the receiver's cognitive experience, and when the hearer expends the effort to accept the invitation, a form of community is acknowledged (6).

However, the intimacy created through metaphorical memories can only be produced if the appreciator is willing to set aside a more rigorously

historical orientation of the past. The audience, or appreciator, of a metaphorical memory has to be able to recognize that the creator of metaphorical memories may simply wish "to say something special, not to arouse,
insinuate, or mislead, and not to convey an exotic meaning, but to initiate
explicitly the cooperative act of comprehension" (Cohen 7). Metaphorical
memory is not a "hijacking" of truth but a move toward shared comprehension, an effort after meaning.

As this essay will show, disputes between academics producing literal
histories of the Crusades and nonacademics crafting metaphorical memories after 9/11 center on these particular historians' failure to recognize
metaphorical acts as creative attempts to connect communities grappling
with traumatic events in the present. In this way, it demonstrates something
that professional students of memory often overlook: that memory is still
sometimes perceived as a threat to meaning and that this suspicion often
accompanies a certain resistance to the promiscuous circulation of the past
that digital media afford.

Philosopher Richard Rorty helps elucidate how metaphorical and non-
metaphorical narratives can be mistakenly viewed at odds with one another.
Rorty describes metaphors as one of the three essential ways that new beliefs
can be added to our previous beliefs (along with perception and inference;
"Philosophy as Science" 212). Drawing on the work of Donald Davidson,
Rorty reminds us that metaphors are not entirely distinct from the literal
language promoted by many contemporary historiographers. Rather, metaphors are adjacent

> ways of producing effects on your interlocutor or your reader, but not ways
> of conveying a [literal] message. To none of these is it appropriate to respond
> with "What exactly are you trying to say?" ... An attempt to state that meaning
> would be an attempt to find some familiar (that is, literal) use of words ... but
> the unparaphrasability of metaphor is just the unsuitability of any such familiar
> sentence for one's purpose. (*Contingency* 19)

Bearing these contentions in mind, what follows is in many ways a
narrative of miscommunication between two parties. When the historians
discussed in this essay mistakenly perceived metaphorical memories of the
Crusades as literal truth claims, they superficially condemned the creators
of those metaphors as deficient in historiographical rigor. Rather than taking these historians' advice and abandoning the creative potential that metaphorical memories possess in their capacity to address the present, many
audiences instead turned to other authors and creators who *were* willing to
engage in figurative language, providing a panoply of alternative historiog-

raphies that arose with their own practical—and often violent—agendas for metaphorical memories of the Crusades.

POLITICAL AND POPULAR CRUSADE METAPHORS AFTER 9/11

Metaphors linking the Crusades and medieval warfare with modern conflict in the Middle East proliferated in the White House, in US-led combat in Iraq and Afghanistan, and in American literature and film after 9/11. Arguably the most remarkable of these was President Bush's use of metaphor on the White House lawn five days after 9/11. After stressing the need for Americans to return to work, Bush announced, "This Crusade, this War On Terrorism, is going to take a while" ("Remarks").

While the White House press secretary apologized for the president's use of this word the following week, Bush nevertheless repeated the Crusade metaphor five months later to describe his "important Crusade to defend freedom" ("Public Papers" 237). In contemporary English, the term "Crusade" is frequently used to describe any "aggressive movement or enterprise against some public evil, or some institution or class of persons considered as evil" ("Crusade"). However, in tandem with the White House's religious and medieval rhetoric and metaphors in the years to follow, it is unsurprising that the use of this figurative language became so controversial.

When not referencing the Crusades directly, White House leaders such as Deputy Secretary of Defense Paul D. Wolfowitz were notorious for their use of medieval metaphors in prepared speeches and interviews. In the months after 9/11, Wolfowitz referred to various Muslim governments and terror organizations as reflecting "a medieval sort of regime," a "medieval view," "a medieval, intolerant, and tyrannical way of life," and "a twisted, medieval notion of what the proper order of things is" (Wolfowitz, interview with *Sunday Telegraph,* interview with Indonesian Television, "Gathering Storm," Hoover Institution Transcript).

Secretary of Defense Donald Rumsfeld similarly described Abu Musab al-Zarqawi, the Jordanian terrorist responsible for a number of bombings during the Iraq War, as personifying a "dark, sadistic, medieval vision of the future—of beheadings, suicide bombings, and indiscriminate killings" (Rumsfeld, "Abu Musab al-Zarqawi Killed"). For Rumsfeld, these medieval metaphors encapsulate a change from the First Gulf War, suggesting that "[our new enemies] combine medieval sensibilities with modern technology and media savvy to find new ways to exploit perceived weaknesses and to weaken the civilized world" ("Senate Appropriations Committee").[2]

Medieval historian Bruce Holsinger underscores the practical nature of Wolfowitz and Rumsfeld's medieval metaphors as they relate to military action. Rumsfeld's particular understanding of Middle Eastern enemies as "medieval," he argues, extends beyond intellectual, moral, or cultural characteristics. Rumsfeld's medieval metaphors tie directly to US military decision making: "The 'medieval sensibilities' of the enemy, then, are tactical, and they must be met with *newly medieval* sensibilities of our own. Our military must be more mobile, its communications infrastructure more adaptable and flexible" (*Neomedievalism* 53).

The practical applications of these medieval Crusade and "holy war" metaphors for the War on Terror stretched beyond White House and Pentagon military actions and were similarly adopted by US military contractors, commanders, and soldiers deployed in these conflicts. US lieutenant general William G. Boykin spoke to church congregations in 2003 in military uniform, exulting in the fact that the United States was engaged in a holy war against Satan in Iraq and Afghanistan (Leung). Former employees of US military contractor Blackwater (now Xe Services) claimed in a 2009 affidavit lodged with a Virginia court that the company founder, Erik Prince, "views himself as a Christian Crusader tasked with eliminating Muslims and the Islamic faith from the globe" ("Erik Prince").

Unofficial military uniform badges replicating medieval Crusade Knights Templar insignia and others with the phrase "Pork Eating Crusader" (written in English and Arabic) were sold through online retailers and worn by US soldiers in Iraq and Afghanistan (Johnsrud, "Adoption of Crusade Imagery"). While these examples are not meant to illustrate a national trend or imply that these metaphors became a dominant part of military discourse, their public and frequent occurrence demonstrates the wide range of individuals and communities who felt that the Crusades had a practical relevance for US and Middle Eastern conflict after 9/11.

Finally, literature and film after 9/11 have also crafted vivid metaphorical memories of the Crusades for American and global audiences (Haydock and Risden; Johnsrud, "Da Vinci Code"). While a number of films and television series after 2001 tell the story of the medieval Crusades,[3] it is noteworthy that many employ anachronistic rhetoric or rely on recent notions of East versus West in ways meant to resonate with contemporary audiences' political vocabulary. Perhaps more remarkable are the ways that the Crusades have been integrated into popular narratives that are set in the present but that rely upon crusading history to understand our contemporary moment. The most widely read and watched narratives of this kind are undoubtedly Dan Brown's novels, such as *The Da Vinci Code* (2003) and the subsequent film version (2006).

Brown's third book in his Robert Langdon series, *The Lost Symbol* (2010), is the first that does more than reference the Crusades; it also repeatedly refers to 9/11 and the War on Terror. In so doing, the novel asks its readers to question American political motivations and ideological intentions (conspiratorial or not) in the same way that the protagonist and Harvard professor of symbology, Robert Langdon, leaves his students "confounded to learn that the true intentions of our nation's forefathers had absolutely nothing to do with what so many politicians now claimed. America's intended destiny has been lost to history" (82). The novel, the only in the series to be set entirely in the United States rather than Europe, also takes seriously the prevailing Crusader and holy war rhetoric in the United States and Middle East after 9/11 and emphasizes rhetoric as a violent act in itself: "From the Crusades, to the Inquisition, to American politics—the name Jesus had been hijacked as an ally in all kinds of power struggles" (327).

Altogether, these brief examples from political and military leaders and popular culture sketch a range of uses of metaphorical memories of the Crusades in the "West," particularly in the United States, uses that were so upsetting to the historians introduced in the following section. To be sure, there are just as many, if not more, vivid examples of Crusader rhetoric applied to cultural products created in other countries, especially in the Middle East. However, it was Americans who, in Christopher Tyerman's words, "ought to know better" ("Modern Crusade Historiography") and who received the harshest critiques from the American and British historians discussed below. It was also prominent American authors and public figures who ignored academic censors and produced controversial, anti-Muslim histories of the Crusades that called for a "tenth Crusade" to reenact a millennial struggle to keep Muslims out of the Western world and its sacred places, texts attended to later in this essay.

ACADEMIC RESTRICTIONS ON DEFINITIONS AND OF METAPHORICAL MEMORIES OF THE CRUSADES

The main critique leveled by historians at attempts to discuss the Crusades in contemporary terms is a definitional one: namely that the medieval Crusades are categorically different from modern conflict. Of course, metaphors *depend upon* difference between the two objects being compared in order to function. However, it is necessary to briefly describe the ways that the Crusades have been traditionally defined, as this insistence on definitive categorical traits is adopted and countered by later popular authors such as Rodney Stark and Robert Spencer.

Historian Jill Claster usefully outlines three prevailing definitions of "Crusades" used by modern historiographers to determine "what counts" as a Crusade, when they began, when they ended, and how many there have been. Claster describes the first camp as "pluralists." This group, including Cambridge historian Jonathan Riley-Smith, argues that all wars initiated by a pope to fight enemies of the Church and Christendom are legitimate Crusades, regardless of the geography of the conflict or its period (4).

The second faction, who Claster terms the "traditionalists," believe that only movements launched by the papacy to recover or preserve the Holy Land for Christendom should be rightly considered Crusades (4). The final group of modern Crusade historians, the "generalists," place Crusades under the umbrella of holy war and study the Crusades as any conflict fought in the name of God (5). It is only by this last group of "generalists," who are the minority among modern Crusade historians, that the wars in Iraq and Afghanistan could be considered a Crusade, and then only if President Bush and other leaders of the conflict could be shown to be fighting—in belief or practice—"in the name of God."[4]

Of course, these definitions are bound by traditional Western historiographic norms. For many Muslim historians, following Sayyid Qutb, Crusade is "a term that can be applied to any offensive including a drive for economic or political hegemony, against Islam anywhere by those who call themselves Christians or are in the Christian tradition" (Riley-Smith 164). This opens up a second major definitional concern: how many Crusades were there, and when—if ever—did these series of conflicts end? Most historians traditionally set the beginning of the Crusades with Pope Urban II's 1095 call to assist the Byzantine Empire in defending Jerusalem's and Europe's eastern borders.

Depending on whether one considers Frederick II's and Louis IX's subsequent staggered campaigns as either one or two separate Crusades, the number of historical Crusades reaches either seven or nine, ending in the late thirteenth century. However, even the most conservative of Crusade historians, such as Tyerman, are willing to extend these dates. In his largest monograph Tyerman argues that Pope Innocent XI's seventeenth-century Holy League war against the Ottoman Empire was the "last formal Crusade" (Tyerman, *God's War* 917). Perceived in this way, the term "tenth Crusade" refers to the notion that there are nine traditional premodern Crusades and that the tenth began with the US invasion of Afghanistan in early 2002.

While these distinctions may seem like parsing hairs to those outside the field of medieval historiography, these definitions matter if they are endowed with authority by those who develop them and who feel an intellectual right to protect them, inside academia and beyond. Yet these categorical and periodization models are also culturally and historically situated within academic norms, trends, and politics. Even Crusade historian Thomas Madden admits that after World War II, for instance, medieval scholars with a newfound aversion to fanatic ideology began to reexamine the Crusades as only nominally ideological and in actuality driven by economic concerns (Madden, *Crusades* 6). However, Madden does not suggest that he or his peers are similarly affected by current events, despite the fact that nearly every major Crusade history written within a decade after 9/11 mentions US conflicts in the Middle East.

Thomas Asbridge, for instance, neglects the correlation in his 2010 book in his closing chapter on contemporary Crusade rhetoric and the Iraq War, and he underscores the contemporary significance of his new interpretation of the Crusades as wars endowed with modern notions of "reciprocal violence," "diplomacy," and an affirmation of "the capacity of commercial interests to transcend the barriers of conflict" (Asbridge 680–81). Considering how institutional disciplines construct and maintain authority (note the term "Authoritative" in the title of Asbridge's book), literary theorist Stanley Fish argues, "Whatever account we have of a work or a period of the entire canon is an account that is possible or intelligible only within the assumptions embodied in current professional practice" (357). In this way, prominent medieval historians of the Crusades, such as Christopher Tyerman, Thomas Madden, Jonathan Riley-Smith, and others, frantically rushed to place limits on what is "possible or intelligible" regarding any scholarly or nonacademic analysis of the Crusades after September 11.

Of all the leading historians of the Crusades to engage with and critique metaphorical memories of the Crusades, Oxford historian Christopher Tyerman is the most impassioned. "To understand medieval crusading for itself and to explain its survival may be regarded as an urgent contemporary task," he argues, but "one for which *historians* must take responsibility," or else the history of the Crusades is doomed to lose its "objective precision in definition, practice, perception, or approval" (*Fighting for Christendom* 6, 10). Without the "objective precision" of an academically trained historian, Tyerman fears the Crusades will undergo the transformation from dead history to living memory, as already "the Crusades no longer just haunt the memory but stalk the streets of twenty-first century international politics, in particular in the Near East" (199). In short, for Tyerman, the distant past should never to be made practically relevant to present sociopolitical circumstances but should remain *in the past,* as he dictates: "There can be no summoning of the past to take sides in the present" (23).

The ferocity of Tyerman's critiques cannot be understated. Many of Tyerman's books on the Crusades published after 9/11 were repackaged and marketed in shorter, more accessible versions for nonspecialists, such as *The Crusades: A Very Short Introduction* (2006) and *The Crusades: A Brief Insight* (2009). Despite the fact that his books were themselves situated in a post-9/11 popular market interested in the Crusades in relation to present conflict, he critiques any texts or products about the Crusades created by nonacademics for the general reader. All nonacademic texts after 9/11 discussing Templar history, he argues in one of his books targeting a general audience, are "championed by obsessive, swivel-eyed anoraks and conspiracy theorists allied to cool money sharks bent on the commercial exploitation of public credulity. The popularity of such tabloid thinkers and the continuing attraction of their fantasies provide a subject for study on their own" (*Fighting for Christendom* 3–4).

While this essay is, in many ways, such a study, it instead aims to circumvent the kind of crude name-calling and pathologizing of the public that Tyerman engages in, in order to understand the characteristics of the contemporary moment that made Tyerman's writings—any writings on the Crusades—significant for so many. Indeed, I contend that academic dismissals like those from Tyerman reflect the voice of conservative factions, who, in Rorty's words,

> speak the old language and have no wish to change, those who regard it as a hallmark of rationality or morality to speak just that language, will regard as altogether *ir*rational the appeal of the new metaphors—the new language game which the radicals, the youth, or the avant-garde are playing … The question of why people speak this way will be treated as beneath the level of conversation—a matter to be turned over to psychologists or, if necessary, the police. (*Contingency* 48)

Tyerman is not the only contemporary Crusade historian to convey a stark, moralizing tone toward "irrational," nonacademic readers.

Like Tyerman, Thomas Madden, professor of history at Saint Louis University, saw his publications on the Crusades boom after 9/11. Unlike Tyerman, Madden directed his disdain for nonhistorians discussing the Crusades beyond academic book manuscripts to news sources and periodicals as early as November 2001. "So, what do the medieval crusades have to do with all this [US and Middle East relations after 9/11]? After all, doesn't the Muslim world have a right to be upset about the legacy of the crusades?" Madden asked readers of *The National Review* before answering his own questions, "Nothing and no" ("Crusade Propaganda"). In so doing, Madden suggests that the average American is (unsurprisingly) less fluent in medieval history than a trained historian. In his cynical assessment, he suggests, "Ask a random American about [the Crusades] and you are likely to see a face wrinkle in disgust, or just the blank stare that is usually evoked by events older than six weeks" ("Crusade Propaganda").

The following year, Madden brought his complaints to print in *American Outlook,* a periodical published by the Hudson Institute, a Washington, D.C.–based conservative think tank. In this piece, Madden provides a list of "the best" and "the worst" books on the Crusade, a necessary exercise in his mind because "the popular media resolutely ignore more recent studies, relying almost exclusively on … highly dated work" ("Crusades of History and Politics").[5] He praises his colleagues, most notably Jonathan Riley-Smith, while lambasting Tariq Ali's 2002 *The Clash of Fundamentalisms: Crusades, Jihads, and Modernity* as "a pitiful attempt to equate the Crusades with the centuries of jihads that caused them and the 'cultural imperialism' of the United States" and Karen Armstrong's 2001 revised version of *Holy War: The Crusades and Their Impact on Today's World* as "an exercise in modern left-wing rhetoric about sensitivity, tolerance, and the evils of Western civilization" ("Crusades of History and Politics").

For Madden, like Tyerman, all efforts to make the Crusades relevant to the present—whether by established historians or not—are either "pitiful attempts" or thinly veiled "left-wing rhetoric" (he notes from his article in a "right-wing" publication). Rather than waiting for the public to hear his critiques in his printed books, which came pouring out later that year, Madden attempted to silence metaphorical memories in the very public-facing venues he and Tyerman held in such contempt. What Madden and Tyerman do not seem to realize is that a denial of historical connection is *also* a form of memory politics, albeit one under the sign of a strategic amnesia.

The list of critiques by historians such as those offered by Tyerman and Madden is substantial. Jonathan Riley-Smith, while more tempered in his criticism of nonacademic Crusade discourse, was one of the first and loudest voices to disavow the notion that the Crusades have any claim to be a living memory today, especially for those in the Middle East. This is a response largely to Amin Maalouf's 1984 popular collection of Arab historical sources of the Crusades, *The Crusades through Arab Eyes,* which includes graphic accounts of medieval Crusader's acts of torture, killing, and cannibalism. Maalouf ends the volume with an epigraph claiming, "There can be no doubt that the schism between these two worlds [the Arab East and the West] dates from the Crusades, deeply felt by the Arabs, even today, as an act of rape" (266). Riley-Smith refutes this claim, which has been echoed in both academic and oral histories in the Middle East, that grievances from the Crusades have left a lingering sense of anti-Western sentiment.

In the second volume of *Crusades,* a journal launched just after 9/11, Riley-Smith dismisses the possibility of this living continuity, insisting, "nothing could be further from the truth" on the grounds that the first known Arab history of the Crusades did not appear in print until 1890 (167). Of course, oral history is not bound to the printing press, and there is no shortage of Crusader castles, statues of famous anti-Crusader heroes like Saladin, and other "sites of memory" throughout the Middle East, in the Levantine states in particular. Suggesting that the first printed Crusader history written by an Arab historian marks the beginning of a cultural memory of the Crusades not only is misleading but reinforces the Western academic legitimacy placed on printed, authoritative sources rather than understandings of the past carried on in alternative or popular forms. Here again, the attack on cultural memory counts as a form of memory politics.

Nevertheless, Riley-Smith is one of the few Crusade historians mentioned here who attempts to escort the discourse beyond institutional norms to acknowledge the cultural, political, and practical resonance of metaphorical memories. "It is somewhat pedantic," he acknowledges, "to engage in argument whether the policies of the developed world are 'crusading' or not. Disputes about the terms we employ will not alter the fact that a very large number of people in the Islamic world, moderates as well as extremists, are attached to a history which satisfies their feeling of both superiority and humiliation" (167).

Along these lines, popular interest in the Crusades in the contemporary Islamic world, the United States, and beyond has created a mass market for the publications produced by scholars of the Crusades. Yet by denying—indeed, ridiculing—the metaphorical impulses that drew readers to their historical writings, many modern historians of the Crusades in fact lost the audiences they were trying to persuade, individuals and groups seeking stories of the past to contextualize and come to terms with living memories in the present. The examples from historians outlined above underscore the ontological confusion between literal and metaphorical, history and memory, along with a fundamental misunderstanding of how individuals present the past through figurative devices for practical, cognitive purposes. Yet others were willing to supply metaphorical memories of the Crusades under the banner of historiography to fill the void so staunchly guarded by academic historians.

POPULAR HISTORIOGRAPHY "FILLS THE VOID"

Cultural historian Peter Knight argues that the rise of alternative histories and conspiracy theories in the United States in the latter half of the twentieth century is due, in part, to "a widespread loss of faith in the 'sophisticated social scientists' themselves, as well as their model of historical causation" (10). In a similar way, the treatment of Crusade metaphorical memories as conspiratorial and invalid after 9/11 reinforced a certain turning away from academic authorities toward alternative sources willing to engage in popular debates.

As a result, the academic discussion was effectively silenced and relegated to journalism (Minugh) and the blogosphere for a number of years,[6] until being carried into popular and often inflammatory historical narratives such as Robert Spencer's *New York Times* best seller *The Politically Incorrect Guide to Islam (and the Crusades)* and Rodney Stark's *God's Battalions: The Case for the Crusades.* By refusing to acknowledge the popular adoption of post-9/11 Crusades metaphorical memories, questions about possible continuities with the present, and conspiracy theories as legitimate forms of cultural knowledge and historical understanding (however inaccurate they may turn out to be), many scholars of the Crusades made themselves inaccessible to American audiences. Instead, they surrendered their authoritative voices to popular realms and digital media that make it possible to establish a historical authority outside of academia proper.

Spencer and Stark both argue that 9/11, and even the Crusades, are indicative of an earlier Ur-conflict between Islam and Christianity, between East and West. At these moments, they draw heavily on the "clash of civilizations" discourse generated by Bernard Lewis and Samuel Huntington in the 1990s. Lewis, a preeminent historian and critic of the contemporary Muslim world, first introduced the notion of a cultural incompatibility between the modern East and West, destined to result in conflict, in his *Atlantic Monthly* article "The Roots of Muslim Rage" (1990). Samuel Huntington later bolstered Lewis's theory in his book *The Clash of Civilizations and the Remaking of World Order* (1996), which also argues that this fundamental "clash" between Western and Eastern civilizations will only be alleviated by Easterners adopting modern, Western ideology.[7]

Robert Spencer is a popular anti-Islamic author and blogger as well as the director of the anti-Islamic website *Jihad Watch*. In 2005, he published *The Politically Incorrect Guide to Islam (and the Crusades)*, part of a larger series that follows the style of the popular *Complete Idiot's Guide* and *For Dummies* series that simplify complex topics and histories for nonexpert audiences. Spencer's book outlines his six key arguments on the front cover with crucifix-shaped bullet points, alongside a photo of a masked militant in camouflage sporting an assault rifle, presumably one of the contemporary "jihad terrorists" the book continually insists are the true face of Islam. The parenthetical title itself, "and the Crusades," bridges the past and present, suggesting that an understanding of Islam and the Crusades are interconnected.

Similarly, the front cover implies that the reader may *think* they know about Islam and the Crusades, yet perhaps upturns their former suppositions by insisting that Crusades were *defensive* conflicts, that Muslim "persecution of Christians has continued for 13 centuries—and still goes on," and that "Today's jihad terrorists have the same motives and goals as the foes of the Crusades." Even a cursory glance at Spencer's initial provocations shows his attempt to bridge the Crusader past with contemporary conflict, albeit with misguided and abhorrent implications for inciting ongoing violence in the present. The Crusade "still goes on," the book jacket informs the casual observer, a claim of historical continuity strictly forbidden by the historians mentioned in the previous section. If you want to understand *why*—why Islamic terrorists attack civilians, such as seen in the 9/11 attacks—the answers are revealed in the crusading past, as "the motives and goals" (back cover) of medieval and modern jihadists are the same, Spencer promises.

The book as a whole is riddled with anti-Islamic, xenophobic, and racist claims, too many to count and too unwholesome to dwell upon. Nevertheless, hundreds of thousands of readers *did* dwell on them—or at least purchased the book, as published book lists like the *New York Times* show. One of Spencer's more striking claims concerns revising traditional notions of what constitutes a "Crusade." This definitional intervention contradicts all of the historians listed above, as Spencer insists that the Crusades be defined as any defensive (or preemptive) strike against an Islamic group, such that the first Crusade actually began four hundred years earlier than 1095, with the rise of Islam itself (xvi). Moreover, Spencer argues that the spread of Islam is an inherently violent act, and so preventing countries—especially the United States and European countries—from reaching an untenable state of Islamic majority *in the future* also falls under the definition of a "Crusade," an interpretation advanced in a terrifying way by Norwegian terrorist Anders Breivik, who cited Spencer heavily in his online manifesto.

Spencer's book was successful in reaching its audience, in part due to the way he places his narrative in contradiction to authoritative histories of the Crusades, as an alternative or supplemental resource for readers who find Tyerman's and Madden's tomes inaccessible or limited in their direct connections to contemporary concerns. "Most textbooks and popular history books," the back cover also argues, "are written by left-wing academics and Islamic apologists who justify their contemporary political agendas with contrived historical 'facts.'" Interestingly, as shown in the previous section, many of the mainstream Crusade academics self-fashion themselves as conservative, in their political leanings, attitudes toward historiographical norms, or both. Either way, Spencer's rhetorical move here is to quickly discount the contemporary archive of academic Crusader historiography, promising the reader that his book holds "all the information you need to understand the *true nature* of the global conflict America faces today" (back cover; my emphasis).

Rodney Stark, a professor of sociology at Baylor University, followed suit five years after Spencer with *God's Battalions: The Case for the Crusades.* Although an academic and self-identified "sociologist of religion," Stark paradoxically seems to draw credit from the fact that he has *not* devoted his career to studying the Crusades. He notes that to cite all the sources for his book would result in a list that "would take most of a page," a page he is unwilling to produce. "I'm one of *you*," Stark implies with these insertions, "and like you, dear reader, I have not time or interest in mundane citations or academic-ese." Instead, he promises to "synthesize the work of these specialists into a more comprehensive perspective, written in prose that is accessible to the general reader" (9).

At first glance, Stark's book—from its binding, cover image, and aesthetics—looks similar to the manuscripts published by historians of the Crusades mentioned previously. In these passages, however, Stark makes clear that his value lies in the ability to synthesize complex ideas and, indeed, to helpfully introduce readers to historiographic norms. He shares with the reader that he is always "careful to fully acknowledge the contributions of the many experts on whom I have depended, some in the text and the rest in endnotes" (9), drawing on the authority of academic conventions more than Spencer does, for instance.

Yet despite stylistic, aesthetic, and generic differences, Spencer and Stark's historical claims and arguments share a remarkable number of similarities, and Stark even duplicates at least 251 quoted passages found in Spencer's earlier book.[8] Both produce self-consciously conservative and right-wing revisions to what Stark perceives to be a post-9/11, liberal, "cynical and sinister explanation of the Crusades [that] has gained popularity ... in the immediate aftermath of the destruction of the World Trade Center by Muslim terrorists" (4). Like Spencer, Stark refutes "most conventional Crusade historians" by arguing that the Crusades actually began "with the rise of Islam and the onset of the Muslim invasions of Christendom" four hundred years earlier (9).[9]

The success of Spencer's and Stark's books is due, in part, to their willingness to engage in creative—if overextended—exercises in historical continuity, figurative language, and counterfactual thinking, thus making the past practically relevant for political decision making in the present. The Crusades ended, Stark regrets, not because the original goals had been met but because of taxpayer "grumbling [which] grew increasingly louder when bloody 'crusades' began against 'heretics' in Europe [and] a *medieval version of an antiwar movement* eventually prevailed; after two centuries of support, the kingdoms in the Holy Land were abandoned" (238).

Just as the Crusades were cut unfairly short by a lack of popular support, he suggests, modern, US-led Crusades in the Middle East run the risk of being forestalled if readers fail to remember this lesson and counteract modern *antiwar movements* (238). Similarly, Stark reminds his American readers that Crusade kingdoms "had survived, at least along the coast, for nearly as long as the United States has been a nation" (245). In metaphorical moves like this, Stark, like Spencer, invokes American nationalism to compare the United States to a Crusader state and beseeches his audience to remember that the United States could also risk being "lost" to Muslims if not defended through tax-based military spending.

Finally, Stark and Spencer both grab their readers' imaginations with counterfactual thought experiments, an analytical practice scorned by many contemporary historians as "epistemological slumming" (Tetlock and Belkin 37). However, while the practice of imagining "what if" may be condemned in contemporary historiography, "the business of imagining such counterfactuals is a vital part of the way in which we learn," argues conservative historian Niall Ferguson, "because decisions about the future are—usually—based on weighing up the potential consequences of alternative courses of action, [and] it makes sense to compare the actual outcomes of what we did in the past with the conceivable outcomes of what we might have done" (2).

Stark and Spencer, indulging their readers in the cognitive work of counterfactual thinking, both cite a thought experiment by eighteenth-century historian Edward Gibbon, who suggested that "if Charles Martel hadn't defeated the Saracens in the Battle of Tours, students at Oxford would be scrutinizing the Qur'an rather than the Bible" (470). Stark and Spencer argue that remembering and practicing this thought experiment and the history it draws upon is fundamental for their readers, and each author proposes his own counterfactuals (Stark 43; Spencer 63).

In the chapter section "The Crusade We Must Fight Today," for instance, Spencer repeats his warning that the United States, along with the entire Western world, is at serious risk of being dominated by Muslims (by which he also means terrorists) in the near future. Drawing upon Gibbon's example, Spencer outlines his own counterfactual visions by demanding all Muslim groups in America explicitly "renounce, in word and in deed, any intention now or in the future to replace the Constitution of the United States with Islamic *sharia*" (230). Like the metaphors employed by these authors, this creative cognitive act of counterfactual thinking—while patently prejudiced, xenophobic, and alarmist—is nevertheless supplied to a readership searching for an imagined Crusader past mediated through figurative language and imaginative work, something leading Crusade historians refused to provide.

In the end, Stark and Spencer succeed in bringing metaphorical memories of modern "Crusades" into printed histories with various authoritative currencies. A good deal of the success of these two books is arguably due to their willingness to engage in creative counterfactual thinking and to respond to a popular desire for practical, metaphorical memories of the Crusades when other historians of the Crusades refused. However, by broadening the definition of a Crusade to the degree of justifying any attack—preemptive or otherwise—against adherents of Islam who threaten Christian dominance of the Western hemisphere, these authors have also contributed to a terrifying rhetorical environment where "holy war," "jihad," and "Crusade" are reduced to a single deployable currency, one that is brimming with ire and violence but bankrupt in lessons from the past that lead toward any sense of tolerance or understanding. In my conclusion, I argue that this situation holds a lesson for memory agents in contemporary mediascapes.

THE JANUS-FACED POTENTIAL OF METAPHORICAL MEMORIES

While making the past practical for the present is a natural cognitive act, this is not to say that it contains an inherent good. Indeed, some of the worst atrocities in recorded history have been justified as retaliations or continuations of previous acts of violence. In the extreme, texts like Stark's and Spencer's have the damaging potential to encourage renewed violence through their propagation of racist and xenophobic ideas.

On 22 July 2011, Anders Behring Breivik electronically distributed his manifesto, *2083: A European Declaration of Independence,* hours before killing eight people in a bombing of government buildings in Oslo, Norway and shooting dead sixty-nine people on the nearby island Utøya. The brutal shootings and bombing of innocent civilians were meant to punish liberal Norwegian citizens and decision makers who were not recognizing the "Crusade" to keep Muslims and Islamic influence out of Europe. In his manifesto, Breivik illustrated the dark potential of metaphorical memories of the medieval Crusades and supported his rambling, often incoherent thesis by drawing heavily from authors like Spencer.

Most of the authoritative historians of the Crusades mentioned in this essay, namely Tyerman and Riley-Smith, do not appear anywhere in *2083*. Breivik also had alleged ties to a contemporary Islamophobic British organization calling itself "the Knights Templar" (Bright). Months after Breivik's crimes, Britain's home secretary made membership to the Islamist group

Muslims against the Crusades illegal, claiming that the group was a suc-
cessor to and front for the already banned Islam4UK and other proscribed
terrorist organizations (Casciani).

These examples illustrate a central insight of memory studies: that the
past can be made into metaphorical memories that can be mobilized to
justify actions in the present. This process, traced briefly in this essay, offers two urgent challenges to those who represent events from the past that
are deemed relevant to the present or near future. First, to recognize that
figurative language like metaphors may indeed distract from rigid historiographical goals if it is misunderstood as an attribute of fiction and enemy
of the "truth." Second, to underscore the fact that metaphorical memories
of the past that emphasize conflict resolution and nonviolence are desper-
ately needed in the contemporary media ecology as counterpoints to the
vicious and damaging rhetoric that individuals like Breivik draw upon and
propagate.

While this essay urges contemporary historians to take up these challenges, it is not meant as a wholehearted critique of the practice of objec-
tively driven historiography itself. As Rorty mischievously reminds us, "Every
sparkling metaphor requires a lot of stodgy literal talk to serve as its foil"
(*Contingency* 42). However, in the end, not only are harsh academic condemnations of popular thinking practices ineffective, but as this essay has shown,
they can have an equally impassioned and opposite effect.

In the social and cultural climate of terrorism and so-called clashes of
civilizations in the twenty-first century, the bulk of Crusading rhetoric certainly falls short of historiographical standards. Yet we can study *why* that is
the case and trace the effects such precedents may evoke as a fundamental
step toward understanding past and future cultural encounters between the
United States and the Middle East. In one sense, it is perhaps unsurprising that the popular American imagination of the Crusades has remained
understudied for so long, as the cultural "texts" displaying it are either sur-
rounded by other vibrant metaphorical frames, considered unworthy objects of study, or discarded as mere fleeting cultural ephemera. Historical
inaccuracies and conspiratorial ephemera, however seemingly anecdotal,
deserve to be studied as an integral part of memory culture and placed
within a larger cultural framework.

Constructing, framing, and ordering narratives of the past are essential
parts of working through traumatic events (Johnsrud, "Putting the Pieces
Together"). Yet the imaginative impulse surrounding popular histories, novels, films, and speeches does more than draw from and reflect an existing
cultural milieu of trauma and representation in a sort of feedback loop. In
terms of Hayden White's conception of "linguistic protocols," metaphorical

memories of the Crusades after 9/11 challenge academic historians' limits of what is "thinkable" by creating new linguistic protocols to characterize the past's relationship with the present *"in their own terms"* (30). Rather than outsourcing that historical engagement to professional academics, these acts of metaphorical memory create new cognitive and historical frameworks that encourage nonacademics to engage in the work of introducing the past to the present to–hopefully–imagine a better future.

Brian Johnsrud is the codirector of the Poetic Media Lab at Stanford University and a researcher in the Center for Spatial and Textual Analysis. His interdisciplinary research combines anthropology and literary and media studies to examine how narratives of the past are mediated in ways that inspire action in the present. His current project examines how Crusade metaphors were employed in the United States and the Middle East after 9/11.

NOTES

1. The Crusades were surely not the only metaphor used to grapple with 9/11 and the ensuing War on Terror. Journey, travel, and roadmap metaphors, for instance, abound in the 2002 US-led "Road Map to a Permanent Two-State Solution to the Israeli-Palestinian Conflict," which was in many ways a primer to the new post-9/11 global political arena (Semino 110).
2. These remarks and other examples of popular Crusade metaphors are quoted in Holsinger.
3. Most notably, Ridley Scott's *Kingdom of Heaven* (2005); Peter Flinth's *Arn: The Knight Templar* (2007); BBC's three-part series *The Crusades* (2012); and Ubisoft's video game *Assassin's Creed* (2007), which is brimming with highly produced cinematic cut scenes and set to be produced as a film in 2016.
4. In fact, George W. Bush did claim, on multiple occasions, that his decision to invade Iraq resulted, in part, from divine inspiration and God "speaking" to him.
5. Ironically, the first selection in his "the best" list is also the most "dated" (Hilaire Belloc's 1937 *The Crusades: The World's Debate*).
6. See especially www.uscrusade.com and Matthew Gabriel's blog modernmedie val.blogspot.com.
7. The vagueness of the term "Western ideology" is used intentionally here to reflect its uncertain and problematic use by Lewis, Huntington, and the rest of the "clash of civilizations" devotees.
8. I created this count using digitized copies of each text run through the text analysis software Novus Scan.
9. Despite these parallels in argument, numerous shared quotations, and identical revisionist timelines tied to contemporary politics, Stark, in his bibliography,

leaves Spencer's earlier book conspicuously absent; he is apparently willing to share ideas but not professional association.

WORKS CITED

Asbridge, Thomas. *The Crusades: The Authoritative History of the War for the Holy Land.* New York: Ecco, 2010.

Belloc, Hilaire. *The Crusades: The World's Debate.* Rockford: Tan Books, 1992.

Bright, Arthur. "Why Does Norway's Breivik Invoke the Knights Templar?" *Christian Science Monitor.* 12 Apr. 2012. Web. 28 Mar. 2014.

Brown, Dan. *The Lost Symbol.* New York: Anchor, 2010.

Bush, George W. "Public Papers of the Presidents of the United States, George W. Bush, 2002, Bk. 1, January 1 to June 30, 2002." Washington, D.C.: US Government Printing Office, 2005.

——. "Remarks by the President Upon Arrival." *The White House Archives.* 14 Sept. 2001. Web. 20 Mar. 2014.

Casciani, Dominic. "Muslims against Crusades Banned by Theresa May." *BBC News.* 10 Nov. 2010. Web. 28 Mar. 2014.

Claster, Jill N. *Sacred Violence: The European Crusades to the Middle East, 1095–1396.* Toronto: University of Toronto Press, 2009.

Cohen, Ted. "Metaphor and the Cultivation of Intimacy." *On Metaphor.* Ed. Sheldon Sacks. Chicago: University of Chicago Press, 1978. 1–10.

"Crusade." *Oxford Dictionaries.* Oxford: Oxford University Press. Web. 3 Sept. 2014.

"Erik Prince and the Last Crusade." *The Economist.* 6 Aug. 2009. Web. 28 Mar. 2014.

Erll, Astrid, and Ansgar Nünning. *A Companion to Cultural Memory Studies.* Berlin: De Gruyter, 2010.

Ferguson, Niall. "Virtual History: Towards a 'Chaotic' Theory of the Past." *Virtual History: Alternatives and Counterfactuals.* Ed. Niall Ferguson. New York: Basic Books, 1997. 1–90.

Fish, Stanley. "Profession Despise Thyself: Fear and Self-loathing in Literary Studies." *Critical Inquiry* 10.2 (1983): 349–64.

Gibbon, Edward. *The Decline and Fall of the Roman Empire, Volume 6.* London: JF Dove, 1821.

Haydock, Nickolas, and Edward L. Risden. *Hollywood in the Holy Land: Essays on Film Depictions of the Crusades and Christian-Muslim Clashes.* Jefferson: McFarland, 2009.

Holsinger, Bruce. *Neomedievalism, Neoconservativism, and the War on Terror.* Chicago: Prickly Paradigm Press, 2007.

Huntington, Samuel P. *The Clash of Civilizations and the Remaking of World Order.* New York: Simon & Schuster, 1996.

Jameson, Fredric. "The End of Temporality." *Critical Inquiry* 29.4 (2003): 695–718.

Johnsrud, Brian. "The Adoption of Crusade Imagery by U.S. Soldiers in Afghanistan and Iraq after 9/11." US Air Force Academy, Colorado Springs. Sept. 2010. Lecture.

——. "The Da Vinci Code, Crusade Conspiracies, and the Clash of Historiographies." *Conspiracy Theories in the United States and the Middle East: A Comparative Approach.* Ed. Michael Butter and Maurus Reinkowski. Berlin: De Gruyter, 2014. 100–20.

——. "Putting the Pieces Together Again: Digital Photography and the Compulsion to Order Violence at Abu Ghraib." *Visual Studies* 26.2 (2011): 154–68.

Knight, Peter. *Conspiracy Culture: From Kennedy to the X Files.* New York: Routledge, 2001.

Leung, Rebecca. "The Holy Warrior: General Called a Religious Fanatic Finally Speaks Out." *CBS News.* 15 Sept. 2004. Web. 28 Mar. 2014.

Lewis, Bernard. "The Roots of Muslim Rage." *Atlantic Monthly.* Sept. 1990. Web. 25 Oct. 2014.

Maalouf, Amin. *The Crusades through Arab Eyes.* Trans. Jon Rothschild. New York: Schocken, 1984.

Madden, Thomas. "Crusade Propaganda: The Abuse of Christianity's Holy Wars." *National Review.* 2 Nov. 2001. Web. 28 Mar. 2014.

——. "Crusades of History and Politics." *Sagamore Institute.* 1 Jun. 2002. Web. 28 Mar. 2014.

——. *The Crusades: The Essential Readings.* Ed. Thomas Madden. Oxford: Malden, 2002.

Minugh, David. "George Bush and the Last Crusade or the Fight for Truth, Justice and the American Way." *Language and Computers* 61 (2007): 191–205.

Nora, Pierre. "Between Memory and History: Les Lieux De Mémoire." *Representations* 26 (1989): 7–25.

Oakeshott, Michael. *On History and Other Essays.* Indianapolis: Liberty Fund, 1983.

Olick, Jeffrey K., Vered Vinitzky-Seroussi, and Daniel Levy, eds. *The Collective Memory Reader.* Oxford: Oxford Universuty Press, 2011.

Radstone, Susannah, and Bill Schwarz, eds. *Memory: Histories, Theories, Debates.* New York: Fordham University Press, 2010.

Riley-Smith, Jonathan. "Islam and the Crusades in History and Imagination: 8 November 1898–11 September 2001." *Crusades* 2 (2003): 151–67.

Rorty, Richard. *Contingency, Irony, and Solidarity.* Cambridge: Cambridge University Press, 1989.

——. "Philosophy as Science, as Metaphor, and as Politics." *The Rorty Reader.* Ed. Christopher J. Voparil and Richard J. Bernstein. Chichester: Wiley-Blackwell, 2010. 211–26.

Rumsfeld, Donald. "Abu Musab al-Zarqawi Killed in Airstirke; Rumsfeld Hold Press Briefing." *CNN.com.* 8 Jun. 2006. Web. 28 Mar. 2014.

——. "Senate Appropriations Committee–Defense." *Defense.gov.* US Department of Defense, 7 Apr. 2005. Web. 28 Mar. 2014.

Sand, Shlomo. *The Invention of the Jewish People.* New York: Verso, 2009.

Semino, Elena. *Metaphor in Discourse.* Cambridge: Cambridge University Press, 2008.

Spencer, Robert. *The Politically Incorrect Guide to Islam (and the Crusades).* Washington, D.C.: Regnery, 2005.

Stark, Rodney. *God's Battalions: The Case for the Crusades.* New York: HarperOne, 2009.

Tetlock, Philip E., and Aaron Belkin. "Counterfactual Thought Experiments in World Politics: Logical, Methodological, and Psychological Perspectives." *Counterfactual Thought Experiments in World Politics: Logical, Methodological, and Psychological Perspectives.* Ed. Philip E. Tetlock and Aaron Belkin. Princeton: Princeton University Press, 1996. 1–38.

Tyerman, Christopher. *Fighting for Christendom: Holy War and the Crusades.* Oxford: Oxford University Press, 2004.

——. *God's War: A New History of the Crusades.* Cambridge: Harvard University Press, 2006.

——. "Modern Crusade Historiography." Hertford College. Feb. 2008. Lecture.

White, Hayden. *Metahistory: The Historical Imagination in Nineteenth Century Europe.* Baltimore: Johns Hopkins University Press, 1975.

Wolfowitz, Paul D. "Deputy Secretary Wolfowitz Interview with Indonesian Television." *Defense.gov.* US Department of Defense 28 Nov. 2001. Web. 28 Mar. 2014.

——. "Deputy Secretary Wolfowitz: Interview with London *Sunday Telegraph.*" *Defense.gov.* US Department of Defense 26 Oct. 2001. Web. 28 Mar. 2014.

——. "The Gathering Storm: The Threat of Global Terror and Asia/Pacific Security." *Defense.gov.* US Department of Defense 1 Jun. 2002. Web. 28 Mar. 2014.

——. Hoover Institution Transcript of Remarks by Paul Wolfowitz at Willard Hotel 5 Jun. 2002. Web. 28 Mar. 2014.

Part IV

Transdisciplinary Memory

Chapter 10

The Agency of Memory Objects

Tracing Memories of Soweto at Regina Mundi Church

Frauke Wiegand

◈

REMEMBERING APARTHEID IN SOWETO

Since the fall of apartheid, South Africa has witnessed an inflationary construction of public commemorative sites and sights, a process that is significantly fuelled by the heritage tourism industry (Marschall 99). This leads
to ever more "memorial upgrades," not least in the townships' urban landscapes, where the "memory boom" often focuses on physical markers of
the liberation struggle (Hlongwane 138). Soweto's "tourism reflexivity," as
Mimi Sheller and John Urry call the global monitoring and development of
a place's touristic potential (3), is booming, particularly since the 2010 FIFA
World Cup that took place in South Africa; theme park–like memory sites
have been established, such as Vilakazi Road, which commemorates the 16
June 1976 uprisings.[1]

In many places this development seems to culminate in monument fa-
tigue on the part of the visitors, who no longer see the past for the monuments (Huyssen, "Monumental Seduction"). In other places, such as the
exhibition discussed in this essay, the unexpected meeting with others' pasts
and memories leads to more dynamic forms of commemoration that are
constantly reanchored in the present. Soweto offers a shifting "memory
assemblage" (Macdonald; Reading) of sights and oversights—a mixture of
celebrated, highly visible, and overlooked or even forgotten everyday memorials and places of memory that are recorded in tourists' photo albums, dis-

tributed on platforms online, sent via email, or digitally shared with family and friends. The essay examines this increasing mobility of memory objects at sites of memory and scrutinizes their mediation in yet new memories, as tourist souvenirs, through a transdisciplinary approach that introduces actor-network theory to the established methodologies of memory studies.

The article zooms in on the site of the small photographic exhibition "The Story of Soweto" and its mediations via tourist snapshots. This exhibition is a rather unimposing documentary exhibition on the balcony of Regina Mundi Church, the oldest Roman Catholic Church in Soweto, which once was a strategic site for the antiapartheid liberation struggle and now serves as a forum for the commemoration of its victims and heroes. Photographs (mainly black-and-white and a few in color) by famous South African photographers Bob Gosani, Jürgen Schadeberg, Jodi Bieber, and Bongani Mnguni are assembled on simple, white, movable walls, displaying everyday life and the joys and struggles of Soweto from the 1950s to the present. Moving closer, one detects the unusual texture of the not so white walls, which are scribbled over and over with notes and names, dates and remarks about the exhibition, South African history, different Black consciousness movements, worldwide freedom struggles, Nelson Mandela, God, and religion as well as local soccer team cheers, declarations of love, and name tags.

These layers of different materials and accounts from different times highlight the palimpsestic nature of memory work at the exhibition space, recalling Huyssen's characterization of the city as a palimpsest "being rewritten while previous text is preserved, traces are restored, erasures documented, all of it resulting in a complex web of historical markers that point to the continuing heterogenous life" of a mnemonic site (*Present Pasts* 81). My focus on the dynamic nature of the memory work at play in the exhibition ties in with recent calls in memory studies to recognize "the superimposition and productive interaction of different inscriptions and the spatialization of time central to the work of memory" (Silverman 4) by finding ways to map the transmedial and transcultural nature of histories and memories and the practices of remembering and remediation tied to them (Erll and Rigney).

My analysis departs from people's ordinary interactions with and appropriations of traces of the past, particularly the past of others as encountered on a tourist trip. Visitors' photo albums of the exhibition and their memories of the visit at Regina Mundi Church as well as my own observations at the site build the background against which the dynamics of this Sowetan memory assemblage are analyzed.[2] The essay follows the ways in which cultural memory is formed through people's ordinary appropriations of objects, sites, and texts of memory; it examines how memorial sites and objects are taken in, transformed, and mediated in everyday life by a range of different people. Additionally, it shows how the new accounts stemming from these encounters feed back into the life and materiality of memories and thereby change the remembrance of, for example, the antiapartheid liberation struggle or postcolonial Africa in transnational discourses.

Sites and objects of memory evoke different perceptions and appropriations. An event or experience made physically manifest by a marked memorial site or object of some kind may be transformed and reevaluated through the acts that give meaning to it and the media in which it is represented. No matter how concrete mnemonic products may be, Jeffrey K. Olick writes, "they gain their reality only by being used, interpreted, and reproduced or changed" (158). Traces of the past are appropriated and transformed in everyday life by a range of different people, both consciously and unconsciously. These inventions take the form of participatory interactions with sites and objects of memory and the cultural forms that mediate and distribute them. They make memory truly transcultural and transmedial.

Tourist accounts reveal how the pasts and memories of others are woven into the tourist's own memorable experience. This is not to imply that every tourist visiting a place and learning about the past is struck by the same events, records the encounter on a range of media, or necessarily becomes a "critical reader" of memory (Bal x). Nor is it sufficient to say that all cultural heritage tourism is simply a form of commodification that has nothing to do with "real" remembrance, a ready-to-consume package of a nation's history that has no impact on its visitors' lives. The relevance and resonance of the tourist experience and the memories it mediates lie somewhere in between the critical and the commodified positions.

In what follows, I use an interpretive framework inspired by actor-network theory (ANT) as developed in Bruno Latour's *Reassembling the Social* (2005), which has in recent years become increasingly influential in the social sciences and the humanities, to demonstrate that tourist accounts may act as mediators setting into motion what an encountered "memory actor," an account or object mediated at a memory site, can mean to other actors in the present. This increasing transmedial and transcultural mobility of memories also requires a research methodology that actively seeks to combine different research tools across disciplines, in this case sociology, anthropology, and visual culture studies.

The methodology that informed the findings of my research in and around Soweto is similar to what Gillian Rose and Divya Tolia-Kelly describe as the "situated eye," "an attunement to the collective, multiple and embodied textures, sensibilities, and productive meanings of the visual through the material, and vice versa" (4–5). I will approach the dynamic of the Sowetan memory assemblage that is initiated and embedded in Regina

Mundi's small exhibition by zooming in on different tourist snapshots and series of snapshots of the space visited. These mundane photographic memories project the photographs and scribbled walls beyond the exhibition space, becoming proper agents of memory themselves, in line with Ariella Azoulay's call for an alternative to the privileged notion of the human agent (the photographer) at the expense of other actors in the event of photography ("Photography" 65). As will be shown, it is especially the material photograph, the wider photographed scene, and the photograph's reintegration in different contexts of reception that is of importance for the dynamics of cultural memory.

Doubtless, the layers of community affiliations tied to different cultural memories are particularly complex in the case I am discussing, as different imaginaries overlap in the tourist experience of South African memoryscapes. Next to the many local practices commemorating the traumatic colonial and apartheid past and the liberation struggle, there is still a tourist imaginary building on a century-old colonial mindset with problematic projections of Africa as Europe's exotic Other (Behdad; Salazar and Graburn). Rather than merely exploring the problematic representation and reproduction of stereotypes and their impact on a colonial cultural memory that has been discussed in postcolonial tourism studies (Wiegand and Knapp), this essay starts from the site of the single memory object, asking how a tourist photograph may function as both a material image and a mnemonic medium and how it acts on the images and imaginaries at play.

Tourism is one of the first practices that comes to mind when we think of a privileged gaze, of the right of the spectator, as Ariella Azoulay explains in *Civil Imagination,* to view others' traumas and difficult pasts (1). Tourism is, moreover, almost unthinkable without the snapshot, the taking of photographs, which, in the case discussed here, includes photographing photographs and visual remnants of others. On the privileged stage of heritage tourism, the visitor's photograph can and does develop a life of its own and adds to the life of the memory inherent to the cultural forms encountered and appropriated on tour, such as the exhibited photograph of a scene of struggle or liberation.

SEQUENCING REGINA MUNDI:
A PHOTO ALBUM CHRONOLOGY

A typical photo album chronology of a tourist's visit to the church (based on an analysis of Flickr and Picasa web albums as well as private collections made available to me) starts with a snapshot of the church from outside. If visitors take a tour of the church with one of the tour guides, the series is followed by photos of the church's physical marks and visible "wounds" from the liberation struggle that the guide introduces: a broken piece of the altar or bullet holes in the roof and windows of the church; further landmarks are the Black Madonna painting and the guestbook showing the signatures of Nelson Mandela and Barack and Michelle Obama. After the tour, the guide usually tells visitors that they are free to visit the exhibition on the balcony. Unaccompanied by the guide and his stories, visitors then choose which photos to take of the exhibition, and, for example, which captions to frame.

Their photo series often start with a snapshot of the information plaque naming the title of the exhibition, its background, and its sponsors—even if this plaque is hardly legible because of the intense tagging. It is typically followed by an image of one of the displayed photographs—most favored are Jürgen Schadeberg's Sophiatown photograph "We Won't Move" (1955) and Schadeberg's "Mandela in His Cell" (1994) in Robben Island (see also Illustrations 10.3 and 10.4). Interestingly, the subsequent photos in the album, often making up the majority of the images, are details of the scribbled walls, close-up views of individual comments or comment narratives, and notes commenting on photos.

I will focus on two aspects of this memory assemblage that become apparent when visiting the site and following its journeys through other media: first, the mobility and transformation of the photographic displays through visitors' appropriations, and, second, the shifting stories told by the sketches on the walls.

POPULATING PHOTOGRAPHS:
TAKING VISUAL WITNESSES ALONG

Tourist photographs feed into the circulating vision and memory of a place or an image. They tell us a variety of things about its author, the time they were taken, the things and people they display, and their agency at large. They reveal what mattered to their author in a certain situation, what looked interesting and was thought to make a memorable impression or can best capture the experience a person had in a particular place. Likewise, and importantly for this essay, they reveal how the photographed scene or actors present in the field of vision caught the photographer's attention, attracted her gaze, and drew her in. Furthermore, a photograph is a stage for everything that was present but unnoticed in the moment the photograph was taken and only potentially noticed at a later point.

These characteristics of the event of photography are of peculiar interest for the dynamics of memory in the exhibition at Regina Mundi, demonstrating the different stages of what Azoulay calls the "activating gesture" of photography ("Photography" 66). This gesture is an act not only of the photographer but of the photographed scene or the material photograph itself. Azoulay promotes photography as "an ontology of the many, operating in public, in motion. It is an ontology bound to the manner in which human beings exist—look, talk, act—with one another and *with objects*" (71; emphasis in original). The photographic memories in and of the exhibition have no end; they are continuously forming new relations.

One visitor's series includes different snapshots of Jürgen Schadeberg's photograph "Avoiding the Pass" (1954), which shows two black men seemingly hiding behind a wall in Johannesburg downtown when two white police officers are approaching.[3] The photographer first captures the whole photograph using a flashlight. As if to improve the image (the camera screen probably revealed the white flashlight bulb mark in the middle of the image), she then captures the same detail without using a flash—with the effect that she is now visible in the act of taking the photograph as a reflection in the glass frame. She finally takes a photo of the photograph's caption, a plaque naming the photographer, title, and year and giving a few words about the people and incident displayed.

In all three photos, bits of extra light and other situational details are written onto the image; in many other similar images of different photographs in the exhibition taken by other visitors, we see blue and yellow reflections of the church windows on the glass frames, reflections of the photographer or other visitors, and flashlight bulbs in the middle of the picture: the original image gets crowded as it gathers experiences, people, and looks, and its texture changes. By appropriating a photo in the exhibition and combining it with other images and impressions in another place, like an online photo album of a trip, the tourist's experience is coacting in this memory assemblage.

As Jean-Luc Nancy writes, "The image touches me, and thus touched and drawn by it and into it, I get involved, not to say mixed up in it. There is no image without my too being in this image" (7). The photographic display as captured in a tourist's image is given a place in the present situation and in encounters with future spectators. All images of images are therefore recontextualizations, appropriations of some earlier or even original image in the life of the photograph, photographer, or spectator. To cite Azoulay again, "The encounter with the photograph continues the event of photography which happened elsewhere" ("Photography" 75).

Furthermore, the represented content of the image connects to other representations of the same image or scene, transforms them, adds to them, and reworks its cultural meaning and form. "The photograph or the snapshot ... appropriate a brief difference," Nancy writes, "an imperceptible alteration that thus becomes perceptible, present, indubitable ... Likewise do I appropriate myself" (101). Though Nancy's is clearly a phenomenological account, he is sensitive to the agency of the material or immaterial photographic image itself—its power to appropriate a difference and visibly change accordingly. In the case of the tourist snapshots of displays in Regina Mundi Church, there is an appropriation of art and memory within everyday life. The tourist snapshot becomes a creative actualization of an earlier photographic event and, as a consequence of this actualization, slightly adjusts the encountered cultural memory, the exhibited photograph, to the new situation.

"The many users of photography," writes Azoulay, "never ceased from inventing new forms of being with others through photography" ("Photography" 67). The very same material, an account of apartheid South Africa, for example, can present itself in different figurations, motivating different appropriations. It is this process of reworking, recognizing, and highlighting some details and playing down or leaving out others that characterizes the work of memory and generates a memory assemblage constituted through relational investments and shared mediations. "The event of photography," Azoulay writes, "is never over. It can only be suspended, caught in the anticipation of the next encounter that will allow for its actualization" (77). In short, I argue that some tourist snapshots of the visit at Regina Mundi Church actualize cultural memory's media and demonstrate what a memory image of a difficult heritage can mean to others in the present. Additionally, they visibly transform the images of the past available to us at this memory site.

INSCRIPTIONS: MEMORY STORIES IN THE MAKING

In their photos, visitors often zoom in on the walls that do not exhibit photos and take a snapshot of a small narrative in the form of a clipping of short dedications and scratches. These inscriptions seem to comment on each other and on the photographs next to them, revealing a further interweaving of different memorial media. "Sedativegunk" from Canada choses such an image for his blog post on Johannesburg and Soweto (see Illustration 10.1). As he notes, "We were fascinated by these photos, so much so that our guide Mandy had to come and find us and drag us out because we were dawdling too much." Although he expresses his fascination for the photos, the image he chooses to illustrate the scene on his blog is one of the scribbled wall. The image focuses on a comment by "Elke from Germany," written

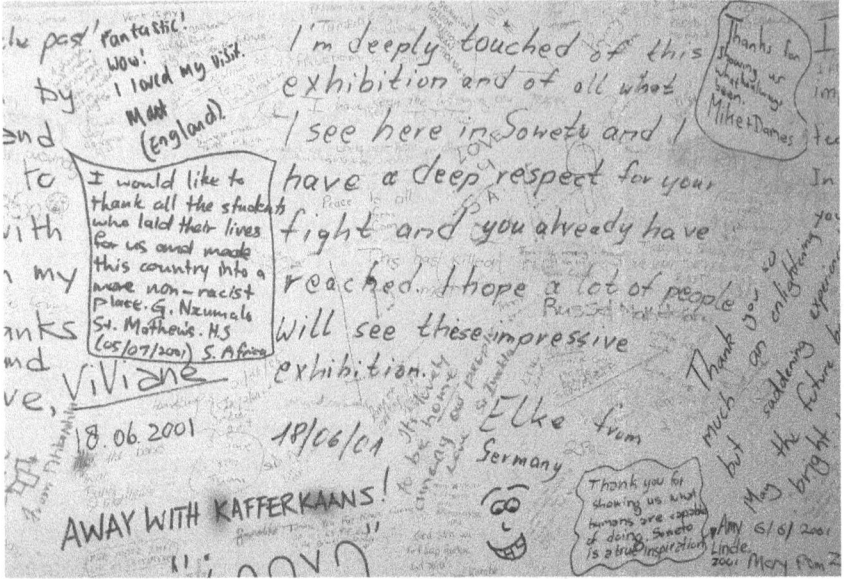

Illustration 10.1. Kevin DeGaust, Messages scrawled in the photo gallery of the church, 16 August 2005, http://sedativegunk.files.wordpress.com/2005/08/sowe to-regina-mundi-church-scrawl-in-photo-gallery.jpg. Courtesy Kevin DeGaust.

in big black letters over many smaller comments, which reads, "I'm deeply touched of this exhibition and of all what I see here in Soweto and have a deep respect for your fight and you already have reached [*sic*]. I hope a lot of people will see these impressive exhibition [*sic*] (18.06.01)."

In between these lines other comments read, "This has killed me" and "I am so extremely moved by what I saw. Thank you for the tour"; "Thank you for showing us what humans are capable of doing. This is a true inspiration, Amy June 2001." Different South African visitors write, "I would like to thank all the students who laid their lives for us and made this country into a more non-racist place. G. Nzumalo, St. Matthews H.S. (05/01/2001), S. Africa," "It's lovely to be home," and "Thanx Nelson Mandela for freedom, Bonolo Madiba 2004." Other quotations read, "God bless you and keep freedom and peace," "Thank you for never giving up makes me proud to be black, Jane, US," or even "I love you Tumi" and "For more info call me on 073-****Jacob Motshabi."

This mixture of international and domestic tourists' as well as locals' expressions of gratitude, belief, and solidarity, entangled with everyday extraordinary or minor joys like declaring one's love or soliciting other business ("call me") is what makes these walls unique mundane—or what Joyce van de Bildt elsewhere in this volume calls vernacular—memorials, working their way into each other's vision. Visitors find in the photo exhibition what Jill Bennett calls "a blurring of memorial spaces and the ordinariness of everyday places" (99).

The ability to move its visitors depends on the openness of this memorial's "mode of engagement" (Jill Bennett 14): the constant transformation of the exhibition walls and the whole memorial space of the church is what makes this a dynamic memorial and a lasting site of negotiation. It is the playful association of vanishing, overwriting, and preserving that the walls exercise, putting in dialogue reflections about an extraordinary past, everyday business, rehearsed commemoration, and future aspirations that many choose to capture in their photographic souvenirs of the church.

While the listing of names and their inscription into stonewalls is a common memorial practice, the distinctive feature of the gallery walls at Regina Mundi is their openness toward new comments and the rather unforeseeable associations each comment enables. The visibility and durability of names and comments depends on a number of random or only partially intended factors, such as the amount and type of light falling on a spot, the quality of the pen used, and the fact that some comment or framed photo overshadows other comments, which also depends on how well liked and welcome a certain comment or critique is. One wonders what distinguishes these walls from other tagged and scribbled walls in public restrooms or bus stops—which they do certainly resemble, not least of all visually.

Most striking is surely their rather unique location. A location such as a church would usually prohibit people's inscriptions in the form of scratches and tags as would a conventional exhibition space or monument, where people's inscriptions are routinely treated as vandalism. Imagine an exhibition space such as a gallery or museum that lets the marks of former displays remain visible—that, for instance, keeps the information plaque of a painting that no longer hangs on the wall in place and lets it interact with exhibitions to come. "The Story of Soweto" does exactly that and allows us to trace back the constant act of overwriting and substitution, renovation and refurbishing that such a cultural display performs, irrespective of whether it leaves visible or decodable traces for posterity. At Regina Mundi, we get a grasp of what was before and what comes after the display of the photos.

Many of the comments, or an earlier layer of such comments, were there before the photographs were displayed in 2003, building the ground for the images displayed today and for visitors' inscriptions that have been added since.[4] As on an advertising pillar, former layers of the wall of remembrance are still visible, photos and comments overwrite one another while constantly forming new narratives, witnessing the different generations and groups performing memory as cultural memory. The stories formed by the notes almost overwrite the photographs themselves, which come to function as source material or catalysts for the ongoing dialogue formed by the various scribbles and scratches.

We no longer know when or why a particular comment has been added: its initial motivation could have been another comment, a photo, the church itself, or a particular event. As traces they are nevertheless incorporated in new stories over and over by their readers and the souvenirs they produce, such as tourist photographs. The inclusiveness of the walls convinces visitors that they are part of this memory work. It is especially the welcoming gesture of the gaps between the comments and the associations between the photographs on the walls and the comments that enable creative appropriations of memories and motivate participation in practices of cultural remembrance: the continuous addition of notes, tags, photos, and remarks displays the nature of cultural memory as an ongoing conversation.

MEDIATORS OF MEMORY: "THE STORY OF SOWETO" AS ACTOR-NETWORK

So what do we make of the complex temporalities and interactions generated by the different materials of the Sowetan memory assemblage and their shifting importance over time? I propose that Bruno Latour's actor-network theory helps us grasp the character of memory work at play: the walls, comments, and photographs of the space become mediators in the sense that Latour discusses in his *Reassembling the Social.* Latour differentiates between an intermediary that simply "transports meaning or force without transformation" and mediators that "transform, translate, distort, and modify the meaning or the elements they are supposed to carry" (39).

A mediator, accordingly, allows for a network of relations between different objects, forms, and actions—the exhibited photograph relates to comments on the walls and, again, to the photographs that are being taken of these walls; as mediators, they are on the move and set other elements on the move. As mediators, memory objects translate the past in and for the present, they transform the figuration of a memory, and they productively distort older discourses—without simply replacing them—to motivate active cultural remembrance.

We can understand the "stuff" of memory—a photograph in an exhibition, a memorial stone, a memory of a trip, a note on a wall, or other kinds of souvenirs—as both an actor, "something that acts," and an actant, something "to which activity is granted by others" (Latour, "On Actor-Network Theory" 5). According to Latour, "Any thing that does modify a state of affairs by making a difference is an actor—or, if it has no figuration yet, an actant" (*Reassembling* 71). In the case of Soweto's church, the exhibition walls are actors granting activity to the visitors; the notes left by previous visitors are at the same time actors granting activity to the present visitor, who in turn adds a note herself and who becomes an actor when sharing a photograph online; this photograph becomes an actor in its own right, granting further activity to the notes and exhibited photographs.

Latour offers the following definition of an actor: "An actor in the hyphenated expression of actor-network is not the source of an action but the moving target of a vast array of entities swarming toward it" (*Reassembling* 46). In any memory assemblage, we are confronted with a vast array of swarming entities and changing positions rearranging themselves in response to new impulses and thereby themselves transforming the array: from the comments on the wall to the different visions that the tourist photographs offer. Looking at the agency of memory objects from the perspective of ANT offers an important means of recognizing the vast range of actors in memory work and underscores their mobility across culture, generations, and media: from material to atmosphere, place, time, and human organization, all actors participate in making memory cultural. Memory work in Soweto's Regina Mundi Church follows the associations and relations made between the different objects and people present and their remediations of memory over time.

Following Latour, we might understand "The Story of Soweto" as an actor-network supported by and giving way to a range of mundane appropriations of memorialization, which are potential actors in the work of cultural memory. The actor-network acknowledges "how many participants are gathered in a thing to make it exist and to maintain its existence" (Latour, "Why Has Critique" 246). The same is true for the dynamic work of memory that is dependent on the acts and scenes of remembering and forgetting; memories depend on inscription, investment, and mediation. In the cultural acts of memory gathered around the Regina Mundi Church, we can follow the complicities and agencies of the stuff of memory and the different actors it draws toward it.

Crucially, cultural acts of memory are not limited to human actions, nor is human remembering simply complemented by objects or props; indeed, the latter work beyond, besides, and through human interventions. In this way, ANT underlines the importance of the mobility and movement inherent in cultural forms—both material and immaterial—that invite appropriation and imagination and lead to mediation. Visitors' photographs of the scribbled walls are momentary snapshots of a memory site in transformation, unrepeatable mundane archival records inviting a range of readings and findings beyond its author's or site's intended message.

In heritage tourism, reminders of the past are usually conceptualized and thought of as intermediaries (in Latour's sense), as static memorials transporting a story, a memory, or a part of history with little or no scope for transformation. By contrast, I argue for the incremental and assembled character of memory in which staged memory objects, appropriated in multifarious ways, act as mediators. They transform the memory of Soweto as a place for the antiapartheid liberation struggle by creatively altering the accounts that give meaning to this memory through a range of media that articulate and connect the memory actors in further networks. Thus, ANT offers a tool to trace the work and agency of memory beyond spatiality, materiality, or temporality only, mapping furthermore its transmedial and transcultural mobility. For the study of complex memory assemblages, memory studies can therefore profit from the sensitizing concepts of ANT.

If an archival photograph's actor-network and, within that network, the tourist's inscriptions—a scribble on a wall, a snapshot, an entry in a guestbook, a memorable experience told in a weblog—"leave a trace," they can become "matters of concern," about which Latour writes: "While uncertain and loudly disputed, these real, objective, atypical and, above all, interesting agencies are taken not exactly as object but rather as *gatherings*" (*Reassembling* 114). In a reading of *Reassembling the Social*, Robert Oppenheim rightly points out that matters of concern are *interesting agencies* in Michel Callon's sense of *intéressement,* a process of enrolling and making others act, in the sense that they "draw actors into complicities with the world and one another" (475).

It is especially the work of the material objects in the exhibition and their digital mediations that draw human actors and places into complicities. This is how a memory of, for example, the antiapartheid liberation struggle, coupled with a memory of a trip to South Africa, gathers sights and sites, people and traces, stories and experiences. The exhibition walls at Regina Mundi Church are the core performers in this network, motivating and gathering appropriations by visitors who in turn change the wall and the exhibition's appearance and cocreate its visuality—and visibility—in different mnemonic communities.

(RE)MINDMAPS: ENCOUNTERING "TALKING WALLS"

With these reflections on the nature of memory actors in mind, we can think of memory objects—like the tourist photograph—as mediators rather than intermediaries. This does not mean simply that we move beyond reading a photograph or note as a representation or an authorial gesture but also that we take its agency seriously, a concern that has been highlighted, among others, by Karen Barad and Jane Bennett. In the eyes of their viewers, the "talking walls" at the exhibition form more or less coherent narratives that make room for a variety of voices and viewpoints, experiences and thoughts.

It is these that actively keep the conversation going. The visitors' photographs capture and transport more than the photographer noticed or intended to photograph, which is important for the later functions of the image as memory, for its durability, and for the network it participates in. This participation happens on a material level but also on the level of meaning and content: an actual debate is taking place between individual comments through their arrangement on the walls and their appropriation in tourists' (and others') snapshots, which in turn make these comments actors in the Latourian sense. I will illustrate this transmedial dynamic by zooming in on a detail of the wall photographed by another tourist (see Illustration 10.2).

The comments in the image read like a summary of the Truth and Reconciliation Commission, parts of which actually took place in the church between 1995 and 1998. The photographer has probably zoomed in on a message spread over the whole image reading, "You are in our hearts we send you love & trust that peace is yours. Keep brave. With our love Frank & Annie Australia 23/06/01," yet this inscription is framed by a series of other comments. In between the lines of this message we read a range of undated criti-

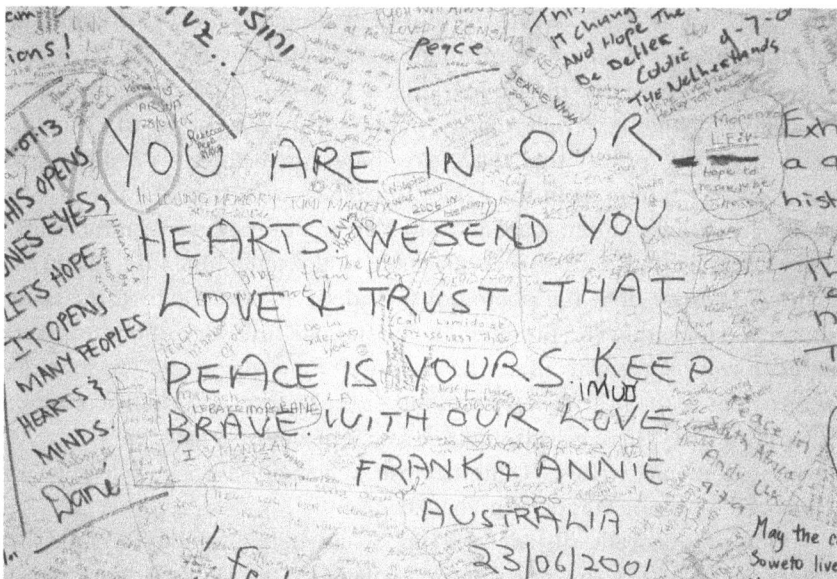

Illustration 10.2. Patrick Delahanty, You Are in Our Hearts, Regina Mundi Church, 17 June 2010, http://www.flickr.com/photos/4-5-43-pat/4756725924. Courtesy Patrick Delahanty.

cal notes on South Africa's past and current ways of coming to terms with the past. One unsigned statement articulates a critique that is only rarely heard in public: "To all the Whites who were involved in any acts during the struggle may you rot in hell and may God never forgive. Bless you!"

A little further down someone has written, "forgive them they know not"; next to that we read, "The day that will never be forgotten June 16"; further down it says in small letters "I'm deeply sorry about those who were victimised, I hope God will bless them and for them to learn to forgive their enemies" (written in a bubble by one N. Vilakazi); next to that, we find a note that is almost indecipherable but that very likely reads, "Fuck the white people" and something almost illegible ostensibly about democracy. In the top of the picture one Toto Molefe writes, "HOPE LIVE & TELL," underlined by "Peace in South Africa, Andy UK" and lots of "I was here" inscriptions. Although one cannot tell for sure whether the comments were originally written to answer or even criticize and correct one other, in the retrospect that this photograph provides they do enter into a debate about how to come to terms with the past.

The walls enable and transport a type of open criticism that is rarely uttered in the public domain, and they offer a temporary forum where seemingly incompatible opinions find a space right next to each other, reminding us of the complex issues at stake and the danger of forgetting the more negative and critical voices. While the official reading of South Africa's nation-building policies is one of reconciliation and amnesty, the walls show that anger and disappointment also mark the active remembrance of this past.

The walls act as an alternative public forum for people to articulate their thoughts, "prove" that they were there, answer other comments, or even "correct" opinions in the exhibition. They are a strange mixture of a public guestbook, a mind map, and a hall of remembrance: a "remind-map." They are integrated into an exhibition but at the same time integrating the exhibited works. Both the photographs and, to a certain extent, the notes situate a past within the present. The quotations link very different places and connect people who share the memory of a struggle and the memory of atrocities in the near past (or present) or the burden and chance of unfinished histories. There are also quite a few transnational calls for solidarity, as when someone writes, "Unite against Apartheid—even in Palestine" or "We need a Nelson Mandela in Venezuela."

One of the walls displays Jürgen Schadeberg's famous Sophiatown chronicle from 1955, showing three men playing Nine Men's Morris in front of a wall tagged "WE WON'T MOVE" just a few days before the black population of what was then Sophiatown was forcefully removed and resettled in the suburb Meadowlands, which would become part of Soweto. Interest-

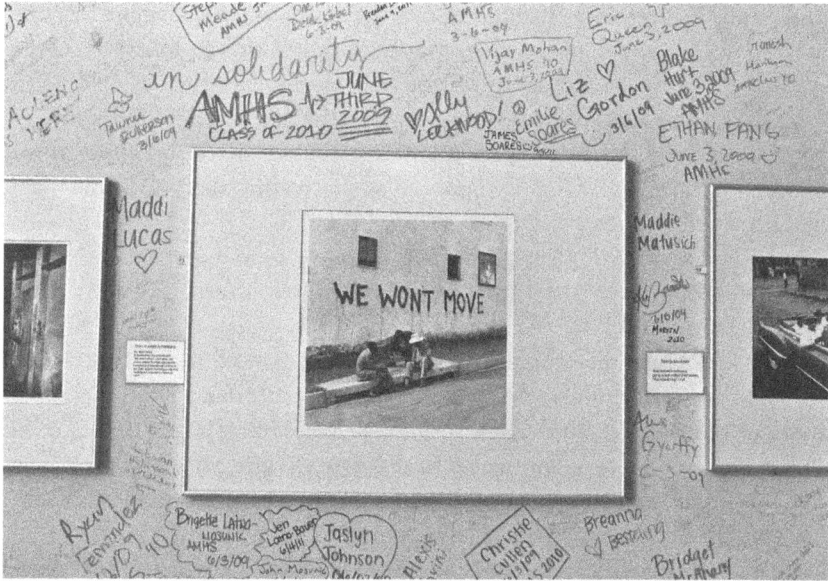

Illustration 10.3. Keeley Kennahan, Soweto uprising exhibit at Regina Mundi Church, 11 October 2011, http://www.flickr.com/photos/hippityhoohah/63129 96665. Courtesy Swahili-Keeley Photography.

ingly, next to the frame someone commented "Same for us in Lebanon" in 2009, with an arrow which points at Schadeberg's photo. Is this author referring to the fact that people in Lebanon face ongoing displacements, or is he or she identifying with the call for resistance in the image? Did the photographer see this connection, and what did she make of it?

What makes these transnational connections meaningful is not only the fact that comments such as this are there, interacting with the images, but also the fact that they draw actors into complicities, motivating other comments and building the focus of further photographs, while finding new audiences beyond the exhibition space. Thus, the actor-network that Schadeberg's photograph is involved in, and the acts it continuously draws toward it, are mediated and thereby maintained by the travelling tourist snapshots in Illustrations 10.1, 10.2, and 10.3, but the snapshots also point to other motions catalyzed by the exhibition setup.

MOVING SIGHTS

The changing constellation of the photos and comments leads to rather unusual physical movements asked of the gallery visitors. One can observe their constant zooming in and out, moving closer and back again, not only to decipher the name of the photographer (written on signs next to the images) but first and foremost to be able to decipher the various comments. One has to kneel down or stand on tiptoe at times to follow the scribbles. What at first sight appears as an amateurish gallery space suddenly evolves into an engaging and moving topography, motivating visitors' involvement and physically moving people's sight.

The photographic displays are on the move as well: not only when appropriated in visitors' snapshots and figuratively travelling over continents through the World Wide Web but also physically when falling off the wall, thereby changing the whole mise-en-scène. The most widely distributed image of the exhibition setup shows a photograph frame that has fallen off the wall, namely Schadeberg's portrait of Nelson Mandela looking out of his cell in Robben Island standing on the ground. Judging from found images of the exhibition online, this frame has fallen off at least twice, and twice this has been read as a metaphorical comment upon the exhibition image and its content. One Flickr user captures the Mandela photo next to a photograph of Walter Sisulu and his wife in a café—both frames standing on the ground—naming the photo "Fallen Heroes (Mandela & Sisulu à terre) [Mandela & Sisulu on the ground]."

As the heroes, Nelson Mandela and Walter Sisulu, referred to in this title were freedom fighters and later politicians, the attribute "fallen" makes an ambiguous remark about, first, that both are no longer "fighting" and, second, the visible fact that the frames that "hold" their images have fallen off the wall. It is also making a conscious or unconscious reference to a comment by one Pakiso right above the frame that reads, "To da Fallen heroes we salute you." This comment might have been there before the frames fell off, earnestly saluting the student heroes who left their lives in the Soweto uprisings of 1976 commemorated in many of the photographs. But it might just as well be directed at the unusual setup of the frames and the fact that the people in the photos, Mandela and Sisulu, "fell" with their frames and left the hero gallery for a while at the same time pointing to the fact that the times of the old freedom fighters are over—and new voices have entered the stage.

The visitor's photograph (Illustration 10.4) thus captures and thereby actively creates an association between otherwise separated actors in the exhibition. The content of the exhibited image—the nation's idols, Mandela and Sisulu—interacts with the changing circumstances of the medium—the glass frame—by which it is carried: the frame has fallen, and, with it, the two former freedom fighters. As the frame mobilizes the photographer, who has to kneel down to take this snapshot, the content also relates to the comment

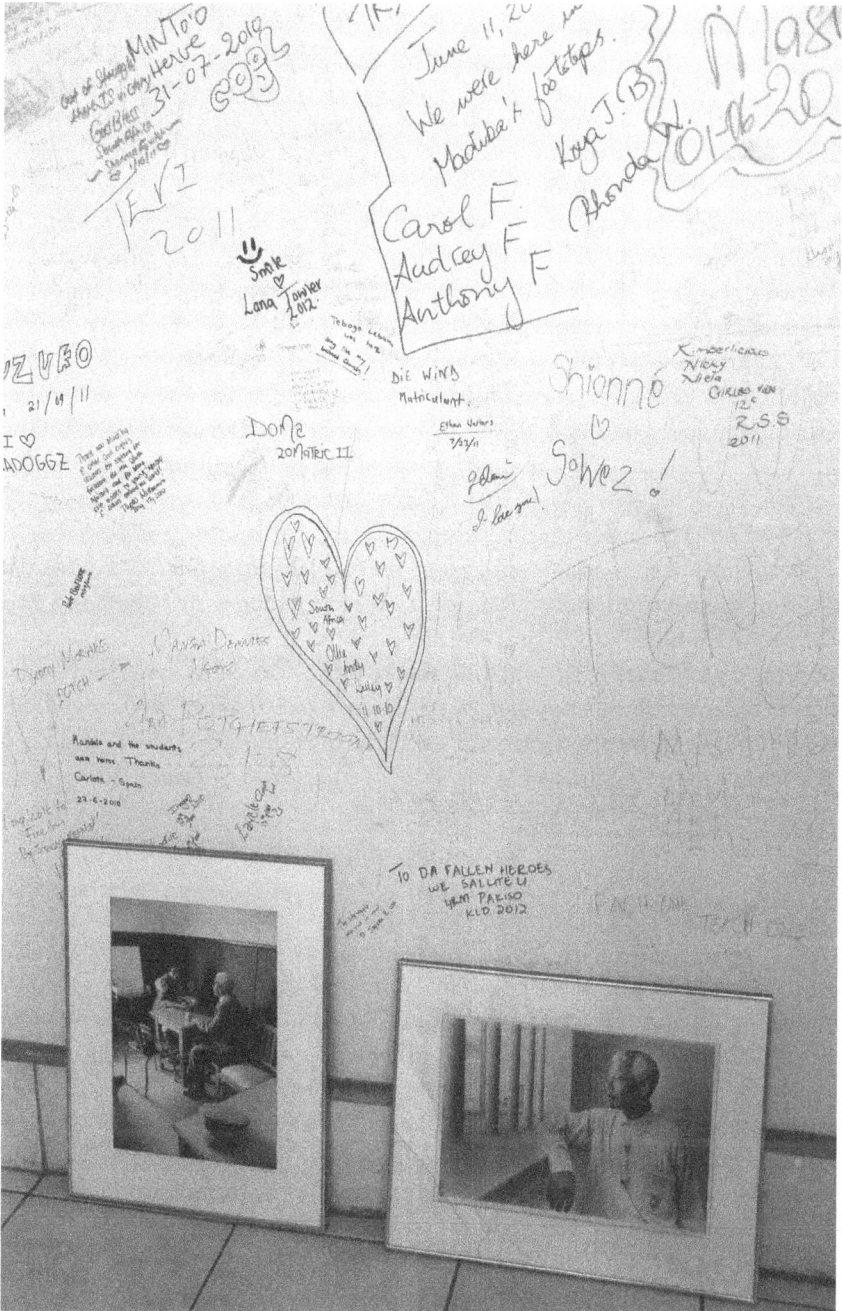

Illustration 10.4. Jean Liou, Fallen Heroes (Mandela & Sisulu à terre), Regina Mundi, Soweto, Johannesburg, Gauteng, Afrique du Sud, 21 July 2012, https://www.flickr.com/photos/tarkastad/7615833040. Courtesy Jean Liou.

above the frame, broadening the actor-network around the memory visualized in Schadeberg's photo. Borrowing from the toolbox of ANT lets us map
and productively read together the mnemonic mobility at stake.

A similar detail was photographed a year later in June 2013 by Dai
Kurokawa for EPA (the European Press Photo Agency) and was reproduced
over and over in July 2013, when it was used in more than fifty online news-
paper articles throughout the world reporting on the former president of
South Africa's hospital stay and lung infection.[5] Remediated in this context,
Pakiso's comment from 2012 seems even more relevant as the frame with
Mandela's image is wrapped in plastic foil, "bandaging" the former president at a time when millions feared for his health. With different captions
in different media, the very same image is used to make a reference to the
critical age and condition of the former president. Dug out of the online
archives for international obituaries when Mandela eventually died in December 2013, it again adopts a whole new meaning.

The fallen frame with the photograph symbolizes the transitoriness of
both the one who is *in* the photo and that which *is* the photo—an archival
record. The appropriations in the form of the accompanying comments, and
the visitors' photos in which it features, reveal the transformative potential
of the image. What I wish to highlight here is the actual *physical* agency of the
actors featured in the snapshot—Schadeberg's photograph, its frame, Mandela (its object), the photographer—and how they interact in the assemblage
the snapshot displays to, as Latour writes, "transform, translate, distort, and
modify" cultural memory.

TRACING SITUATED MEMORY WORK

In the case of "The Story of Soweto," following cultural formations as they
evolve in situated practices in a specific site and moving from this site to
other places can lead to an understanding of the dynamics of memory work
in situ. This is an understanding that does not postulate the prior impact of
structures of difficult heritages and unequal power relations between, for instance, visitors and guides, tourists and locals, or exhibited images and tourist snapshots; rather, it recognizes the unfinished histories and imaginaries
that meet in this space as nondetermining, potentially but not necessarily
mediated in present relations and associations. It is surely very different
actors whose comments meet in this postapartheid encounter.

People make references to all sorts of individual experiences and ordinary needs they are reminded of or want to share with others. The main
purpose of this essay is not to judge the meaning of these articulations and

their authors' positions and intentions but to trace and reflect how they interact with the other elements present in the encounter and present in the images—how they and their acts transform the whole memory assemblage as an actor-network connecting a range of different people and ideas. The interplay of photographic image and text or scribbled image creates a dynamic mnemonic space that prevents a fixation in any visible figuration. As the scribbled text creates more space for the memory of the photograph, the photograph draws visitors' attention toward the notes assembled around it.

The physical and symbolic movement that both the notes and the images afford enhances the creative work of memory transported and transformed in visitors' mediations. Latour's actor-network theory offers us a tool to recognize all these motions and interactions: what is on the move, swarming and gathering in Soweto's Regina Mundi Church, is more than just a nation's designed tourist memoryscape and a human actor's consumption of it. Within this actor-network setup, tourists' appropriations and especially snapshots actualize what a mediated memory has to say in the present.

Frauke Wiegand is a postdoctoral fellow at the University of Copenhagen. Her Ph.D. thesis "Tracing Cultural Memory. Holiday Snapshots at Sites of Memory in an Actor-Network Perspective" investigates the visuality of cultural memory work in an ANT perspective. Her main research interests are cultural memory, postcolonial thinking, actor-network methodology, and vernacular photography. She is a coeditor of a three-volume anthology on visual culture studies titled *Transvisuality: The Cultural Dimension of Visuality* (Liverpool University Press, 2013–2017).

NOTES

1. Although most of the memory sites are situated in the middle of Soweto, they seem detached from the township's everyday life, which makes them appear to be different stations in a memory theme park. This impression is even enhanced by an overuse of colorful signposts.
2. Fieldwork was undertaken in Soweto in June and July 2012 in the form of a mixture of observation and interviews with local and domestic tourists and tourism professionals in Soweto.
3. See http://www.flickr.com/photos/17285281@N07/with/4454990502
4. Personal conversation with the curator Claudia Schadeberg.
5. See, for example, Tracy Connor, "'Difficult Time': Nelson Mandela in Critical Condition in Hospital," *NBC News,* 23 June 2013. Accompanied by the original EPA caption: "A portrait of former South African president Nelson Mandela rests against the wall as messages written by visitors are seen on the wall at Re-

gina Mundi church in Soweto township, a flashpoint during the anti-apartheid struggle, in Johannesburg, South Africa, on Sunday."

WORKS CITED

Azoulay, Ariella. *Civil Imagination: A Political Ontology of Photography.* London: Verso Books, 2015.

——. "Photography." *Mafte'akh: Lexical Review of Political Thought* 2 (2011): 65–80.

Bal, Mieke. "Introduction." *Acts of Memory: Cultural Recall in the Present.* Ed. Jonathan Crewe, Mieke Bal, and Leo Spitzer. Hanover: University Press of New England, 1999. vii–xvii.

Barad, Karen. "Posthumanist Performativity: Toward an Understanding of How Matter Comes to Matter." *Signs: Journal of Women in Culture and Society* 28.3 (2003): 801–31.

Behdad, Ali. *Belated Travelers: Orientalism in the Age of Colonial Dissolution.* Durham: Duke University Press, 1994.

Bennett, Jane. *Vibrant Matter: A Political Ecology of Things.* Durham: Duke University Press, 2010.

Bennett, Jill. *Empathic Vision: Affect, Trauma, and Contemporary Art.* Stanford: Stanford University Press, 2005.

Connor, Tracy. "'Difficult Time': Nelson Mandela in Critical Condition in Hospital." *NBC News.* 23 June 2013. Web. 5 June 2016.

Erll, Astrid, and Ann Rigney. *Media and Cultural Memory: Mediation, Remediation, and the Dynamics of Cultural Memory.* Berlin: De Gruyter, 2009.

Hlongwane, Ali Khangela. "Commemoration, Memory and Monuments in the Contested Language of Black Liberation: The South African Experience." *Journal of Pan African Studies* 2.4 (2008): 135–70.

Huyssen, Andreas. "Monumental Seduction." *New German Critique* 69 (1996): 181–200.

——. *Present Pasts: Urban Palimpsests and the Politics of Memory.* Stanford: Stanford University Press, 2003.

Latour, Bruno. "On Actor-Network Theory: A Few Clarifications." *Soziale Welt* 4 (1996): 369–81.

——. *Reassembling the Social: An Introduction to Actor-Network Theory.* Oxford: Oxford University Press, 2005.

——. "Why Has Critique Run Out of Steam? From Matters of Fact to Matters of Concern." *Critical Inquiry* 30.2 (2004): 225–48.

Macdonald, Sharon. "Reassembling Nuremberg, Reassembling Heritage." *Journal of Cultural Economy* 2.1–2 (2009): 117–34.

Marschall, Sabine. *Landscape of Memory: Commemorative Monuments, Memorials and Public Statuary in Post-Apartheid South Africa.* Boston: Brill, 2010.

Nancy, Jean-Luc. *The Ground of the Image.* New York: Fordham University Press, 2005.

Olick, Jeffrey K. "From Collective Memory to the Sociology of Mnemonic Practices and Products." *Cultural Memory Studies: An International and Interdisciplinary Handbook.* Ed. Astrid Erll and Ansgar Nünning. Berlin: De Gruyter, 2008. 151–61.

Oppenheim, Robert. "Actor-Network Theory and Anthropology after Science, Technology, and Society." *Anthropological Theory* 7.4 (2007): 471–93.

Reading, Anna. "Digital Media, Global Memory: Developing an Epistemology for the Globital." *On Media Memory: Collective Memory in a New Media Age.* Ed. Oren Meyers, Motti Neiger, and Eyal Zandberg. Basingstoke: Palgrave Macmillan, 2011. 241–52.

Rose, Gillian, and Divya P. Tolia-Kelly, eds. *Visuality/Materiality: Images, Objects and Practices.* Farnham: Ashgate, 2012.

Salazar, Noel, and Nelson Graburn, eds. *Tourism Imaginaries: Anthropological Approaches.* New York: Berghahn Books, 2014.

Sheller, Mimi, and John Urry. "Places to Play, Places in Play." *Tourism Mobilities: Places to Play, Places in Play.* Ed. Mimi Sheller and John Urry. London: Routledge, 2004. 1–10.

Silverman, Max. *Palimpsestic Memory: The Holocaust and Colonialism in French and Francophone Fiction and Film.* New York: Berghahn Books, 2013.

Wiegand, Frauke, and Marcela Knapp. "Wild Inside: Uncanny Encounters in European Traveller Fantasies of Africa." *Tourism and the Power of Otherness: Seductions of Difference.* Ed. David Picard and Michael Di Giovine. Bristol: Channel View Publications, 2014. 158–75.

Chapter 11

Cultural Memory Studies in the Epoch of the Anthropocene

Richard Crownshaw

❧◆❧

In a seminal essay of 2009, Dipesh Chakrabarty hypothesizes the reconceptualization of historical thinking in the Anthropocene, the relatively new geological epoch marked by anthropogenic climate change. The essential definition of the Anthropocene, Chakrabarty argues, lies in its determination of humans as possessing geological force or agency (200–01, 206–07). That agency can be dated to the inception of the Industrial Revolution but has had the greatest impact since the second half of the twentieth century. It is from the eighteenth century that humanity's interaction with nature has been superseded by the actualization of humanity as a force of nature (207), particularly when the consumption of renewable sources of fuel (wood) gave way to the large-scale use of fossil fuels (coal from the 1750s, oil and gas from the twentieth century). The increase in carbon dioxide emissions through the burning of fossil fuels and its effect of global warming, which has left a geological record (as shown by polar ice core samples that date from the mid to late eighteenth century), has prompted Paul J. Crutzen (2002) and Eugene F. Stoermer (with Crutzen 2000) to signal the end of the previous geological epoch, the Holocene, the warmer period of ten to twelve millennia that succeeded the ice age of the Pleistocene. Crutzen and Stoermer have identified the Anthropocene, as succeeding the Holocene, to designate a new era of anthropogenic climate change, the geological evidence for which dates back to James Watts's invention of the steam engine in 1784 (Chakrabarty 208–10).

The notion of the Anthropocene has gained remarkable traction across the academic disciplines in the last few years. Taking a geological turn, the humanities, and more specifically literary and cultural studies, has begun to explore, scrutinize, assess, and theorize the limits and possibilities of representing and conceptualizing life in the Anthropocene. The humanities has been taking stock of the cultural and theoretical resources available to understand the catastrophic conditions that render that life (be it human or nonhuman) and its environments precarious, if not unsustainable and devastated, through the effects of climate change; energy insecurities; the potential and realization of species extinction; unprecedented levels of pollution, waste, and toxicity; and the social disintegration brought about by the depletion of resources. In the face of the Anthropocene, the humanities has found itself theoretically depleted, given the cognitive and representational challenges issued by these unfolding and interrelated catastrophes. As we shall see, it is the scale and materiality of these catastrophic environmental processes that demand of cultural memory studies a truly transdisciplinary approach, informed by, for example, the study of geology as much as by cultural understanding.

So, in keeping with this volume's collective exploration of the transcultural, transmedial, and, particularly, transdisciplinary dynamics of cultural memory, this chapter explores what role cultural memory studies might play in that geological turn and how it might be recalibrated in relation to the Anthropocene. It does this by examining the cultural memories staged by the American novelist James Howard Kunstler. Kunstler's trilogy of novels— *World Made by Hand* (2008), *The Witch of Hebron* (2010), and *A History of the Future* (2014)—envisages a post-oil world (America) brought on by a disastrous war in the Middle East fought to secure American oil supplies, the consequent detonation of nuclear devices on the American homeland by "jihadist" terrorists, and the resulting collapse of existing economic, social, and political structures. What emerges is something akin to a vision of nineteenth-century frontier life, with the racial warfare, indentured labor, states of authoritarianism both benign and criminal, healthcare, daily violence, life expectancy, and gender politics characteristic of that period. Still, this story world is imagined as a pastoral vision of environmental stewardship, artisanal industry, and mostly local patterns of production, consumption, and exchange. Different social configurations and ways of life to those organized by petrocapitalism are suggested, different relations to resources considered, and different resources and forms of energy used. Kunstler's novels identify a history of geopolitical, socioeconomic, and cultural causes that explain the conditions experienced by his protagonists—in terms of a world without oil—and imply a wider, ecological context that implicates the history of the United States' fossil-fueled modernity in extreme climatic events (flood and hurricane) that have devastated coastal parts of the United States in this novel. That the relationship between petrocapitalism and climate change remains implicit and unarticulated—in fact, these environmental catastrophes occur at the margins of the plot and have no structural significance or effect on the narrative—is obviously problematic and something to which this chapter will return. Kunstler's future anterior dramatizes an etiology of the conditions that are imagined in the future but that are unfolding in the present of this literature's production and consumption; in this way, the novel suggests a cultural memory of the Anthropocene. The problematic nature of this cultural memory is useful to this enquiry, as it illuminates the conceptual challenges of representing and remembering the Anthropocene.

The theorization of cultural memory studies has of late taken a transcultural (Bond and Rapson; Crownshaw), transnational (De Cesari and Rigney), multidirectional (Rothberg, *Multidirectional Memory*), postcolonial (Craps, *Postcolonial Witnessing*), and global (Assmann and Conrad; Levy and Sznaider) turn, but, as Tom Cohen points out, the scales of "mourning theory" (as he terms it), are still calibrated to a humanist logic. For Cohen, cultural memory studies is preoccupied with the defense of human "cultures, affects, bodies and others" through their reconstruction in representations of the past (15). This is a defense mounted, in Judith Butler's use of the future anterior, to frame lives from their beginnings as "grievable" and so "sustained by that regard" but, in anticipation of their potential precariousness, recognized as lives and so subject to grievability and testimony (15). In sum, the "apprehension of grievability precedes and makes possible the apprehension of precarious life ... [that is,] living, exposed to non-life from the start" (15). For Cohen, these humanist grounds of remembrance and its theorization secure "political" and "epistemological" "homelands": political in the sense that human habitats, domains, or territories are remembered and thereby delimited; epistemological in the sense of our modes of cognition that cannot think beyond these delimitations. Failing to think ecologically, to apprehend the imbrication of human and nonhuman (or more-than-human) worlds, means, for Cohen, deferring addressing "biospheric collapse, mass extinction events, or the implications of resource wars and 'population' culling" (15–17). More specifically, a reconfigured cultural memory studies is needed in the face of radical changes in atmospheric, hydrospheric, lithospheric, and biospheric conditions brought about by climate change that reveal the interconnectedness of human and more-than-human worlds through their mutual devastation.

The remembrance of environmental catastrophe cannot then be enclosed by just human experience (humans as victims and perpetrators of, for example, anthropogenic climate change); instead, cultural memory studies must account for the wider, ecological dimensions of human actions. In fact, the very idea of an anthropogenic, catastrophic environmental event—its "eventness"—needs to be rethought, given the ways such events unfold unevenly across time and space, their slowly violent effects often dislocated temporally and spatially from their causes. This is particularly complicated in the example of climate change, the feedback loops of which turn effects into causes of further climatic transformation, and with atmospheric thresholds crossed and tipping points met those transformations can be dramatic, sudden, not necessarily predictable or gradual. More generally, in the "slow" (to use Rob Nixon's term) as well as fast violence of environmental catastrophe, human activity sets in motion a chain of action that exceeds human control and in which the environment itself is lent a catastrophic agency. Jane Bennett's "vibrant materialism" is useful here in its identification of "the capacity of things ... to act as quasi agents or forces with trajectories, propensities, or tendencies of their own," which means that the "locus of agency is always a human-nonhuman working group," an ad hoc "assemblage," and that causality is more "emergent than efficient, more fractal than linear" (ix, viii, viii, xvii, 3, 9, 23–24, 30, 33, 37). Therefore, cultural memory studies must resist grounding the memory of environmental damage or devastation, delimiting the degraded as a discrete, lost, and static object to be reconstituted and restored through remembrance. Rather, cultural memory studies must track emergent causalities, ad hoc assemblages of agentive matter, and mutating patterns of change in predictable and unpredictable, calculable and incalculable ways. Thinking expansively across space and time, matter and life—and the multiscalar referents of climate change—calls for a "derangement," as Timothy Clark might put it, of the scales of cognition, remembrance and representation, for which the "humanist enclosures" (Cohen 17–18, 21) of cultural memory studies are ill equipped.

Having said that, the innovations and potential reach of a globalized cultural memory studies to date should not be overlooked, particularly in relation to global capitalism. Cohen complains that the exclusive preoccupation of "mourning theory" (and critical theory in general) with human precariousness was intensified by the economic crisis of 2008. The remembrance of the precariousness of life lived under capitalist regimes of inequity meant that, for cultural memory studies, the planetary scales and dynamics of capitalism stood in for an ecology of the imbrication of the human and more-than-human world. Again, this served to construct "political" and "epistemological" "homelands" while overlooking other forms and realms of dispossession as well as the precarious ecological contexts that enable those "homelands" in the first place (Cohen 15–16). Despite the validity of this posthumanist critique and its illumination of the imbrication of human and more-than-human worlds, cultural memory studies still needs to account for the human subject's interpellation by capitalist economic regimes (and their attendant ideologies) as well as the wider ecological implications of that hegemony; it needs, in other words, to address the humanist *and* posthumanist enclosures of memory. Conversely, Cohen decrees the diremption of the humanist and the posthumanist in his identification of the need for critical theory in general and mourning theory in particular to resist the temptation to construct climate change as theory's other: an "ethical attention to otherness relies on a metaphorics of the home[land] ... that can only play on the borders of the bounded" and cannot intimate a radically unbounded and ungrounded way of thinking; the apprehension of difference ends up reifying and regrounding the homeland (24). To move beyond naming "climate change" as other from the confines of that homeland necessitates an ungrounded (not-at-home) "asubjectal" perspective from which is uttered an equally ungrounded "ephemeral non-phase 'climate change'" (Cohen 24). How the asubjective is achieved remains open to question but, in theory, it would foreclose the investigation of humanity's gathering of geological force and agency through its hegemonic economic activities—the very fundament of the Anthropocene. It is by looking to the innovations of globalized cultural memory and trauma studies that the empirical groundwork for bridging the humanist *and* posthumanist can be found.

Take, for example, Stef Craps' consideration of the temporality of traumatic experience—not in terms of the belated registration of the event itself but rather in terms of its duration. To contextualize that duration, Craps scrutinizes the ways that dominant conceptions of the traumatic have marginalized the experiences of "non-Western or minority cultures" through the universalization of Western models of trauma at the expense of a transcultural recognition of trauma and grievable life ("Beyond Eurocentrism" 50). Key to widening the concept of trauma is moving beyond the narrow definitions of Post-Traumatic Stress Disorder as propagated by the American Psychiatric Association through the *Diagnostic and Statistical Manual of Mental Disorders* and disseminated in the wider culture, originating in a "sudden, unexpected, catastrophic event," a "devastating blow" or "acute stab that breaks the protective shield of the psyche." Not only does such an approach to trauma pathologize the victim rather than attend to the cultural, social, and historical structures that caused victimization in the first place, it overlooks the normative, quotidian, and structural forms, effects, and affectiveness of oppression (Craps, "Beyond Eurocentrism" 49–50). Put otherwise, such a Western understanding of trauma privileges European genocide, particularly the Holocaust, in its various forms, over non-European genocide and the genocidal over other, slower, structural forms of violence and oppression experienced in colonial and postcolonial scenarios.

Similarly, Michael Rothberg has also questioned the trauma paradigm, seeking an interpretive flexibility to relate trauma to "*other* disruptive social forces" and to think of the trauma category as "*necessary but not sufficient*" in addressing forms of violence trauma theory has historically overlooked ("Beyond Tancred and Clorinda" xiii; emphasis in original). Its interpretive remit widened by a more accommodating dialogue with a range of disciplines, trauma studies would be better equipped to recognize "structural," quotidian violence endured in the institutions and systems of global capitalism, in which, for example, a "sociological" understanding of life under capitalism might be complemented by trauma studies' understanding of "psychic effects of systematic exploitation" and trauma studies' "event-based models" of violence modified by sociology's attentions to the structures of violence (xiv–xv). Revealed, those structures enable the mapping of global capitalism's "uneven" and simultaneous distribution of "experiences of trauma and wellbeing" and thereby of the ways in which the beneficiaries of that distribution are implicated in violence (Rothberg, "Beyond Tancred and Clorinda" xv).

Rothberg's structural understanding of the "implicated subject" informs his theoretical gestures toward the "slow violence" (Nixon) of environmental catastrophe generated by global capitalism, or what might be called Anthropocene trauma. In seeking, then, a model of trauma that can encompass the distribution of environmentally mediated causes and effects of trauma across space and time, Rothberg looks to the ways in which implicated subjects can be the perpetrators of slow violence as, for example, agents of climate change and its effects on the global South but also potential victims, as climate change belatedly threatens the developed, industrialized world from which it originated ("Beyond Tancred and Clorinda" xv). In short, Rothberg arrives where Chakrabarty's argument departs: the conceptual and theoretical frameworks needed to think about capitalism in relation to the Anthropocene.

Chakrabarty asks how a critical analysis of global capitalism—a system inextricable from the epoch of the Anthropocene and an epoch in which environmental catastrophe accentuates the inequalities of that system— might address the causes and effects of the Anthropocene (211–12). More precisely, how might a capitalism-inflected Anthropocene be historicized? As Chakrabarty puts it:

> The problematic of globalization allows us to read climate change only as a crisis of capitalist management. While there is no denying that climate change has profoundly to do with the history of capital, a critique that is only a critique of capital is not sufficient for addressing questions relating to human history once

the crisis of climate change has been acknowledged and the Anthropocene has begun to loom on the horizon of our present. (212)

The Anthropocene designates an entanglement of human and natural history that, along with the critical climate conditions it explains, will outlive the current phase of global capitalism and its subsequent modulations or variations (212). A deeper sense of history (one that extends beyond humanity's chronicling of itself) allows the differentiation of the Anthropocene from the warming of the climate during the Holocene, the preceding epoch, and so the identification of the threshold for conditions under which human life flourishes—conditions that, of course, predate capitalism and industrialization. A deeper sense of history also identifies the conditions under which life becomes precarious in the past, in the present, and in the future (Chakrabarty 213, 217). Put otherwise, a deeper sense of history allows the consequences of climate change to be mapped: the "ensuing crisis for humans is not understandable unless one works out the consequences of that warming" (213). While existing critiques of global capitalism can historicize scenarios of lived economic precarity (inequitable life), they do not, argues Chakrabarty, have the temporal reach to think about the survival of life *per se*; they are not calibrated to think in terms of the duration (or not) of the human species (213). The Anthropocene necessitates thinking together "the planetary and the global; deep and recorded histories; species thinking and critiques of capital" (213).

That is not to say that humanity is homogenized, essentialized, or universalized by species thinking. Rather, species thinking can be characterized as the (our) species' historical self-consciousness as a (differentiated) species and our self-consciousness of our species' place in a wider and deeper planetary history and possible future—a sense of "a shared catastrophe that we have all fallen into" (Chakrabarty 214–16, 218). In this schema, "species" becomes "a placeholder for an emergent, new universal history of humans that flashes up in the moment of the danger that is climate change." "Species thinking" produces not a dialectical arrangement for understanding all of history, akin to the teleologies of capitalism, but "a figure of the universal that escapes our capacity to experience" and understand the world in all its "particularities" (Chakrabarty 221–22).

So, while Cohen problematizes what he perceives as cultural memory studies' failure to grasp the multiscalar, nonlinear trajectories of environmental catastrophe, cultural memory studies' proclivities for apprehending the Anthropocene as other, and, in general, critical theory's reconstitution of the ecological solely in economic terms, I propose that it is cultural memory studies' global turn and corresponding reconceptualization of trauma that has laid the groundwork for the recognition of the implication of sub-jectivity in the Anthropocene. This is an "implicatedness" that is correspon-dent with Chakrabarty's call to think "simultaneously on both registers, to mix together the immiscible chronologies of capital and species history" (221–22).

What forms might cultural memory take if it is to think backward and forward in time with Chakrabarty and expansively across spatial, let alone social and cultural, boundaries not respected by the planetary systems of critical environmental change? Ursula Heise might suggest the "eco-cosmo-politan" literary narrative of risk as a form that can register, and indeed remember, "species" and "capital" as they unfold unevenly and ecologically across time and space. Heise finds in deterritorialized and mobile global-ized culture the capacity to represent "how political, economic, techno-logical, social, cultural, and ecological networks shape daily routines" and local experiences—in other words, how a sense (and the actuality) of place is mediated by a sense (and the actuality) of the "planetary." In this deter-ritorialization lies the potential for an "environmental ethics" and an "eco-logical consciousness." Put otherwise, this is a matter of scale, the cognition of which enables a "more nuanced understanding of how both local cul-tural and ecological systems are imbricated in global ones," informing an "environmentally orientated cosmopolitanism," an "eco-cosmopolitanism" (Heise 55, 59). In exploring what cultural forms enable communities to see their relation to a planetary community, Heise focuses on the potential of literary narratives to convey an eco-cosmopolitanism through literature's en-gagement with the perception and actuality of risk. To be more precise, it is the risk of environmental catastrophe, although differentially distributed across the planet, always culturally mediated and experienced in different ways and to different degrees, that registers a shared potential precarious-ness of living in the Anthropocene.

That risk is always mediated is underlined by the financialization of the risk of environmental catastrophe through, for example, the emergent derivatives market in climate futures, which, Ben Dibley and Brett Neilson have argued, has contributed to an affective form of governance, the forma-tion of political subjectivities, and the securitization of sovereign territory. Subjectivity and territory are secured through the orchestration of risk—that is, risk mediated by its culturally specific perception, its calculability, and its incalculability. Under this affective regime, or "actuarial imaginary," those individuals, communities, corporations, and states that perceive themselves at risk, and that are financially enabled, can preempt and financially survive catastrophe while participating in and maintaining the fossil-fueled econ-omy structurally responsible for the catastrophes that befell them in the first place. The intended effect of financialization is to stave off social discontent, political instability, and economic collapse by insuring against and profiting from the environmental future—the realities of global economic and financial apartheid notwithstanding. As Dibley and Neilson put it, the "actuarial imaginary ... effects ... not only the prevention of the trauma of the unmediated future, but of the trauma of a future that does not have its resolution in protection and profit" (152).

Given the financialization of risk, its mediation of Anthropocene trauma, and its securitization of homelands, it is unsurprising to find the literary narrative of risk implicated in a financialized thinking of species and capital. Indeed, the literary narrative of risk demonstrates the proximity of the future anterior to financial speculation, complicit in and illuminating the ways risk is mediated. The narrativization of risk can draw on the cultural power of generic templates to render "intelligible and meaningful" environmental information in disruptive or reifying ways (Heise 138). As this chapter argues, Kunstler's *World Made by Hand* (2008), exemplifying the trilogy of which it is a part, demonstrates the ways that narrativization of risk adheres to the generic template of the pastoral, which in the context of a catastrophic, post-oil future finds a political and economic solution to the predicament it narrates in—as Heise might put it—a detoxifying return to the premodern (122)—or, at least, that is its intention.

Set in the near future, *World Made by Hand* is located in New York state after nuclear devices, detonated in Washington and Los Angeles in an act of "jihad," have contributed to the collapse of the American economy and its ability to participate in global trade, after war in the "Holy Land" has failed to secure oil resources for the United States, after the collapse of federal and state government, and where governance and social order either takes the form of benign plantocracy, Puritan-like religious community, mafias presiding over local resources and infrastructures (like landfills or river ports), or, at best, local town democracies. Without fossil fuels, computers, digital technology, and automobility, industry, technology, and production are characteristically nineteenth century (but practiced locally rather than on the scale of the Industrial Revolution), with a few working remnants of the twentieth and twenty-first centuries (the occasional, stray electrical current and radio signal) and with trade, transport, and information exchange more regional than national. Little is known of the nation and almost nothing of the outside world. Globalization is a thing of the past. Although the narrative is set in a post-oil and now virtually zero-emission America, the climatic legacies of fossil fuel use are still felt. When national news does filter through from time to time, it is of the devastation of coastal regions due to floods and hurricanes.

Essentially, the plot of this novel centers on local power struggles, and moral integrity, community spirit, social and cultural tolerance, hard work, and technical ingenuity generally determine who survives and prospers, and who does not, in this post-oil world. The novel's moral economy does not detract from the violence of the world depicted, where the exercise of law and order resembles that of a frontier town of the American West. Nor does the novel shy away from the human costs of the transition from an oil-based world to the conditions of this "long emergency" (Kunstler, *The Long Emergency*) following the oil war in which the withdrawal of resources, technologies, and infrastructures and therefore of the securities of civic life was felt most poignantly in lethal epidemics. Nonetheless, the reversion to what might be described as a settler society is inflected by a pastoralism, even if Kunstler claims that his imagination of post-oil society is not wishful thinking and not a utopian corrective to petrocapitalism (*The Long Emergency*). That pastoral idealism is found in the moral economy already mentioned in which good local government means the sustainable and equitable distribution of local resources, in which industry, production, and trade benefit the common good (even if some sections of society, such as the local plantocracy and religious community, are not democratically organized), where the act of labor for oneself or others (in exchange for goods, services, sustenance, or accommodation) is never alienating, and where consumption (of mostly locally produced and prepared food in ordinary or celebratory circumstances) is relished and described with mouthwatering relish.

As Heise might put it, in the fictional world of Kunstler's novel (and the trilogy of which it is a part), the local is an effect of the global, even if the wider world, its human and more-than-human forces, are seen as a disruption to the sense of place cherished by the novel and often consigned to the past as the narrator remembers a historical, globalized world. The narrative of risk in this case registers both the ecological and the economic—"capital" and "species"—in the intertwining of disasters and in the cognitive and cultural difficulties of thinking and representing both at the same time. Even if not sufficiently comprehensive and articulate, the narration of risk in the case of Kunstler's novel captures the difficulties of tracing the causal connections across space and time between human industrial and economic activity and its environmental effects, the difficulties of predicting where, when, and to what degree environmental damage will manifest itself in systemic ways (across global systems) and through cumulative, local environmental degradation (Heise 152, 158–59).

In its staging of an anterior future, a past that will have taken place by the time of the novel's present, Kunstler's work demonstrates the difficulties of remembering the Anthropocene—a difficulty brought about by a melancholic attachment to a capitalist world fueled by oil. The lives of most of the characters in this book span the era of fossil fuels and the post-oil age. This means that the local and regional landscape is palimpsestic, as its inhabitants are able to project onto it personal losses of loved ones and livelihoods but also industrial and economic histories that date from the birth of the republic to the late twentieth century. Overgrown and reclaimed by nature—if not recycled by humans—roads, bridges, abandoned houses, factories, municipal buildings, and more recently built malls, shops, and offices are potential sites for the aestheticization of the ruins of modernity—despite the narrator's prefatory comments about his disdain for romancing ruins (*World Made by Hand* 11)—an aestheticization that threatens to subsume the history of a fossil-fueled era, the legacies of which are currently being lived. This passage offers an example:

> Waterford began its existence as the gateway to the Erie Canal system, the first stretch of which was built to bypass several waterfalls on the Mohawk River. But the locks there no longer functioned because they were rebuilt and enlarged in the early twentieth century to open and close on electric power. Now there was no way to operate them. They were too big for human or animal power ... By and by, we crossed an old commercial highway strip with its complement of dead gigantic discount stores, strip malls, and defunct burger barns. The buildings were all in various stages of disassembly as materials of value were stripped from them—copper pipes and wires, aluminum sashes, windowpanes, steel girders, and cement blocks. The parking lots seemed especially desolate with nothing in them but mulleins and sumacs poking through the cracked pavements.
>
> At Waterford, the bridge connected two bluffs about a hundred feet above the surface of the Mohawk River. It was one of those engineering marvels from the early twentieth century that could never be replaced now, any more than the Coliseum in Rome could be rebuilt by the most talented subjects of Frederick Barbarossa. (137–38)

While the ugly remains of the late-twentieth-century suburban sprawl metonymically and metaphorically figure socio-economic collapse, the monumental remains of the earlier architecture of industrial capitalism aesthetically transcend their implication in an equally fossil-fueled modernity. Elsewhere the ruins of the industrial landscape are subsumed by an unfolding natural history, as in the description of "the railroad tracks along the Battenkill":

> On the steel bridge where the track crosses the river a half mile outside town, I stopped for a while to watch the river... I watched an osprey rise off the stream with a good twelve-inch trout in his talons. When he was gone with his prize, plenty more trout were finning in the feeding lanes in the shadow of the bridges, trusses and girders. (238)

It is the narrator-protagonist of Kunstler's novel who historicizes *and* aestheticizes the landscape, who sketches out the geopolitical context of America's economic and political collapse, who marvels at the excesses of his previous corporate lifestyle and its auto- and aeromobility, and who teaches those too young to remember the concept of fuel (*World Made by Hand* 22–23, 244–45, 247–48). However, aside from its aestheticizing tendencies or potential, this historical consciousness is haunted by more than just personal losses suffered during the long emergency—the death of his wife and daughter. The embodied memories of "living oil," as Stephanie LeMenager might put it, or of a resourced culture, seem equally haunting and disquieting.

At one point, the protagonist "hit the power button on the old stereo. In doing it, I was conscious of putting something behind me: the expectation that things would ever be normal again. There was a kind of relief in it. I also turned off the electric lights so they wouldn't come on and scare anybody again" (Kunstler, *World Made by Hand* 196). Such actions point to the embodied practices of consumption as well as the apparent mourning of that life. However, the alarming possibility of the return of electrical light also intimates an affective if not cognitive reaction to the possible return of the old fossil-fueled regime. A related scene suggests the unconscious manifestation of that anxiety:

> I was sitting in a comfortable padded chair gliding swiftly over the landscape in a way that felt supernatural yet oddly familiar. I did not feel any wind in my face, despite the speed, which was much faster than anything I was accustomed to. I was deeply at ease in my wonderful traveling chair and thrilled by the motion. Familiar sights whizzed by: the Larmon farm on the Battenville Road, Holyrood's cider mill, the old railroad overpass outside the village of Shushan, pastures and cornfields, hills, hollows, and houses I had known for years. In the dream, I came to realize that I was moving inside some kind of protective envelope, not just sitting in a wonderful chair. Then, a dashboard resolved before me with its round glowing gauges, and then the steering wheel… I am driving a car! It had been so many years since I had done that! It was a dream-memory of something that now seemed hardly different from the magic carpets of my childhood storybooks. But then the speed picked up alarmingly and I was no longer at ease. I careened around curves in the road just missing gigantic trees. I couldn't remember what to do with my feet. I had lost control. (19)

Ostensibly, this is all rather obvious: a literal and figurative dream image of the out-of-control and catastrophic petroculture that explains the present condition. Although perhaps more rhetorical, it provides no more historical information than the narrator's usual historicizing purview. The pleasure derived from the sensation of driving perhaps indicates a melancholic attachment to a fossil-fueled life of which he is not normally conscious, and such a reading might be supported by his failure to reflect further on the dream and its contradictions to his archaeological object lessons in fossil-fueled modernity, the concept of fuel, and the geopolitics of the Anthropocene.

The precarious trajectory of automobility continues in a bizarre scene of automobile suicide in *World Made by Hand.* Traveling to Albany in a rescue party to retrieve some local men who, trading there, were falsely imprisoned by the mafia who control the river port city, the narrator's party's journey is interrupted by the startling sight of an automobile, the elderly driver of which has refused to adjust to the new reality. Proclaiming the virtues of the automobile age and berating a now nonexistent state for failing to maintain the decaying roads, he is a mobile anachronism. But this is also his swan song: trundling through the party and onward, his car leaves what is left of the road and crashes as the driver shoots himself while behind the wheel. Astonished, the narrator witnesses, albeit in condensed form, what had remained on the verge of consciousness. For all his astonishment, the narrator finds the incident disturbing, even if (or because) he does not recognize what he has in common with the old man.

This "petromelancholia," as LeMenager would describe it, is not the narrator's alone. As he makes explicit in his nonfiction (*The Long Emergency*), Kunstler finds in localism an appropriate spatial reconfiguration for living without (or with less reliance on) fossil fuels. In the world of his novels, energy is derived mainly from the muscle power of humans and animals, from burning wood, occasionally from wind and water power, and very occasionally from biofuels. Productivity is mainly agricultural, taking place on large farms and plantations—large only by nineteenth-century standards—and small holdings, and where technical it is artisanal in scale. The purchase and exchange of surplus goods and labor mostly take place within the limits of community, but regional trade is possible (dependent on waterways and what is left of the roads). Kunstler, I argue, provides us with a new geography of post-oil energy consumption, but at work is what we can call a geographical uncanny.

Productivity in the post-oil world begins at home, and Kunstler's novels are replete with pleasing descriptions of orderly self-sufficiency taking place in sturdy and resilient small-town homes built in the nineteenth century (as opposed to the now ruined, serially produced dwellings of suburbia). Here old materials are recycled, and new artefacts are fashioned using traditional methods and rediscovered technologies. Such industrious households are well provisioned by food grown and reared at home or bought and bartered for locally. Those who succeed in Kunstler's world are, in effect, the producers of their own lives, and these lives are very much powered by human labor. It is these novels' fetishization of localized acts of human labor, the energy produced by that labor, and the things crafted by that labor—in the absence of modern technology, industry, and mass production—that screens the long history of the fossil-fueled and energized society, which, disavowed by pastoralism, has not been sufficiently mourned. More precisely, such a fetish disavows the sheer amount of energy production and consumption upon which precatastrophe America relied and in which Kunstler's energized subjects were implicated (Nikiforuk). Kunstler's petromelancholic premediation of the environmental future means that his literary speculations about the future are still all too governed by something akin to an actuarial imaginary—that he is, in effect, speculating on the futures market of the postapocalyptic imaginary and that the ecological has inadvertently collapsed into the economic.

Demonstrating the challenges faced by cultural memory studies in its exploration of the future anterior, the limits of Kunstler's attempts to think beyond oil are still useful, because as well as foregrounding economic, affective mediations, they also return us to the problem of scale and the difficulties of imagining deep history and planetary space, capital *and* species. In recent literary criticism, the turn to a geological time scheme has enabled the long histories of environments to be indexed and the effects of human activities, which have futures beyond the parameters of national historiography, to be imagined. However, as Mark McGurl has recently commented, this scaling up of the literary imagination can risk rendering the operations of culture meaningless if framed within a "vaulting largeness" that becomes absolutely indifferent to the idea and actuality of nations that have now become, relatively speaking, insignificant. What is more, the "deep time" into which the nation is plunged threatens to become irrelevant to national understanding. The framing of environmental futures needs to stage a "negotiation" between "expansion and contraction" to give both ends of the scale meaning and form in relation to each other (McGurl 540). Even if life in the post-oil world of Kunstler's novel is precarious, and populations are contracting, social organization is regressive, technology hardly modern, and nonhuman life ascendant, sometimes predatory and reclaiming of human spaces, the novel only gestures toward such a larger temporal scheme. Nonetheless, as McGurl might argue, the literary imagination can only think beyond the homeland in a meaningful way if that homeland remains in its purview. Grounded in petromelancholia, Kunstler's novel at least stages a recognizable departure for the deep time of the Anthropocene.

Rick Crownshaw is a senior lecturer in the Department of English and Comparative Literature at Goldsmiths, University of London. He is the author of *The Afterlife of Holocaust Memory in Contemporary Literature and Culture* (Palgrave Macmillan, 2010), the editor of *Transcultural Memory* (Routledge, 2014), and a coeditor of *The Future of Memory* (Berghahn, 2010; paperback 2014). He is currently working on a monograph, *American Fictions of the Anthropocene,* which focuses on the potential of cultural memory and trauma studies for representing climate change, alongside narratives of extinction, the resourcing of war, American petrocultures and post-oil imaginaries, and climate change communication and cognition.

WORKS CITED

Assmann, Aleida, and Sebastian Conrad, eds. *Memory in a Global Age: Discourses, Practices and Trajectories.* Basingstoke: Palgrave Macmillan, 2012.

Bennett, Jane. *Vibrant Matter: A Political Ecology of Things.* Durham: Duke University Press, 2010.

Bond, Lucy, and Jessica Rapson, eds. *The Transcultural Turn: Interrogating Memory between and beyond Borders.* Berlin: De Gruyter, 2014.

Butler, Judith. *Frames of War: When Is Life Grievable?* London: Verso, 2009.

Chakrabarty, Dipesh. "The Climate of History: Four Theses." *Critical Inquiry* 35.2 (2009): 197–222.

Clark, Timothy. "Derangements of Scale." *Telemorphosis: Theory in the Era of Climate Change, Vol. 1.* Ed. Tom Cohen. Ann Arbor, University of Michigan Library: Open Humanities Press, 2012. 147–62.

Cohen, Tom. "Introduction: Murmurations–'Climate Change' and the Defacement of Theory." *Telemorphosis: Theory in the Era of Climate Change, Vol. 1.* Ed. Tom Cohen. Ann Arbour, University of Michigan Library: Open Humanities Press, 2012. 13–42.

Craps, Stef. "Beyond Eurocentrism: Trauma Theory in the Global Age." *The Future of Trauma Theory: Contemporary Literary Criticism.* Ed. Gert Buelens, Sam Durrant, and Robert Eaglestone. London: Routledge, 2014. 45–61.

——. *Postcolonial Witnessing: Trauma Out of Bounds.* Basingstoke: Palgrave Macmillan, 2013.

Crownshaw, Rick, ed. *Transcultural Memory.* London: Routledge, 2014.

Crutzen, Paul. "The Geology of Mankind." *Nature* 415 (3 Jan. 2002): 23.

Crutzen, Paul, and Eugene Stoermer. "The Anthropocene." *Global Change Newsletter* 41.1 (2000): 17–18.

De Cesari, Chiara, and Ann Rigney. *Transnational Memory: Circulation, Articulation, Scales.* Berlin: De Gruyter, 2014.

Dibley, Ben, and Brett Neilson. "Climate Crisis and the Actuarial Imaginary." *New Formations* 69 (2010): 144–59.

Heise, Ursula K. *Sense of Place and Sense of Planet: The Environmental Imagination of the Planet.* Oxford: Oxford University Press, 2008.

Kunstler, James Howard. *The Long Emergency.* New York: Atlantic Monthly Press, 2005.

———. *World Made by Hand.* New York: Atlantic Monthly Press, 2008.

———. *The Witch of Hebron.* New York: Atlantic Monthly Press, 2010.

———. *A History of the Future.* New York: Atlantic Monthly Press, 2014.

LeMenager, Stephanie. *Living Oil: Petroleum Culture in the American Century.* Oxford: Oxford University Press, 2014.

Levy, Daniel, and Natan Sznaider. *The Holocaust and Memory in the Global Age.* Philadelphia: Temple University Press, 2005.

McGurl, Mark. "The Posthuman Comedy." *Critical Inquiry* 38.3 (2012): 533–53.

Nikiforuk, Andrew. *The Energy of Slaves: Oil and the New Servitude.* Vancouver: Greystone Books, 2012.

Nixon, Rob. *Slow Violence and the Environmentalism of the Poor.* Cambridge: Harvard University Press, 2011.

Rothberg, Michael. "Beyond Tancred and Clorinda: Trauma Studies for Implicated Subjects." *The Future of Trauma Theory: Contemporary Literary Criticism.* Ed. Gert Buelens, Sam Durrant, and Robert Eaglestone. London: Routledge, 2013. xi–xvii.

———. *Multidirectional Memory: Remembering the Holocaust in the Age of Decolonization.* Stanford: Stanford University Press, 2009.

Chapter 12

"Filled with Words"

Modeling the September 11 Digital Archive and the Utility of Digital Methods in the Study of Memory

Jessica K. Young

Jessica K. Young

> It is as if the sign of disaster, this irrefutable, brutal absence revealed in and at ground zero, demands that "the hole in the real" ... not be allowed to remain empty: that it be filled with words, stories, anecdotes, testimonies, biographies, images ...; that it become a site of memory and remembrance, a place of disaster made meaningful by the representations–personal, collective, commemorative, spontaneous, official–that follow catastrophe, a writing of disaster that is also a re-membering (a recalling and a reconstruction) of disaster.
>
> —Richard Stamelman

As the field of memory studies reflects on the possibilities and liabilities digital media pose for the collection, preservation, and global circulation of individual and collective memories, it has to confront methodological problems posed by the sheer volume of data these digital technologies make available. Given the ingrained habits of close reading that define many traditional humanist disciplines, memory scholars, including Richard Crownshaw in his chapter on oil memory in this volume, have sought new transdisciplinary methodologies in order to make sense of the increasing scale of memory, in this case the "indigestible immediacy of digital data dumps" that define the digital storage and circulation of memory (Hoskins 269). Yet, within the context of memory studies, the development and analysis of an alternate methodology to study the material collected en masse by digital media is still in its nascent stages.

Complementing the methodological issues raised by Joyce Van de Bildt elsewhere in this volume, this essay seeks to understand what the tools engineered by the emergent interdisciplinary field of digital humanities can offer in the study of a large corpus of personal stories collected in increasingly popular online user-generated digital memorial archives, specifically what these tools can add to the analysis of a collective memory of trauma. As a case study, I use a form of "distant reading" called Latent Dirichlet Allocation (LDA) topic modeling, a form of statistical analysis, to examine 12,500 personal responses collected by the September 11 Digital Archive. As the largest user-generated digital memorial archive, the September 11 Digital Archive is representative of a new form of interactive public memorialization that demonstrates the difficulties digital memory scholars face when assessing and analyzing the accumulated mass of digital memories circulating across global digital networks. An LDA analysis identifies trends within digital archives and tracks how individual responses are correlated and how they unfold over time, providing critics with a detailed quantitative study of the temporal dynamics of digital remembrance as well as data to validate or modify theories of the collective response to trauma. Ultimately, topic modeling allows memory scholars to examine how certain topics capture the imagination of responders at certain points in time and how they emerge and evolve to reflect the needs of a changing present, thus turning the mass of digital memorial data into a meaningful engagement with collective memory.

DIGITAL MEMORY STUDIES AND THE "INDIGESTIBLE IMMEDIACY OF DIGITAL DATA DUMPS"

Richard Stamelman, in his essay "Between Memory and History," examines the memorial culture surrounding September 11, arguing that it marked a new wave of commemoration unprecedented in its rapidity and volume. The physical and emotional holes—the gaping wound at Ground Zero as well as the wound in the individual and cultural psyche—left in the wake of the attacks, Stamelman notes, quickly began to fill with "words, stories, anecdotes, testimonies, biographies, [and] images" in order to recall and (re)construct what was lost (15). The process by which September 11 became commemorated occurred at an extraordinary rate; whereas "the metamorphosis of a locus of history into a site of memory usually requires ... the passage of decades, generations, even centuries," Stamelman finds that with September 11 "the event itself and the landscape of the event have ... rapidly been transformed into a memory site" (15).

According to Stamelman, the expedited memorialization could have been due to "the speed with which objects, events, and persons in the post-modern age of rapid communication, immediate globalization, and instantaneous commodification are transformed into symbols and icons," thereby speeding up the process by which significant sites traditionally become, in Pierre Nora's terms, *lieux de mémoire* (Stamelman 15, 14). When critics note that September 11 was "one of the most mediated disasters in history" and the first "truly digital event of world historical importance," it becomes clear that we are entering a new age of memorialization with new technologies of commemoration whose influence on collective memory needs to be assessed and analyzed (Brier and Brown 101; Haskins 408). I draw on Stamelman here not only to evoke the ways in which commemorative practices in the age of globalization and digitization have been transformed but also to draw attention to the ways in which these new forms of posttraumatic (re)con-struction allow various official and vernacular forms of memorial responses to exist side by side. In the digital age, a disaster like September 11 provokes a proliferation of "representations—personal, collective, commemorative, spontaneous, [and] official" (Stamelman 15), and it is because of the digital that these diverse forms of memorial representation can be preserved en masse and circulated globally.

In order to understand what meaningful contribution digital human-ities might make to the interpretative approaches to posttraumatic digital memorial archives, it is first necessary to briefly outline the ways in which memory studies scholars have conceived of the storage and flows of memory across digital and networked technologies and to offer a brief history of the emergence and rise of online digital memorial archives. Memory scholars, including Astrid Erll, have noted the increasing impact mass media and new media have on the study of memory. As Erll observes:

> Since the turn of the millennium we have witnessed the rapid development of a host of new concepts in memory studies which address media, specifically mass media and the new media. The reasons for this are arguably to be found in the ever-increasing and accelerating, worldwide dissemination of images and narratives about the past through mass media ... which now shape the everyday experience of most people, at least in the western world. (131)

One important vein of inquiry that has developed within digital memory studies is the reconceptualization of the archive in the digital era, when increased storage capacity meets with new possibilities in the circulation and dissemination of memory across the globalized digital world. As the editors of the collection *Save As ... Digital Memories* note, "There is currently a digital archive fever at work, fuelled by memory-hungry technologies, increased memory capacities of databases and faster, more reliable network connections" (Garde-Hansen, Hoskins, and Reading 130). The capacity and connectedness afforded by digital archives have significantly increased the availability of data and played an important role in the formation and understanding of memory in the digital era. At the same time, this capacity results in a methodological problem in that we are faced with the challenge of studying the vast amount of material the digital makes available.

As Andrew Hoskins points out, "There is an emergent tension between the scale of material that can be made available online and the decreasing capacity of anyone to consume it, or to make sense of it" (269)—a tension that, as Aleida Assmann argues in this volume, affects the inherent link between the concept of memory and conditions of scarcity. This inability to examine the contents of digital data collected in online archives, the actual memorial substance being recorded and maintained, leads digital memory scholars to seek methodological alternatives. As Anna Reading notes, "The globital memory field requires new grounds of knowledge for the study of media memory that implicates research designs for the study of memory, as well as the development of more transdisciplinary and traveling methodologies that reconfigure forms of analysis" ("Memory and Digital Media" 251). What is needed, then, is a new way to assess the data collected in order to see how memory is being preserved and circulated in the digital present.

Such a transdisciplinary methodology may specifically shed light on the massive accumulation of data in online user-generated archives created to memorialize traumatic events—data that have been consistently difficult to assess and study, especially in the case of September 11 with its massive global and digital response. Jennifer Howard finds that over the past decade, online user-generated digital archives have become ubiquitous in the memorialization of traumatic events. Howard specifically examines Our Marathon, a crowd-sourced digital archive created to collect born-digital materials responding to the 2013 Boston Marathon bombings as a recent iteration of the trend, which also includes the September 11 Digital Archive. Archives such as Our Marathon and the September 11 Digital Archive generally ask users to submit first-person accounts of events and their aftermath, and as these archives have grown more sophisticated, users can now upload photographs, emails, videos, and social media artifacts such as tweets and Facebook status updates to their collections. These archives have similar stated purposes, including collecting and preserving "born-digital often evanescent material" produced in the wake of tragedies, providing a site where "members of the community can find comfort and solidarity through storytelling," and acting as a resource for future research that can "fill ... in the gaps left by news-media coverage," allowing scholars access to individual perspectives on these historic events (Howard).

More broadly, however, these archives reflect the rise of what Erika Doss describes as "memorial mania," in which there is a proliferation of memorials reflecting "an obsession with issues of memory and history and an urgent desire to express and claim those issues in visibly public contexts" (2). While Doss primarily examines traditional "brick-and-mortar" memorials that are permanently situated at significant sites of remembrance, the impetus behind memorial mania, the "heightened anxieties about who and what should be remembered," also seems to fuel the creation and maintenance of these digital archives (2). This memorial mania, the "excessive, frenzied, and extreme" process of memorial creation Doss describes, is especially apparent in the attempt of these archives to preserve ephemeral digital material en masse before it becomes lost, ensuring that the data remain available for future generations (13).

Digital archives, however, differ from traditional memorials in that they are not physical edifices tied to a significant location but are digital and intangible, housed on the Internet and available via high-speed networks around the globe. Still, this fundamental difference in memorial medium only intensifies already existent commemorative practices and cultural anxieties about remembering the past. As Andrew Hoskins notes, the memorialization of traumatic events has been significantly accelerated due to the increase in digital storage capacity coupled with the contemporary trend toward memorialization, leading to a "memorial-media boom" in which "a compulsive culture of digitization and connectivity—driven by availability, portability and pervasiveness of digital devices—converges with a memorial culture determined to (selectively but excessively) reconsume past conflicts and catastrophes" (270). As a commemorative practice, digital archives intensify the memorial mania Doss describes through their ability to store near-infinite amounts of information, and through their very storage capacity they encourage the digital collection and preservation of data beyond the point of easy recall or accessibility. In this way, these digital archives are complex memoryscapes that, as Frauke Wiegand's earlier chapter argues, require a rethinking of human and object interaction in the mediation and remediation of events.

Even though there is a similar manic *impetus* that fuels the creation and preservation of these archives, the memorialization *practices* differ between traditional memorials that tend to reflect and reify official commemorative discourses and unofficial crowd-sourced digital memorial archives. Doss finds that traditional memorials are often nationalist projects reflecting national anxieties about how certain events should be remembered and that they are established in order to "control ... particular narratives about the

nation and its publics" (2). This is especially the case with memorials commemorating the aftermath of terrorism; Doss further notes: "America's terrorism memorials embody widespread public fears about the state of the
nation and the vulnerability of its citizens. While they ostensibly counter
those fears with particular security narratives geared toward national unity
and social stability, they also reinscribe them" (119–20). According to Doss,
terrorism memorials especially conform to "nationalist narratives of social
stability, unity, and endurance," and they do so precisely at the cost of any
alternative readings of the traumas they commemorate (122–23). Refuting
in this instance the idea, often associated with Cathy Caruth's work, that
trauma may open up "new modes of reading ...; new concepts of evidence
and interpretation in history; new narratives of identity and purpose in the
national imaginary," Doss finds that these memorials instead offer "superficial" representations "orientated toward the restoration of social order and
the revitalization of presumably shared national norms" (133). "Trauma's ...
transgressive possibilities," Doss argues, "are generally overlooked, if not entirely ignored" (133). Traditional memorials, then, tend to reflect and perpetuate hegemonic state discourses about the events they are commemorating
and, in the case of terrorism memorials, preclude the possibilities opened up
by the trauma for alternative readings and forms of meaning making.

Despite Doss's claims about traditional forms of memorialization and
Hoskins's assertion that the "memorial-media boom" leads to "selective"
but "excessive" preservation of digital memorial material, many proponents
of online user-generated archives view this memorial practice as a more
democratic form of commemoration, able to collect and preserve disparate
voices beyond the political and cultural hegemony of the state; this is what
Van de Bildt, in her analysis of digital media memory in this collection, calls
"vernacular memory." For example, Ekaterina Haskins argues that digital
archives in particular allow for the side-by-side display of official and unofficial discourses regarding traumatic events: "Instead of only official accounts
disseminated by mainstream media and the government, all kinds of stories
can now become part of an evolving patchwork of public memory" (405).
In fact, Haskins finds that digital archives encourage this discursive diversity *because* of their almost infinite storage capacity: "Online memorializing,
thanks to the technology's capacity for virtually unlimited storage and potential to engage many diverse audiences in content production, appears to
mitigate against the ideological ossification associated with official memory
practices" (418). Lee Jarvis further posits that archives such as the September 11 Digital Archive "represent ... a significant social memory project precisely as a refusal of efforts to forge one, singular narrative of the attacks. If
nothing else, we have here a cacophony of stories, each competing to narrate

the attacks from individual and highly personal standpoints" (814). In their ability to include multiple, often conflicting, discourses surrounding traumatic events, online archives, for critics like Haskins, seem to have a "democratic potential" instilled in them by their very digital nature that allows the sheer unlimited collection of a "plethora" of personal responses (419, 411). However, the capacity of digital archives also leads to the difficulty to "read" and assess their contents, due to their sheer size and to their topical and thematic diversity.

As online user-generated digital archives continue to gain prominence as a way to publicly memorialize national tragedies, their role in the commemorative process needs to be assessed. What is more, these archives are a poignant example of the prolific volume and diversity of the digital memorial data that are collected and circulated across the globe every day, and thus they highlight the analytical difficulties digital memory scholars face when assessing the increasing influence digital technology plays in the contemporary memory field. For this study specifically, I use the algorithmic tools developed in the field of digital humanities to read the contents of one of these archives in order to track the public response to trauma and the commemorative structure of these archives.

I argue that an algorithmic analysis of the September 11 Digital Archive exposes how the public transitioned over time from narratives of posttraumatic rupture toward narratives of historical continuity in order to process and come to terms with these overwhelming events. In essence, this analysis can demonstrate the ways in which the public moves, to use Dominick LaCapra's influential terms, from "acting out," where there "is a tendency [to] compulsively repeat traumatic scenes" in an "uncritical" or even "valorized" manner, to "working through," where a "critical distance" from the trauma can be achieved in order "to distinguish between past, present, and future" (143). In doing so, I will also outline how this type of analysis gives us insight into the structure of these digital archives while also evaluating the claims of their democratic potential. I then reflect on the efficacy of analytical algorithmic tools in the study of digital memory, assessing their present limitations while looking forward to future possibilities. It is in developing and assessing new digital methodologies, I argue in my final section, that a critical analysis of not just these archives but digital memory more generally can be forged.

THE SEPTEMBER 11 DIGITAL ARCHIVE

To demonstrate the utility of topic modeling for the study of digital memory, I examine the September 11 Digital Archive as a model for the potential of this form of analysis. The September 11 Digital Archive, one of the first and by far the largest of the crowd-sourced archives, is an ongoing project created by the Center for History and New Media at George Mason University and the American Social History Project/Center of Media and Learning at the City University of New York Graduate Center.[1] The archive was created to "collect, preserve, and present the history of September 11, 2001 and its aftermath" through user-generated personal stories, emails, and images of the events so that scholars could continue to "assess ... how history is being recorded and preserved in the twenty-first century" (September 11 Digital Archive). This preoccupation with collection, preservation, and future assessment is clear not only on the archive's homepage but in its very inception. As Stephen Brier and Joshua Brown, two of the founding architects of the archive, recount:

> [Building the archive] challenged us to think about what historians fifty years from now would want to know about the September 11 events and what data they would want to have access to in order to construct a full historical narrative of what transpired. The foundation's staff was concerned that without a coherent and deliberate plan to capture, archive, and preserve digital materials related to the September 11 attacks—particularly the stories of individuals who had personally experienced the events—such materials would be lost to future generations. (102)

The archive, then, anticipates future interpretation and reflection on the disparate public voices amassed in its corpus as a way to create a more comprehensive narrative of the attacks and their aftermath for posterity. As Brier and Brown make clear, "We believed ... that such digital materials would prove central to any future understanding of September 11 and the larger political, social, and economic meanings of that epochal historical moment" (103).

Given the mass of digital data this archive preserved, there results a tension between the archive's stated goals of preservation and scholarly assessment: the capacity of the archive has ensured that everyone's story can be collected and maintained, but this has resulted in a corpus size that resists traditional humanist methods of interpretation. In lieu of an "other mechanism" for reading the massive corpus of personal responses, scholars combing through the September 11 Digital Archive have found themselves limited in their reading capacities (Haskins 419). Haskins, for example, focuses primarily on the structure and democratizing potential of the archive over the content of the corpus. She gives her readers brief glimpses into the "collage of perspectives" contained within the archive yet highlights few specific themes that permeate and structure the responses, nor does she track how these themes appear in the archive over time (Haskins 412). Similarly, Timothy Recuber focuses on the production of user-generated content and limits his lens of interpretation to the "self-help" nature of the responses in the September 11 Digital Archive and the Hurricane Digital Memory Bank (531). Jarvis, in his study of WhereWereYou.org, a much smaller but similarly structured digital archive responding to September 11, also has difficulty assessing the nuance of the archive's diverse thematic structure, categorizing most responses as meditations on the "abrupt rupture" of the events instead of identifying the smaller unique topics that together create this sense of a "temporal, cognitive and discursive" break (800).[2] If "public memory is, in fact, an evolving process," it has not been possible thus far to assess the nuanced nature, diversity, and temporal flux of the public memory collected by the September 11 Digital Archive through traditional close reading methodologies (Haskins 414).

   While limited in their ability to thoroughly read digital archives, especially in the case of the September 11 Digital Archive, Haskins, Recuber, and Jarvis are some of the few critics who have examined the personal responses—the "stories, anecdotes, testimonies, [and] biographies" that circulated following the attacks and comprise the memorial substance of these archives (Stamelman 15). Indeed, personal narratives by the public have largely been neglected by literary critics, who instead broadly place these personal responses within the overarching generic unfolding of September 11 literature from shorter nonfiction to longer literary works, without examining their content or specificity (Keniston and Follansbee Quinn; Randall). Considering that these personal responses are a window into the public reaction to, and digestion of, the traumatic events of September 11, this critical oversight is significant. It is understandable, though, as the unevenness of their quality, their tremendous quantity, and their dispersion across various media, websites, and archives all make it especially difficult to attempt an extended close analysis of the mass of personal responses through traditional humanist methodologies. As Franco Moretti observes, "The trouble with close reading ... is that it necessarily depends on an extremely small canon" (57). Given these limitations, one would only be able to review a limited portion of the personal responses spread across the Internet and print media. However, with the tools developed by digital humanities, it is possible to attempt a "distant reading" of a large corpus of personal essays, "where distance ... *is a condition of knowledge* [that] allows [one] to focus on units that are much smaller or much larger than the text," uncovering "devices, themes, tropes—or genres and systems" that may shed light on a culturewide posttraumatic response process (Moretti 57). In order to posit the future utility of digital tools for the field of memory studies, I use these methodologies to retrieve and read these responses, examining how they act as modes of memorial (re)construction, creating and reflecting collective memory trends over time as the traumatic events are assimilated into a narrative of continuity.

A MODEL OF DISTANT READING: AN LDA ANALYSIS OF THE SEPTEMBER 11 DIGITAL ARCHIVE

In order to read 12,500 responses collected by the September 11 Digital Archive, I apply Bayesian, or probabilistic, LDA topic modeling. Because the archive asks all contributors to reflect on the same event yet gives very little overall structure to the collection, LDA provides us with a methodology that can identify unique underlying topics that are present in the archive. The LDA model uses a generative process to identify and cluster data points, in this case correlating words across the corpus of the archive and assigning them to a group. In other words, topic modeling identifies specific words that consistently appear together, grouping them in a cluster known as a "topic," which one can then track across the corpus.

Matt Burton reminds us that far from the standard definition of a "topic" within literary studies, "in the domain of language models [a topic] means a *probability distribution* over a vocabulary of words." A topic, then, is not a coherent narrative, but a list of words that require further investigation and analysis. "Given that topics are merely lists of words," Burton continues, "any topic modeling exercise requires some interpretative effort to discern if the model is a reasonable representation of the corpus and what that representation means. Thus, a close and careful reading of the relationship between topics and documents is necessary to fully understand and contextualize what the words of topic really *mean.*" What is more, as David Blei and John D. Lafferty note, "Topics are not known in advance" of running an LDA analysis, so "our goal" then becomes "to learn from the data" and interpret the findings of our results (3). In upending the ways in which humanists usually approach texts, topic modeling, according to Blei and Lafferty, opens up new possibilities for traditional humanist methodologies: "By discovering patterns of word use and connecting documents that exhibit similar patterns, topic models have emerged as a powerful new technique for finding useful structure in an otherwise unstructured collection" (1). Given the data collected by the archive and accessed through such an analysis, we can track these topics over time as they rise and fall in popularity, making it possible to retrieve and identify trends within the corpus to see how the responses to September 11 develop.[3]

An LDA analysis identifying the top fifty topics of the September 11 Digital Archive makes it clear that despite the professed democratic potential of online user-generated archives, many of the archive's most popular topics actually reflect and reproduce the hegemonic cultural and political discourses that proliferated in the wake of the attacks.[4] For example, Topic 20, which correlates words such as "never," "will," "day," "forget," "ever," and "always," seems to reiterate the common posttraumatic refrain "always remember, never forget" that circulated through the political and cultural rhetoric surrounding the events and was reproduced on numerous posters, bumper stickers, and billboards across the United States in the months following September 11. Similarly, Topic 42, which correlates words such as "god," "bless," and "America" with words such as "pray" and "prayed," seems to reproduce the ubiquitous exclamation of "God bless America" that was similarly reiterated in the wake of the attacks. According to Recuber, "Some of the most frequently expressed sentiments left at ... the archive ... were explicitly religious. Thirty-three percent of the September 11 Archive messages contained religious references," even if "some [of these references] were simply phrases like 'God Bless America'" (Blei and Lafferty 541). Given the prevalence of the phrases "always remember, never forget" and "God bless America" used by the media and political figures in their responses to September 11, their ubiquity and their presence in the top fifty topics is expected.[5]

While these topics seem to confirm the infiltration of hegemonic political and cultural discourses into the archive, their inclusion does not necessarily preclude the democratic potential of the archive, as they may exist beside other discourses that refute or dispel these same hegemonic refrains. In fact, the ability to assess the archive, to "reflect ... on whether and which official interpretations of 9/11 entered public consciousness more broadly, how they did so, and when" might give us substantive insight into how the public interacts with, adopts, appropriates, and subverts these hegemonic discourses, and an assessment of these topical trends may yet give us an understanding of, if not the democratic potential of these projects, then at least their potential for preserving a plurality of commemorative efforts, both official and vernacular (Jarvis 797).

I want to highlight two topics in particular that are generally seen as part of the post-September 11 discursive hegemony that may give us insight into not only the plurality of the archive but also the means by which the public encounters and processes trauma. By examining these two topics over time, we can begin to see how a national narrative of posttraumatic continuity slowly emerges through individual remediations of hegemonic national discourses following the attacks, while simultaneously demonstrating how such trends can be identified and studied through an LDA analysis.

The first topic I would like to discuss, Topic 29, seems to identify the surge of patriotism that immediately followed the attacks, correlating words such as "our, country, America, we, nation, united, proud, us, freedom, flag, together, great, stand." A sampling from the individual entries categorized in Topic 29 confirms that these responses are preoccupied with patriotic themes. In one entry correlated with the topic, for instance, the responder writes, "This indeed was a terrible event, but we as a nation have proven to be steadfast and dedicated to the principles of freedom ... I will always and forever be proud to say: 'I am an American.'" Echoing almost verbatim this language is another correlated entry: "I was extremely shocked and did not really think much of my patriotism until that day ... I will forever remember September 11, 2001, and will forever be proud to be an American." This type of patriotic rhetoric was ubiquitous throughout the national discourse following September 11, and its appearance in the archive thus seems inevitable.

Beyond identifying the expected presence of patriotism in the archive, topic modeling traces the trajectory of the cultural popularity of this patriotic rhetoric following September 11. The graphical representation of Topic 29 relative to the size of the corpus over time makes it clear that the popularity of patriotism as a response mechanism peaks early in the response process, between the first and second anniversaries of the attacks, and drops precipitously until the months leading up to the fifth anniversary, when, predictably, there is a brief resurgence (see Illustration 12.1).[6] What this trend suggests is that patriotism provides an immediate counter to the emotional rupture of September 11. It seems to be a discourse that reestab-

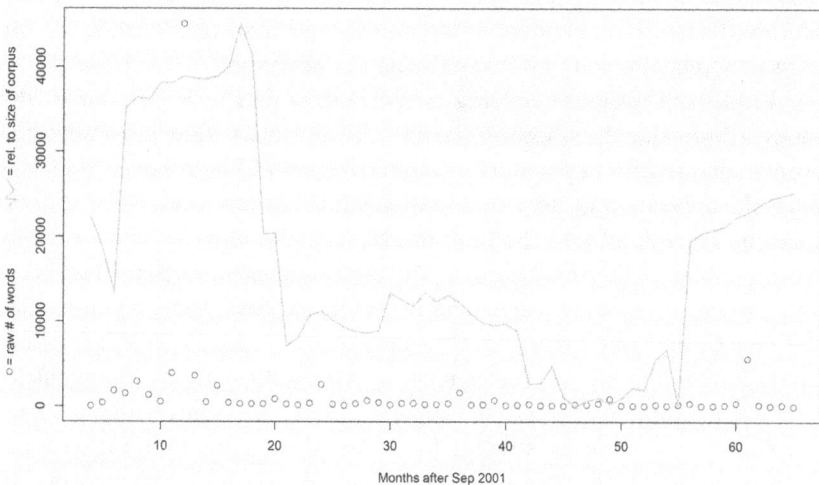

Illustration 12.1. Graph of Topic 29 ("Patriotism") over time.

lishes, however superficially, the constancy of the nation in the aftermath of a violent attack, as individuals use temporal words such as "forever" and "steadfast" in conjunction with the rhetoric of patriotism as a way of projecting a tenuous national continuity. As time progresses, however, patriotism as a response mechanism ebbs in popularity, suggesting that this uncritical hegemonic discourse is of limited utility in creating a lasting coherent narrative about the attacks and their aftermath.

If patriotism was popular in the early days after September 11, it is important to see what topics emerge later in the response process that may move the cultural discourse toward a more lasting narrative of continuity. One such theme seems to emerge in Topic 5, which correlates words associated with September 11, such as "attack," "9/11," and "terrorist," with words pertaining to time and other historical events, such as "after," "Pearl," "Harbor," "America," "bombing," "generation," "Kennedy," and "infamy." Upon closer examination, the responses correlated with Topic 5 attempt to situate the attacks and their aftermath within a larger historical national narrative, as can be seen in the following entry:

> There is only one event I can think of that can even compare to 9/11 and that is the attack on Pearl Harbor. That attack caused devastation and it was a leading cause for the US to enter World War 2. Like Pearl Harbor, 9/11 was also a leading cause to the war in Iraq ... Pearl Harbor and the attacks on September 11th have and probably always will be remembered as some of the lowest points in American history.

Like other responses that correlate with Topic 5, this response seeks to understand September 11 through a national-historical lens, focusing as much on the specific circumstances of the attacks and their aftermath as on the ways they relate to other events in the nation's history.

Unlike the responses relying on patriotism that were popular in the months immediately following the attacks, responses that historicize the events seem to gain in popularity. The prevalence of Topic 5 over time thus takes the opposite trajectory of Topic 29: while initially there is a moderate spike in Topic 5 around the first anniversary, the topic becomes steadily more popular at the third, fourth, and fifth anniversaries (see Illustration 12.2), whereas Topic 29 reached its height in the first twenty months after the attacks and only experienced a moderate resurgence at the five-year mark. Examining the two topics together makes it clear that where patriotism was an initial reaction to the attacks, placing the events within a historical context is a response strategy that attempts to come to terms with the trauma imposed by September 11 by refusing the event's incommensurability, moving from a narrative of rupture to one of continuity.

Topic 5 : attack 9/11 attacks terrorist

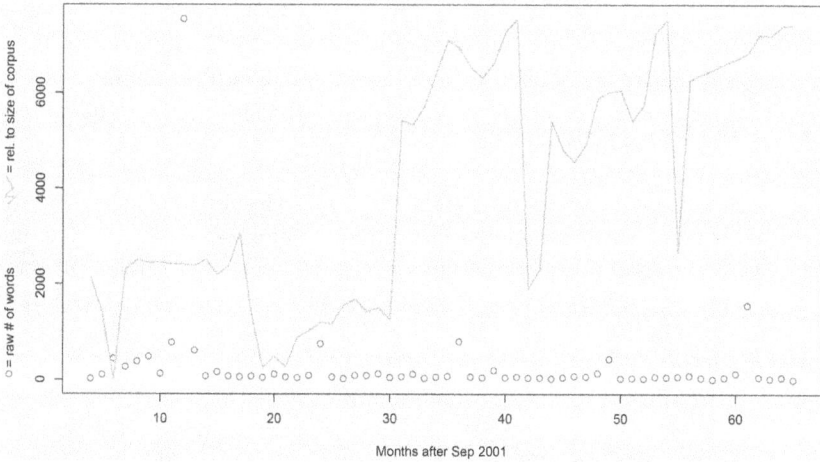

Illustration 12.2. Graph of Topic 5 ("Historicizing") over time.

At the same time, in comparing September 11 and its military consequences to the attack on Pearl Harbor and World War II, the respondent
is drawing on a hegemonic narrative that proliferated in the news media
following the attacks; given the temporal delay from the narrative's public
deployment to the response's appearance in the archive, it is clear that the
respondent is remediating a collective national memory to make sense of
their own present moment. In this way, the respondents that historicize the
events later in the response process may be "working through" the trauma
of September 11 in an attempt to "gain critical distance" from the events
and "distinguish between past, present, and future" (LaCapra 143). As time
wears on, we can continue to track how these responses to September 11
evolve to reflect the present collective memorial state, telling us as much
about our current moment as about our past.

DIGITAL METHODOLOGIES AND
THE STUDY OF DIGITAL MEMORY

As a transdisciplinary methodology, LDA topic modeling allows us to take
a critical look at the interpenetration of traditional and digital media with
the memorial needs of the collective and the individual on a scale and temporal register not available to past media studies on memory. Whereas previous media studies have identified many of the topics uncovered in my
LDA analysis and have specifically commented upon the use of historicizing

narratives in a limited collection of print and digital news media sources
(Brown et al.; Damphousse, Hefley, and Smith), they all see this trend as a
static fact of the archive rather than a constantly evolving remediation of
the events, which take hold of the collective imagination at certain points in
time. Michelle Brown and her coauthors note that historicizing narratives
occur often across Internet news sites dedicated to September 11:

> Because the archive subscribes immediately to the historicizing impulse, it per-
> mits the conceptualization and inscription of one's own experience into the
> canon of historical registry. In this respect, the frequent invocations of Pearl
> Harbor and the assassination of John F. Kennedy in the context of the loss of
> American innocence post-September 11 demonstrate how the archive serves to
> sustain the unifying drive of history. (111)

These scholars see the pervasive use of historicizing narratives within the
archive of Internet news media as indicative of an immediate mediation of
the trauma that "sustain[s] the unifying drive of history"; however, a closer
examination of the personal responses to September 11 demonstrates that
the adoption of this narrative by the public was not immediate but rather
appeared later in the memorialization process. As Garde-Hansen, Hoskins,
and Reading remind us, "In terms of digital practices, users are remediating
memory. They now have at their disposal a digital toolkit that allows them to
refashion memories and histories in multiple ways in order to tell multiple
versions of events" (129). It is in this way that LDA topic modeling charts how
these archives preserve a plurality of perspectives. By allowing us to examine
the ways in which individuals internalize mediated events, adopting forms of
remediation as their own at distinct times in order to describe, make sense of,
and remember trauma in their present, this digital tool uncovers the unique
form of public memorial engagement at work in these archives.

While LDA analysis gives us insight into the processes of mediation and
remediation by the public, it is yet to be seen how far such an analysis can
take us in the study of transnational memory flows as they connect distant
and disparate users across the temporal registers of digital time. As it stands,
this methodology proves that there are alternate temporalities within the
digital landscape. Whereas our current digitized and globalized world is
often characterized by the compression of time, Reading reminds us that,
in addition to "compression and speed, there is the 'slow' and the 'long,' a
'generous' time that is very much part of each citizen's lifeworld and subsequently is an important dimension within any process of commemoration"
("London Bombings" 309). The contributions by Crownshaw and Wiegand
to this volume further underline the complex rhythms and temporalities of
memory when it is considered in geological time, in the case of Crownshaw,
or at the interface of the human and the nonhuman, in the case of Wiegand.

This analysis demonstrates that certain remediated digital responses have a lifecycle and trajectory all their own, rising and falling, emerging and evolving in the days, months, and years that follow a traumatic event. As digital methodologies evolve, it is hoped that they can be modified to examine the temporal and connective possibilities opened up by what Reading terms "globital time," or the possibilities of connections, interactions, and incitements that circulate among globalized digital worlds to form the memories collected in digital archives. Reading defines globital time "not ... in terms of 'the assemblage,' or the heterogeneous composition [of the memory or response] in itself, but in terms of the potential of aqueous volubility, the 'incitements' between the elements of an assemblage" ("Globital Time" 152). The potential of LDA analysis, then, goes beyond simply tracking the popularity of certain topics over time, but rather resides in the methodological possibilities it may one day possess to shed light on how certain responsive topics emerge, circulate globally, combine with other topics, transform, and die out on a mass scale, giving us the ability to read from a distance and discover the complexities of our personal responses to tragedy.

Jessica K. Young is a Ph.D. candidate and Distinguished Fellow in English at the University of Illinois at Urbana-Champaign. She is a cofounder of the Future of Trauma and Memory Studies group at the University of Illinois and a coeditor (with Michael Rothberg) of *Days and Memory,* the blog of the Initiative in Holocaust, Genocide, and Memory Studies. Her work examines biopolitics in contemporary South Asian literature and the transmission of transcultural memory.

NOTES

I would like to extend my gratitude to the September 11 Digital Archive, a project run by the Center for History and New Media at George Mason University and the American Social History Project at the City University of New York Graduate Center, for granting me access to Archive's data. I am especially indebted to Jim Safley, Tom Scheinfeldt, and Sharon M. Leon, as well as the Roy Rosenzweig Center for History and New Media. I would also like to acknowledge Ted Underwood's contribution to this project in organizing the transfer of data from the September 11 Digital Archive and for his invaluable programming skills.

1. The initial version of the archive was launched 11 January 2002, and the site went fully public on 11 March 2002. Although the "active collecting phase" of the archive ended in 2003, the site is still available to view and is still accepting submissions. In the first two years of its existence alone, the archive "collected a total of nearly 150,000 individual digital items, including 45,000 personal narratives" about 9/11 (Brier and Brown 106).

2. WhereWereYou collected a total of 2,500 entries, much less than the September 11 Digital Archive (Jarvis 795). WhereWereYou also only collected responses for a year, which makes it impossible to track the popularity of the underlying topics over a significant amount of time.

3. The September 11 Digital Archive added a timestamp to each entry, which makes it possible to track the responses over time. The archive also attempted to collect the zip codes of responders, but this information was voluntary and was inconsistently offered. As digital archives become more sophisticated, geo-tagging may become standard, allowing future algorithmic analyses to include a locational distribution of topics.

4. The number of topics generated is determined by the size of the corpus, the researcher's goals, and the analysis of the results. As Burton notes, "While mainly a science, topic modeling has aspects of an art form. There are several parameters that we must specify before estimating the model. The most significant of these parameters is the number of topics ... The number of topics is a subjective selection dependent upon the size and shape of the corpus." If the algorithm searches for too few or too many topics, it "can affect the interpretability of the results," leading to "very broad" topics or "uninterpretable topics that pick out idiosyncratic word combinations" (Steyvers and Griffiths 441). Given the corpus size, it was determined that we would run the algorithm to generate fifty topics, which resulted in distinct and interpretable topics.

5. Here, perhaps, is one limitation of an LDA analysis: if one is searching for the most popular topics that structure a memorial archive, one is likely to find the popular and hegemonic discourses that have thus far defined the events being commemorated. However, an LDA analysis can also show us the unique temporal dynamics of these popular and hegemonic discourses, giving us an insight into their remediations by the public. It is also possible to run the algorithm again looking for more topics in order to find less popular forms of response, although expanding the topics under review can, as I remarked in the previous note, also muddy the results.

6. Brier and Brown found that "the real burst of online submissions came on the six-month and one-year anniversary of the attacks. More than one hundred thousand visitors accessed the site on the first anniversary, and we received thirteen thousand new personal stories during the next few days" (105). It is clear from the distribution of topics over time that the anniversaries continue to mark increases in user-submitted responses.

WORKS CITED

Blei, David M., and John D. Lafferty. "Topic Models." *Text Mining: Classification, Clustering, and Applications*. Ed. Ashok Srivastava and Mehran Sahami. London: Taylor and Francis 2009. Web. 20 April 2015.

Brier, Stephen, and Joshua Brown. "The September 11 Digital Archive: Saving the Histories of September 11, 2001." *Radical History Review* 111 (2011): 101–9.

Brown, Michelle, Leia Fuzesi, Kara Kitsch, and Crystal Spivey. "Internet News Representations of September 11: Archival Impulse in the Age of Information." *Media Representations of September 11*. Ed. Steven Chermak, Frankie Y. Bailey, and Michelle Brown. Westport: Praeger, 2003. 103–16.

Burton, Matthew. "The Joy of Topic Modeling." *Mcburton.net* 21 May 2013. Web. 7 Jan. 2014.

Caruth, Cathy, ed. *Trauma: Explorations in Memory*. Baltimore: Johns Hopkins University Press, 1995.

Damphousse, Kelly R., Kristen S. Hefley, and Brent L. Smith. "Creating Memories: Exploring How Narratives Help Define the Memorialization of Tragedy." *Media Representations of September 11*. Ed. Steven Chermak, Frankie Y. Bailey, and Michelle Brown. Westport: Praeger, 2003. 135–57.

Doss, Erika. *Memorial Mania: Public Feeling in America*. Chicago: University of Chicago Press, 2010.

Erll, Astrid. *Memory in Culture*. Trans. Sara B. Young. Basingstoke: Palgrave Macmillan, 2011.

Garde-Hansen, Joanne, Andrew Hoskins, and Anna Reading. *Save As . . . Digital Memories*. Basingstoke: Palgrave Macmillan, 2009.

Haskins, Ekaterina. "Between Archive and Participation: Public Memory in a Digital Age." *Rhetoric Society Quarterly* 37.4 (2007): 401–22.

Hoskins, Andrew. "7/7 and Connective Memory: Interactional Trajectories of Remembering in Post-Scarcity Culture." *Memory Studies* 4.3 (2011): 269–80.

Howard, Jennifer. "For Comfort and Posterity, Digital Archives Gather Crowds." *Chronicle of Higher Education* 18 Nov. 2013. Web. 27 Nov. 2013.

Jarvis, Lee. "9/11 Digitally Remastered? Internet Archives, Vernacular Memories and WhereWereYou.org." *Journal of American Studies* 45.4 (2011): 793–814.

Keniston, Ann, and Jeanne Follansbee Quinn. "Introduction." *Literature after 9/11*. Ed. Ann Keniston and Jeanne Follansbee Quinn. New York: Routledge, 2008. 1–15.

LaCapra, Dominick. *Writing History, Writing Trauma*. Baltimore: John Hopkins University Press, 2001.

Moretti, Franco. "Conjectures on World Literature." *New Left Review* 1 (2000): 54–68.

Randall, Martin. *9/11 and the Literature of Terror*. Edinburgh: Edinburgh University Press, 2011.

Reading, Anna. "Globital Time: Time in the Digital Globalized Age." *Time, Media and Modernity*. Ed. Emily Knightley. Basingstoke: Palgrave Macmillan, 2012. 143–62.

——. "The London Bombings: Mobile Witnessing, Mortal Bodies and Globital Time." *Memory Studies* 4.3 (2011): 298–311.

——. "Memory and Digital Media: Six Dynamics of the Globital Memory Field." *On Media Memory: Collective Memory in a New Media Age*. Ed. Oren Meyers, Motti Neiger, and Eyal Zandberg. Basingstoke: Palgrave Macmillan, 2011. 241–52.

Recuber, Timothy. "The Prosumption of Commemoration: Disasters, Digital Memory Banks, and Online Collective Memory." *American Behavioral Scientist* 56.531 (2012): 531–49.

September 11 Digital Archive. Center for History and New Media and American Social History Project/Center for Media and Learning June 2004. Web. 20 May 2012.

Stamelman, Richard. "Between Memory and History." *Trauma at Home.* Ed. Judith Greenberg. Lincoln: University of Nebraska Press, 2003. 11–20.

Steyvers, Mark, and Tom Griffiths. "Probabilistic Topic Models." *Handbook of Latent Semantic Analysis.* Ed. Thomas K. Landauer, Danielle S. McNamara, Simon Dennis, and Walter Kintsch. New York: Routledge, 2011. 427–48.

Index